St. Louis Community College

Forest Park
Florissant Valley
Meramec

Instructional Resources
St. Louis, Missouri

SEXUAL HARASSMENT

POINT/COUNTERPOINT

Philosophers Debate Contemporary Issues
General Editors: James P. Sterba and Rosemarie Tong

This new series provides a philosophical angle to debates currently raging in academic and larger circles. Each book is a short volume (around 200 pages) in which two prominent philosophers debate different sides of an issue. Future topics might include the canon, the ethics of abortion rights, and the death penalty. For more information, contact Professor Sterba, Department of Philosophy, University of Notre Dame, Notre Dame, IN 46566, or Professor Tong, Department of Philosophy, Davidson College, Davidson, NC 28036.

Political Correctness: For and Against
>   Marilyn Friedman, Washington University, St. Louis
>   Jan Narveson, University of Waterloo, Ontario, Canada

Humanitarian Intervention: Just War vs. Pacifism
>   Robert L. Phillips, University of Connecticut
>   Duane L. Cady, Hamline University

Affirmative Action: Social Justice or Unfair Preference?
>   Albert G. Mosley, Ohio University
>   Nicholas Capaldi, University of Tulsa

Religion in the Public Square: The Place of Religious Convictions in Political Debate
>   Robert Audi, University of Nebraska
>   Nicholas Wolterstorff, Yale University

Sexual Harassment: A Debate
>   Linda LeMoncheck
>   Mane Hajdin, University of Waikato

SEXUAL HARASSMENT

A Debate

Linda LeMoncheck
and
Mane Hajdin

ROWMAN & LITTLEFIELD PUBLISHERS, INC.
Lanham • New York • Boulder • Oxford

ROWMAN & LITTLEFIELD PUBLISHERS, INC.

Published in the United States of America
by Rowman & Littlefield Publishers, Inc.
4720 Boston Way, Lanham, Maryland 20706

12 Hid's Copse Road
Cummor Hill, Oxford OX2 9JJ, England

Copyright © 1997 by Rowman & Littlefield Publishers, Inc.

British Library Cataloguing in Publication Information Available

Library of Congress Cataloging-in-Publication Data

LeMoncheck, Linda.
    Sexual harassment : a debate / Linda LeMoncheck and Mane Hajdin.
        p.   cm.—(Point/counterpoint)
    Includes bibliographical references and index.
    ISBN 0-8476-8424-5 (alk. paper).—ISBN 0-8476-8425-3 (pbk. :
alk. paper)
    1. Sexual harassment of women.   2. Sexual harassment.   I. Hajdin,
Mane.   II. Title.   III. Series.
    HQ1237.L46   1997
    305.42—dc20   96-43497
                                                                        CIP

ISBN 0–8476–8424–5 (cloth : alk. paper)
ISBN 0–8476–8425–3 (pbk. : alk. paper)

Printed in the United States of America

⊗ ™ The paper used in this publication meets the minimum requirements of
American National Standard for Information Sciences—Permanence of Paper for
Printed Library Materials, ANSI Z39.48–1984.

Contents

Preface

This volume is a collaborative contribution to contemporary debates on sexual harassment, covering a broad range of moral and legal issues that we consider central to an informed discussion of the topic. We have developed our own respective views on sexual harassment, as well as represented many of the viewpoints most widely discussed among scholars and the general public alike. The text's point/counterpoint style gives us each the opportunity not only to present our own views on sexual harassment but also to respond directly to one another's line of reasoning. Such an exchange allows readers to see the ways in which two moral philosophers from very different theoretical perspectives tackle this contentious issue. We have written the book for a broad audience of generally educated readers who are curious or puzzled about what sexual harassment is and what is wrong with it. We hope that the book will also be useful as a starting point for classroom discussions in college courses dealing with sexual harassment. While we approach our topic as philosophers, we do not presuppose that our readers have any background in philosophy.

Even though we agree that a broad spectrum of what is referred to as sexual harassment is wrong, we disagree over many other questions, including exactly what is wrong with sexual harassment and what should be done about it: Is men's sexual harassment of women best understood as an injustice to women as a class or as a personal injury to individual women? Do all instances of sexual harassment constitute sex discrimination? Are particular instances of it better understood as nothing more than sexual attraction gone wrong? Do social policies aimed at eliminating sexual harassment in the workplace violate freedom of expression or liberate working relationships between women and men? Because the answers to these questions affect how people morally evaluate sexual harassment, how the law regulates it, and how social policies are implemented to address it, we believe that sexual harassment deserves the reflective and critical inquiry that is a philosopher's stock-in-trade.

When philosophers who belong to the analytic tradition approach a moral issue, they tend to devote a great deal of energy to analyzing the concepts that people use when they express their moral views on that issue. Philosophers do this sort of conceptual analysis not only because they regard it as fascinating in itself but also because they believe that better understanding of these concepts is often an important step in the direction of reaching some kind of agreement or viable compromise on the moral question at issue. Such careful analysis is particularly called for when dealing with a topic in which there are complex relationships between the concepts individuals use and the judgments they make by means of them. Philosophizing about sexual harassment is an excellent case in point. As our readers will discover, we have incorporated both conceptual analysis (the examination of the meanings of words) and normative analysis (the examination of values) into our discussions of sexual harassment, since, even if discerning that sexual harassment is wrong were a relatively straightforward task, discerning precisely what is wrong with sexual harassment and how it is wrong would depend upon what women and men mean when they identify particular cases as harassing. The latter discernment requires examining sexual harassment in a variety of settings and from a variety of points of view. Such an examination, in turn, generates an evaluation of what community censure or legal prohibition, if any, should be involved in condemning particular cases.

For example, a professor who coerces a graduate student into sex in exchange for a job recommendation and a professor who tells "dumb blond" jokes in class may each be guilty of sexual impropriety, but should they both be regarded as guilty of sexual harassment? Even if many women and men answer "yes" to this question, do those with apparently concurring opinions mean the same thing by the expression "sexual harassment"? Is the moral wrong the same in each case? Should responses by academic administrations to each type of conduct be the same or different, and what, if anything, should these responses be? Should the same legal prohibitions apply to each case? Should *any* legal prohibitions apply to such cases? What if a professor tells the same jokes at a church social? As moral philosophers who regard part of our professional responsibility to be the exploration of such questions in our analyses of sexual harassment, we have tried our best to address these and related issues in each of the essays in this volume.

Many feminist philosophers have tried to expand traditional analytic models by arguing that conceptual and normative examination of contemporary moral issues must include an analysis of the ways in which individuals and institutions are influenced by what feminists regard as pervasive and deeply entrenched stereotypes of masculinity and femininity. It has been argued that these stereotypes can generate unchallenged expectations in both women and men that women are the normal and proper subordinates of men in public and private life. Many feminists contend that without disclosing and transforming the prevailing politics of these gender stereotypes, women's lives and experiences will remain bound by the needs and values of men. From this feminist perspective, gender stereotypes are further complicated by the particular race, class, sexual orientation, ethnicity, or age, among other factors, of those whose conduct or experience is under investigation, such that what is wrong about certain behavior becomes a function of a variety of oppressive social constraints not necessarily limited to gender. Many feminist philosophers are thus committed to exploring how philosophical analysis can provide conceptual and normative clarity to women's and men's experiences without narrowing the cultural diversity or complexity of those experiences.

On the other hand, there are philosophers, both progressive and conservative, who believe that such a perspective paints a misleading or distorted picture of contemporary moral problems, either by overemphasizing the oppressive nature of stereotypical conceptions of race, class, gender, and sexuality or by underemphasizing the ways in which the moral wrongs feminists worry about can be adequately addressed in the absence of such a perspective. Many philosophers critical of what has been called a "gendered" approach to moral dilemmas believe that conceptual and normative analysis can be successful only if it remains removed from the distorting political biases that the feminist socio-cultural perspective described above would, according to these critics, impose upon it. Given this tension within philosophy, the essays in this volume introduce our readers to perspectives on sexual harassment, from both inside and outside the feminist movement, that variously embrace or criticize an emphasis on gender politics.

Above all, we have endeavored to stimulate our readers' thinking about the issues involved in sexual harassment and to show our readers how reflective and critical thinking can advance the dialogue on contemporary moral problems, even if that dialogue does not fully resolve them. We wish to thank Rosemarie Tong and Jim Sterba, the series editors, for giving us a professional forum for a respectful, candid, and open discussion of sexual harassment, and we gratefully acknowledge the energy and efficiency that Rowman & Littlefield's acquisitions editor Jennifer Ruark has devoted to this unique series of philosophical publications. We encourage our readers to take the following dialogue on sexual harassment beyond the pages of this book and into a world of public discussion and debate, where still new ways of understanding this very complex, fascinating, and troubling subject may be forged.

LINDA LEMONCHECK
MANE HAJDIN

Taunted and Tormented or Savvy and Seductive? Feminist Discourses on Sexual Harassment

Linda LeMoncheck

I leave this institution not with malice, but with love.

—*former U.S. Senator Bob Packwood*[1]

- In a parking lot in Eugene, Oregon, Senator Bob Packwood allegedly pulls a campaign worker toward him, forces his tongue into her mouth, and invites her to his motel room.

- In his Senate office, Packwood allegedly grabs a staff member's shoulders, pushes her onto a couch, and kisses her on the mouth as she repeatedly tries to push him off her and get up.

- In the Capitol's basement, Packwood allegedly walks a former staff assistant into a room where he corners her against a desk, pushes himself against her, and forces his tongue into her mouth.

  —*Three of eighteen instances of alleged sexual harassment by former Senator Bob Packwood*[2]

- A picture of a woman's pubic area with a meat spatula pressed on it.

- A dartboard picturing a woman's breast with the nipple as the bull's-eye.

- Graffiti painted prominently on the workplace walls: "lick me you whore dog bitch," "pussy," "cunt," and "eat me."

  —*Examples of sexual imagery in the workplace environment of a female welder*[3]

It's pointless to have rules saying what harassment is and isn't since people know that 99.9 per cent of cases are just mistakes. When a charge is made against you there's the attitude that it's not enough to say, "Sorry, you misunderstood my intentions," because she is after your blood.

—*Anonymous man accused of sexual harassment*[4]

For the millions of women in the United States who are sexually harassed each year, sexual harassment could not be less ambiguous: a degrading and debilitating sexual assault on their moral dignity and physical vulnerability, the unacceptable, unwanted, and nonmutual nature of which is indicative of personal violation.[5] Indeed, part of the insult of sexual harassment for many women has been the presumptuous and self-serving claim by more than a few men that a woman's being grabbed by the breasts, subjected to crude sexual jokes, stalked by a persistent suitor, howled at by a street gang, surrounded by sexually violent pornography, or forced to taste a man's tongue in her mouth involves some sort of complicated sexual misunderstanding that would never have happened had she simply made her sexual feelings better known and her sexual intentions less ambiguous. Corporations and campuses have responded to women's complaints about sexual harassment with an array of policies and procedures designed to identify "unwanted sexual conduct" and to establish guidelines for in-house investigation and sanction. The law has responded by making sexual harassment in the workplace and in education a type of sex discrimination in violation of Title VII of the Civil Rights Act of 1964 and Title IX of the Education Amendments of 1972; legal cases have established precedents on the basis of widely accepted, albeit variously interpreted, definitional guidelines authored by the U.S. Equal Employment Opportunity Commission (EEOC) with whom claims against employers are filed. Despite the relatively recent formal recognition of sexual harassment as a legal offense,[6] feminists continue to fight for women's freedom to go to a movie, walk the streets, go out on a date, sit in a classroom, or work diligently at their jobs without being sexually violated or victimized. Thus, it would appear that what has been a historically tolerated sexual abuse of women by men is now deemed, from many disparate social quarters, to be both morally unacceptable and legally prohibited.

Such an apparently proactive and positive response to the pervasive problem of sexual harassment in a variety of social settings is not without its problems, however. While many victims of sexual harassment say they know it when they feel it, not every woman classified by social researchers as a victim of sexual harassment would identify her own treatment as harassing, and women, even after being given formal policy guidelines, disagree among themselves as to which behaviors in which settings count as harassing. Many women change their views about it over the course of their own lives depending upon their economic circumstances or their experience of victimization.[7] While both women and men continue to disagree over whether or not current Supreme Court Justice Clarence Thomas did in fact sexually harass Anita Hill during Thomas's chairmanship of the EEOC, African American women still differ among themselves over both the offensiveness of Thomas's alleged conduct and Hill's propriety in publicizing it, particularly since a black man's nomination to the Supreme Court was at stake.[8] The offensiveness of sexual coercion ("Sleep with me or I'll fire/demote you"), sexual bribery ("Sleep with me and I'll hire/promote you"), and unwanted sexual touching is less contentious among both women and men than that of sexual jokes, gestures, or pictures because in the former cases, as with assault and battery, the question at issue is whether the abuse occurred, not whether what occurred was abuse. However, sexual innuendo, comments on general appearance, sidelong glances, and persistent requests for dates are much more controversial among and between members of both genders. As one lawyer has put it, "Something highly offensive to Minnie Pearl might be an inviting dare to Madonna."[9] Many women and men complain that the workplace, which is commonly regarded by single employees as an appropriate venue for meeting potential partners, has become completely devoid of the kind of easy repartee that makes much of the workday palatable and coworkers approachable. With sexual harassment that creates a "hostile environment" actionable under EEOC guidelines, men are afraid to compliment a woman on her new haircut, and women are afraid to laugh at an off-color joke for fear of harassing *other women*.

Moreover, the process of sexual harassment can be subtle, even if its effects are not, making the treatment itself often very difficult to isolate and categorize: An instructor's compliments in class about a female student's "perceptive reading of Tennyson" can lead to invitations to private office hours to "become better acquainted." Such invitations can be followed by intrusive and embarrassing questions about the student's sexual habits and personal life, which are later justified by the instructor as innocent and spontaneous responses to a seductive student's requests for intellectual "stimulation" in an atmosphere designed to foster "spiritual growth." Plum assignments and workplace bonuses that are perceived by a woman on her way up the corporate ladder as rewards for work well done can result in subtly expressed expectations, but not outright demands, that she will be sexually available to her boss at the next corporate convention. Such circumstances are especially disconcerting because they can leave women who are socialized to be the sexual gatekeepers against men's advances, and so supposedly responsible for men's sexual conduct, feeling guilty and ashamed for "not catching it sooner" or wondering what they must have said or done to encourage such expectations.

What I believe is frustrating, and ultimately misleading, about characterizing sexual harassment for purposes of identifying particular cases and assessing liability is trying to stipulate the range of behaviors that will pinpoint *any harasser* and *any victim* in *any and all* circumstances. This is especially true if we take the feminist aphorism seriously that "the personal is political" and examine the complex of organizational hierarchies, gender role expectations, cultural bias, and economic discrimination that variously inform sexual harassment depending upon the time, place, and people involved. Some women in supervisory positions sexually harass their male employees. Teens harass other teens for sport or spite, inside the classroom and outside it. A harasser may be a persistent suitor pleading for attention through an Internet E-mail address, a clumsy boss "just trying to be friendly," or a hostile machinist determined to distract and denigrate the women on his assembly line.[10] African American women often complain that white feminists are fighting for a presumption of sexual credibility that has historically been at black men's expense. Women of all colors complain that glass ceilings and wage and job discrimination make them easy targets for men's sexual harassment, since many women are desperate to keep the precious jobs they have. Harassment of gay men or lesbians may be a function of sexual pursuit, heterosexism, or homophobia. Dating games reinforce mixed sexual messages when a woman's "no" means "yes" to men used to interpreting women's hesitancy to have sex as a socially appropriate, but sexually repressed, display of femininity; and women and men of various races, classes, sexual orientations, ages, and physical abilities continue to disagree with each other over what each wants out of personal relationships, in which contexts, and why.

Given the variety of types of sexual harassment victims, perpetrators, and interpretations of the fault lines, it should come as no surprise that we feminists profoundly disagree among ourselves over the nature and prevention of sexual harassment and how women should respond to the victimization they experience. A common feminist complaint is that sexual harassment is not really about sex at all, or at least not about sexual pranks, misunderstandings, or miscues, but about *power*, the power of men within male-dominated social and economic institutions to violate and victimize women. Indeed, from this view, sexual harassment is but one instance of the ubiquitous and systemic oppression of women under a patriarchy whose hierarchies of authority, status, and privilege are designed to advantage men. As such, sexual harassment is an example of the gender dominance over, and discrimination against, women, to be handled, not by trying to "work things out," since men's greater credibility and organizational power over women make women's private resolution of the problem unlikely, but by filing sexual harassment claims in a court of law. Other feminists are convinced that such a characterization of sexual harassment betrays feminism to be largely populated by a group of victim-obsessed, antimale sexual puritans who see a sexual predator in every man and who would thus excise heterosexuality from contemporary life. From this view, the solution to sexual harassment is a renewed sense of personal responsibility and sexual self-confidence that encourages women to stop the harassment where it starts, with a curt "Knock it off!" So-called gender hierarchies that invest men, simply by virtue of being men, with oppressive patriarchal power are perceived by critics as condemning women to the very sexual violence and victimization that feminists should be vehemently combating.

The irony in this feminist standoff is that when combined with the disagreements mentioned earlier over the form and function of sexual harassment, it gives men precisely the ambiguity and confusion they need to excuse their unacceptable sexual behavior. Without some consensus on what counts as sexual harassment, men cannot be expected to know what is required of them; and worries about miscarriages of justice are made legitimate precisely because vague or conflicting descriptions of what counts as sexual harassment can breed arbitrary and prejudicial applications of these descriptions. Even with consensus on what a general policy description of sexual harassment should contain, the terminology is often so ambiguous as to make a mockery of the practical value that sexual harassment policies are meant to offer. Thus, men accused of sexual harassment under policy guidelines that prohibit "unwanted sexual behavior," "offensive conduct," or a "hostile environment" charge feminists who support such policies with victimizing men. Specifically, they charge those feminists with encouraging so-called hypersensitive, paranoid, or vindictive women to bring capricious lawsuits well after the fact for unintentional slights and thereby to discriminate against men in violation of due process.

Moreover, clarity and closure on what counts as sexual harassment is important *for feminists*, not only to warn potential harassers of unacceptable treatment, but also to help individual women recognize sexual harassment when it happens to them, identify their accusers, and make their claims legitimate without fear of successful countersuits for defamation of character or economic damages. Workplaces and educational institutions would certainly benefit from a clearer sense of the problem, in order to promote public discussion of the issues and evaluate particular experiences. What I wish to argue in this essay is that we need a way to negotiate the tensions and advance the dialogue among competing views in ways that recognize the practical need of individuals, policy makers, and legislators for mutual understanding about what sexual harassment is and does, without forcing the phenomenon of sexual harassment into a rigid definitional grid that cannot account for its cultural complexity and contextual variation.

To accomplish this, I offer a description of sexual harassment as a dialectical process of sexual politics, whose regenerating and interpretive character reveals itself in the interplay of victimization and empowerment that informs the sexual lives of women and men. I argue that the relevant question to ask with regard to sexual harassment is not whether a given act is harassing but by whom and under what cultural conditions is the assessment of conduct being made. I believe it is a mistake to make definitive and universally binding distinctions among sexual misconduct, sexual harassment, and sexual assault, since such distinctions depend upon partial and historicized assessments of sexual propriety, whose primacy of place in any discourse on sexual harassment will depend upon the social power and collective process of the voices expressing them.

This way of understanding sexual harassment reflects a complex of organizational hierarchies and cultural stereotypes that inform a Western industrialized world much of whose authority, priority, and credibility still lie in the hands of educated, Anglo-European, heterosexual men. I wish to expand this picture further by situating sexual harassment within a patriarchy in which the *politics* does not obfuscate the *sex* in sexual harassment, the *practice* does not obfuscate the *process* of sexual harassment, and the *victim* of sexual harassment does not obfuscate the *sexual subject* of a politically aware and socially responsible life. As such, this characterization is designed to reflect the male power and privilege that is reified by men's sexual harassment of women at the same time as it underscores the sexual misunderstandings and miscues that cultural stereotypes about women and men foster. Its dialectic can simultaneously accommodate a woman's clarity that she has been harassed and her ambivalence about why it has happened to her or what she should do about it. Indeed, one of the strengths of this characterization is that it acknowledges what I think is a dynamic and often contradictory sexual landscape. This characterization is also meant to address the experiences of those women and men who have confronted their harassers and transcended their harassment, as well as those who wonder what the fuss is all about. In this way, I believe feminists can speak to the wide variety of women and men who experience sexual harassment, thereby obviating some of the criticisms and allaying much of the disillusionment that has accompanied contemporary discussions of sexual harassment in recent years. At the same time, my goal is to incorporate the wide variety of sexual harassment that exists within a framework for thinking and talking about the problem, which can guide judges, juries, human resource specialists, campus administrators, and others in their assessments of sexual harassment claims and their formulation of social policy.

I am also firmly convinced that while sexual harassment must be understood within the patriarchal institutions that inform both its sexual and organizational politics, the way this message is often conveyed leaves feminists open to criticism that they are undermining the very liberation that feminism is meant to facilitate. Therefore, in the next section, I outline some of the common feminist discourse defining sexual harassment as a paradigm of the sexual violence and victimization of women under patriarchy. In the second section, I offer a review of the feminist counterclaims that this paradigm exaggerates men's sexual harassment of women and dogmatically asserts questionable claims about institutionalized male dominance in ways that bash men, trash sex, and victimize women.

In the third section of the essay, I offer my own nuanced account of sexual harassment that is sensitive to both the gender politics of sexual harassment and the liberating possibilities for a self-identified sexual subject. Understanding sexual harassment as a dialectical and regenerating process of sexual politics, I show how and why some feminists' political analyses of sexual harassment appear as anathema to other feminists. In so doing, I hope to create a new forum for advancing a feminist dialogue otherwise stalled by incompatible views. Moreover, by identifying sexual harassment as a violation of sexual integrity whose intrusiveness is identifiable but also interpretive, I prepare the way for guiding legislation and formulating social policy as discussed in the fourth section.

In that section, I endeavor to balance the burden of persuasion in sexual harassment cases between alleged perpetrator and victim. I argue against the usefulness of either an "unwelcomeness" test or a "reasonable woman standard" for sexual harassment. Agreeing with other feminist legal theorists, I believe such standards inevitably put the conduct of the victim, not the perpetrator, on trial and expose women to considerations of "special protection" that militate against the success of sex discrimination suits understood as eliminating unequal treatment. Current EEOC guidelines have been used to set a variety of interpretive precedents, despite a discrete list of sufficient conditions purportedly conducive to a more objective assessment of claims. My own characterization of sexual harassment is no less open to the wide-ranging interpretations of particular judges and juries than current guidelines but is more broadly construed within a context that requires both empathy and political sensibilities to recognize the cultural diversity and sexual politics that inform sexual harassment cases. Therefore, I include in the fourth section an outline of how politically aware and socially responsible workplaces and academic institutions can play an essential and preemptive role in identifying, investigating, and sanctioning sexual harassment.

In the concluding section, I outline how some of women's and men's objections to sexual harassment can inform a feminist sexual ethic sensitive to the value of care and collaboration in sexual relations circumscribed by the dynamics of gender politics. By embracing, as opposed to reducing, the tensions among women's and men's assessments of sexual harassment, I wish to recognize the importance of dissension and difference to any meaningful and self-consciously feminist evaluation of the problem and to advocate that consensus may be more a matter of process than of resolution. My ultimate goal is to convince women and men otherwise skeptical of feminism's efforts to contribute to contemporary discourse on the status of women, that understanding sexual harassment as informed, but not determined, by a culturally sensitive sexual politics will ultimately benefit the personal relationships of us all.

Feminist Objections to Sexual Harassment:
The Case against Patriarchy

[T]he central concept of sexual harassment is the misuse of power, whether organizationally or institutionally, in a manner that constructs a barrier to women's educational and occupational pursuits.

  —*Louise F. Fitzgerald, Sandra L. Shullman, Nancy Bailey, Margaret Richards, Janice Swecker, Yael Gold, Mimi Ormerod, and Lauren Weitzman*[11]

You can only understand sexual harassment if you take a hard look at gender roles and who controls who in the workplace.

  —*Anonymous woman recounting her experience of being harassed*[12]

Sexual harassment is not about sex, it's about sexism.

  —*Billie Wright Dziech and Linda Weiner*[13]

Feminists have long recognized that when women's oppression becomes an expected and everyday feature of women's lives, it becomes something to tolerate, not something to contest. Moreover, if the normality of women's oppression can be made into the natural or the inevitable, then women will not even consider contestation, since their condition will be regarded as unalterable. Indeed, since what is natural is often associated with what is valuable or what is good, women will come to believe that there is something wrong with them if they consider their condition to be unacceptable, intolerable, or harmful. Thus, feminists have argued that if sexual harassment is understood as a normal and natural feature of women's lives, stemming from the inevitable misunderstandings and miscues that inform sexual relationships gone awry, women will accept their harassment without complaint.

On the other hand, if sexual harassment is understood not as a private and personal injury to individual women but as a very public and political injury to women as a class, then sexual harassment becomes contestable as a socially constructed harm designed to advantage men at women's expense. Sexual harassment understood in this way becomes a matter of a male-biased gender politics, in which authority, priority, and credibility are conferred on men because they are men and in which women are concomitantly delegitimized, degraded, and distrusted because they are women. From this perspective, sexual harassment is a power issue because it is a gender issue. Men's advantage over women is a political one, since men are perceived as morally superior people with superior knowledge who say and do superior things—all of which give men the status and privilege required to maintain power over, and control of, women, whose words and deeds are regarded as inherently second class. Male dominance becomes institutionalized by being protected, promoted, and normalized in the rules, practices, terms, and conditions of the institutions that inform cultural life. "Customary and appropriate" behavior in business, academia, law, medicine, government, science, the arts, and the family will favor men whose power to define what is customary and appropriate maintains and reinforces men's power base.

According to this view, sexual harassment is an example of the patriarchal oppression of women because it maintains and reinforces in the workplace, in education, at home, in the shopping malls, on the streets, indeed everywhere, what is perceived as the normal and proper subordination of women to men. A woman's economic subordination under patriarchy compels her to tolerate her sexual harassment rather than lose her precious wages or chances for advancement by refusing or reporting her harasser, and the psychological tension and unease caused by her harassment insure continued wage and job discrimination against her by making it more difficult for her to do her work. Her lowered ambitions, decreased job satisfaction, and impaired job performance are then cited as evidence that she is simply not capable of doing the work required of her. Her low productivity may also be used to rationalize the demotions or poor performance reviews that are, in fact, retaliation for her refusals to comply with her harasser's demands. Many women experience being hounded, badgered, plagued, baited, tormented, and worn out by persistent and unrelenting invasions of their personal space. Simply the threat of sexual harassment acts as a kind of terrorist blackmail to force a woman to quit, transfer, or suffer in wary silence, not knowing when she will be harassed next, by whom, or how. Political conservatives argue that American women's median income is roughly 75 percent of men's income because women *choose* to care for children, and so tend to *choose* lower-paying and part-time jobs to accommodate their domestic needs and limited job experience. However, many feminists counter that women typically *become* the primary caretakers of their children, without freely or self-consciously *choosing* to do so, because they seldom have the wages and job opportunities to accommodate alternative day care and that if they do have sufficient wages and opportunities, women are socially stigmatized as guilt-free "bad mothers" for single-mindedly pursuing careers while leaving their families in the care of others.[14]

In short, the gender oppression that keeps women in lower-status jobs or hard-won management positions makes them more vulnerable to harassment along organizational lines. From this perspective, gender hierarchies facilitate and exacerbate men's dominance within organizations, making sexual harassment a pervasive and intractable feature of business and educational institutions. While men may exploit their favored positions within organizational hierarchies to extract sexual favors from women on lower rungs of the economic ladder, many feminists argue that sexual harassment is a function of the ubiquitous and systemic oppression of women under the gender hierarchies that define patriarchy. Men's economic dominance and social privilege thus conspire to keep women from achieving economic and social parity with men. When 90 to 95 percent of all harassers are men and 90 to 95 percent of all those harassed are women, and when individual women are victimized more often and more severely than individual men, particularly when women's jobs involve more than filing or typing, feminists argue that we must identify gender roles, not organizational power positions exclusively, as indicators of who will harass whom.[15]

While sexual harassers come in all shapes and sizes, they tend to be older than their victims, male, married, and sexually unattractive to their victims; the higher the male-to-female ratio in the workplace, the greater and more severe the harassment. Gay and straight men harassing other gays is much more pervasive than lesbians harassing women. Moreover, when women do successfully and sexually harass men, it is typically their organizational power, as professors or employers, that makes the harassment successful, whereas male students, coworkers, dates, and perfect strangers with no obvious positions of institutional authority over women continue successfully to harass women. Women in positions traditionally confined to men are "put in their place" with dismissive comments about their "real" talents for sex and reproduction, with pornography and sex toys strewn throughout their work areas, and with sexual coercion made real with threats of demotion, poor performance reviews, or lukewarm recommendations if women make public their harassment. Ironically, women in the more traditional and economically vulnerable jobs of secretary or housekeeper are harassed precisely because they are doing the less prestigious work that their more nontraditional sisters are harassed for *not* doing. Thus, the vulnerability and visibility of both traditional and nontraditional work for women appear to attract sexual harassment. Bribes of advancement in exchange for sex are coercive, since harassed women cannot know what will become of their positions no matter how they respond. If they do comply, harassed women are often accused of unfairly "sleeping their way to the top" by seducing, in a manner unavailable to men, an unsuspecting but susceptible male boss. Indeed, women who are the most competitive for traditionally defined "men's work" are the women most often subjected to sexual harassment, and to its most egregious forms.[16]

Gender hierarchies also explain the phenomenon of coworker or peer harassment, where women continue to be the most common targets and the gender most profoundly affected.[17] Even if a woman complains about her harassment, the gender politics of her situation insure that either (1) her complaint will not be taken seriously ("Boys will be boys!"); (2) her complaint will be ignored ("Don't you think you're being overly sensitive?"); or (3) her complaint will not be believed ("He's too high up in the company to stoop to such things" "He wouldn't risk doing something that could get him fired"). At worst, she will be accused of provoking her harassment by her dress, speech, or manner. When sexual harassment policies and procedures are under the auspices of the very men whom a woman suspects of tolerating abuse, or when such policies fail to identify what she has experienced, she will feel she has no recourse but silence. Legal cases are expensive, time consuming, and almost unthinkable if she wants to keep her job. She may even try to empathize with her harasser, having been socialized to "smooth things over" rather than be the "bitch" that belligerently confronts him, believing it best not to hurt him if she can handle the hurt herself. Under such conditions, it is no surprise, then, that many women believe that no good can come from reporting their harassment, despite feelings of humiliation, sickness, fear, embarrassment, self-blame, self-doubt, wracked nerves, frustration, anger, anxiety, denial, and helplessness over their predicament.[18]

Sexual harassment in colleges and universities has its own special characteristics and problems, which are exposed rather than disguised by the gendered analysis specified here. Undergraduate women and men are in constant and regenerating supply in an environment that many of them would happily admit is a primary dating ground, providing open season for hunting sexual partners. Yet students are also in school, after all, and so provide feedback and affirmation of their professors' academic expertise, autonomy in the classroom, and superior knowledge in their fields. Indeed, in a setting where mind meets body(s), professors in contemporary academia are expected not only to impart their knowledge to their students but also to nurture students' intellectual and moral maturity. This expectation, when combined with professors' academic authority and credentials, can make a heady impression on an undergraduate woman flattered with the sexual attentions of a male professor who could purportedly choose *any* student he wished with whom to align his power and prestige.

Moreover, the academic freedom and autonomy accorded professors can tempt them to speak and behave irresponsibly. Professors have tremendous power over students in the assignment of grades, the writing of recommendations, and the direction of tutorials and graduate theses. Like the power to hire and fire, this power combines with the gender credibility and, in this case, the academic authority of a largely male intellectual establishment to act as a sexually coercive instrument against female students. With the expectation of intellectual bonding, particularly from graduate students, and with the plethora of young, emotionally available, sexually active, and relatively transient women with whom to form noncommittal relationships, campuses can become hotbeds of both subtle and blatant sexual intimidation and exploitation. Between 20 and 30 percent of college women report sexual harassment by male faculty, ranging from obscene gestures and unwanted touching to outright threats or bribes. Such numbers translate into well over a million sexually harassed female undergraduates, with a new group enrolling in college every year. Moreover, this statistic does not account for repeat offenses or for sexist remarks or materials used in the classroom.[19]

Male faculty are much less likely than female faculty to label jokes, sexual teasing or innuendo, gestures, or suggestive looks as harassing; much more comfortable with consensual sexual relations between faculty and students; and much more likely to expect female undergraduates to be able to handle sexual advances by professors. They are also more eager to think that such students encourage their professors' advances.[20] While, as Billie Dziech and Linda Weiner point out, some students are bound to get crushes on professors and "hassle" them for attention, such women are not in a comparable power position to destroy the intellectual self-confidence, question the moral credibility, and instill the fear of academic reprisal in their professors. Thus, many, if not most, campus administrations warn against liaisons between faculty and students, particularly students currently taught or supervised, because of the unequal power differential between the partners. This differential, it is argued, not only makes a female student's sexual consent suspect but can also work to the detriment of the student should the relationship sour. Moreover, others outside the relationship, watching women get "special treatment" by their professors, may see it as unfairly manipulative. Some universities outrightly prohibit student-faculty relationships inside instructional contexts.[21]

Like their counterparts in the workplace, female students are often prevented from reporting their harassment to authorities because of the risk of interrogation and painful self-disclosure. Many students simply do not know of the existence of their campuses' sexual harassment policies and procedures. Others are afraid of being held responsible by the perpetrator or of not being believed by the administrators and other faculty to whom they are often asked to answer (and who may be colleagues of the perpetrator and harassers themselves). Feminists who advocate a gendered perspective on sexual harassment contend that young women are taught by a patriarchal status quo to trust male authority figures and may not be in an emotional or practical position to withstand the pressures of confrontation. Rebuffs of a professor's sexual harassment can mean lower grades; humiliation or isolation in the classroom; disappointing recommendations for research appointments, fellowships, or academic posts; false rumors spread to other faculty; and the inability to form professional networks in the field of one's choice. As a result, women switch classes, change majors, drop master's and doctoral programs, and transfer to other schools to avoid their harassers, literally forfeiting research and career goals rather than submit to their continued harassment. (So much for women "choosing" to stay home!)

Professors defend their behavior by privatizing the conduct with complaints about being misunderstood, being penalized for responding to the sexual overtures of an assertive coed, or being persecuted for their political views. Through denying or ignoring the inherent power differential between faculty and student, male faculty can avoid their responsibility for pressuring women with their sexual advances and can maintain the fantasy that students are attracted to *them* and not merely their credentials. When accused of sexual harassment, academics may project their own power and authority onto their accusers and assert that it is the student, as seducer and betrayer, who has all the power, while the professor is the victimized one. Taxed by committee work, administrative duties, large teaching loads, diffident colleagues, unappreciative students, or rejecting book publishers, many professors may feel that they have very little power of their own. Indeed, many professors experience midlife crises or professional burnouts for which the sexual attentions of an appreciative and attractive young student can provide a mediating palliative. And there is no underestimating the "nerd factor," when tenured faculty, having painfully experienced their sexual awkwardness in youthful pursuit of academic success, attempt to make up for lost ground by coming on to their students.[22] Colleagues are often unwilling to report one of their own or oversee the work of a student fleeing another professor's mistreatment, especially when faculty are given the responsibility of retaining and promoting each other. A penchant for tolerating a fair amount of "eccentricity" among faculty makes sexual harassment appear to be just one more dip into the (cess?)pool of academic freedom.

Women faculty performing academic work that is unconventional for women are also harassed with relative impunity, when women's already tenuous professional status and credibility are on the line. Many such women self-consciously "dress down" so as not to attract sexual attention in an effort to maintain academic credibility, only to find that their colleagues have dubbed them sexually frustrated, dowdy, or "unapproachable" for doing so. While faculty women depend on male colleagues for retention, tenure, and promotion, most academic women are automatically suspect as interlopers on male turf and will be expected to "take their lumps" in a man's world while maintaining their equanimity. The professional risks involved in either reporting their own harassment or supporting the claims of students are often perceived to be too high to do much about. Indeed, from the gendered perspective outlined here, a patriarchal climate encourages a woman to believe that the cost of being "one of the boys" means turning her back on "one of the girls."[23]

Moreover, it is argued that a gendered perspective on sexual harassment explains why, according to researchers, "women perceive a wider range of behaviors as threatening, particularly those that could create a hostile work environment."[24] When women constitute the vast majority of sexual harassment victims, their sense of the range and variety of sexual harassment tends to be greater than that of men whose gender dominance and power positions within organizations make sexual harassment easier for such men to overlook. Boys as well as men tend to see themselves as more confrontational and less willing to take abuse than women, even as men misperceive the abuse they dish out. As one male teenage harasser reports, "I'd beat the crap out of someone if they touched me like that."[25] Gender politics also informs Deborah Tannen's comment that for men, the fear of sexual harassment is the fear of the false charge, while for women, it is the fear of male violence. If men value their power base enough to harass women into compliance with them, they will also fear losing it to women regarded as both savvy and devious enough to convince others of their case.[26]

In fact, feminists like Nancy Ehrenreich and Stephanie Riger argue that unless more women recognize that gender hierarchies are firmly entrenched to the advantage of men, plurality and consensus concerning what counts as sexual harassment will inevitably and invisibly reinforce a patriarchal status quo by disguising men's power to define the discourse on sexual harassment. Given a hierarchy of credibility in organizations where those higher up the corporate ladder define the terms and conditions of the workplace, combined with a gender hierarchy in which men tend to hold positions of power within those organizations, "men's judgments about what behavior constitutes harassment, and who is to blame, are likely to prevail."[27] Common critical complaints that feminists' objections to sexual harassment constitute an intolerance for diversity and a violation of freedom of expression thus appear as men's legitimate laments against an overbearing feminism that would deny important democratic liberties in the name of moral prudery, sexual totalitarianism, and ideological dogma.[28]

In contrast to this critical view, many feminists argue that sexual harassment is an example of sex discrimination, not just because a harassed woman, in virtue of being a woman, is treated differently from men in the same or similar circumstances, but because sexual harassment contributes to the continued subordination of women as a class.[29] Accordingly, the sexism that pervades contemporary American society reinforces a view of women as the natural and proper subordinates of men, a gender-conventional stereotype of women that does not require that all men treat all women in the same way, only that some women—as it happens, many, if not most, women at some point in their academic or working lives—be denigrated, degraded, or devalued because they are women. Thus, women are not socialized under patriarchy to define and validate their experiences for themselves; rather, they are socialized to defer to others to validate those experiences for them. As a result, sexual harassment trades on many women's uncertainty about their own lived experience. Naomi Wolf asserts that "some women, for whatever unfortunate reason, cannot yet say no so that it can be heard" and "[t]he other side of the feminist demand for men to learn to listen should be the feminist responsibility for women to learn to speak."[30] However, from the feminist perspective outlined above, without a moral and epistemological authority comparable to men's under patriarchy, even the most vociferous, articulate, and well-reasoned complaints will fall on deaf male ears, including the ears of many women convinced of the unerring authority of men.

Such discrimination may combine with educated, white men's race and class dominance to make the sexual harassment of women of color particularly distressing, since such women's economic prospects and sexual credibility tend to be even lower than their white sisters'. Ironically, the struggle of many black women to care for their children and to be free of men's physical assault often makes black women less sympathetic to complaints, such as those brought by educated professional women like Anita Hill, against the "hostile environment" type of verbal harassment. Yet black women may see the oppression of sexual harassment more clearly than white women precisely because of the African American experience of white racism. When white women claim to be harassed by black men, they often find themselves in conflict with black women. In such cases, white feminists' demands for credibility often ring hollow to black women whose cultural history includes lynchings of black men resulting from white women's false accusations of rape. On the other hand, some white women harassed by black men have watched their complaints reduced to charges of racism by men who take advantage of the credibility of their gender to discredit their accusers. African American women are often asked to think of the cohesion of their race before they file suit against a fellow black. Although harassment of grade-school children is reported to be more common among African American students than among whites, Anita Hill is considered a traitor to her race by some black women precisely because she aired the dirty laundry of black discontent before a white public eager to find new ammunition for denigration and distrust of blacks.[31]

Thus, from the feminist perspective outlined here, exposing the gender politics of sexual harassment becomes a matter of exposing the power, and not the sex, in sexual harassment, that is, exposing the powerlessness of the harassed to stop the harassment or to make good her accusations, and the power of the harasser to believe he can get away with it. Many feminists argue that if sexual harassment were nothing more than a matter of sexual misunderstanding or a sexual prank, then women would not suffer retaliation and further intimidation for their refusals to "go along" and that if sexual harassment were merely sexual attraction gone wrong, when individual women asked harassers to stop their behavior, they would. Turning sexual harassment into a joke makes sexual conduct funny. The harasser becomes a hail-fellow-well-met with a good sense of humor, while his victim looks like a moralizing prude unable to take a joke. Depoliticizing "the game" of sex makes it into something that is supposed to be fun for everyone (hence the popularity of wet tee-shirt contests and "spin the bottle" stripping games). Thus, women who complain about their alleged harassment are perceived to be spoiling the fun. According to this view, depoliticizing the problem also simplifies it, by making sexual harassment into a misnamed nonevent instead of a socially inscribed, contextually sensitive, and complexly motivated power play.

Moreover, it is argued that since women as a class are charged with the responsibility for negotiating and facilitating personal relationships, if sexual harassment is reduced to the personal, women will be blamed, and will blame themselves, for the failure of those relationships. Particularly in the realm of sex, where women are expected to be the gatekeepers against men's sexual advances (while keeping their own desires in check), sexual harassment will be women's fault because they failed to stop men sooner. Indeed, according to this view, women become the root cause and motivation for men's untoward conduct in virtue of women's very existence as heterosexual objects of male desire. The most charitable reading of sexual harassment, qua imperfect sexual signals imperfectly received, asserts that neither party is at fault (because both are complicitous) and, therefore, that neither party is a victim, effectively eviscerating women's experience of humiliation and distress. This is especially galling, given the array of physical and psychological symptoms, from nausea, headaches, muscle spasms, and eating and sleep disorders to depression, distraction, and paranoia, that many women victimized by their harassment have reported. Nevertheless, we are supposed to be "good girls" and respond to men's sexual attentions with grace, generosity, and good humor ("Don't you *like* being told you're sexy?" "Well, you don't have to be a bitch about it").[32]

In this depoliticized picture, the harasser is no longer a manipulator and dominator of the action under social conditions that facilitate his success but a victim of a wily seductress, neurotic flirt, or vindictive bitch out to give men their comeuppance. If she is sexually attractive, she egged him on; if she is sexually unattractive or undeniably chaste, the harassment could not have happened; and even if it did (there were witnesses), it was no big deal, proving that women have no sense of humor and are downright Victorian in their public attitudes about sex. Susan Estrich wryly refers to these rationalizations as the "slut," the "nut," and the "so what?" defenses against sexual harassment.[33] Women are characterized as asking for their treatment in the way they dress, speak, or behave, and women are characterized as wanting their treatment, since, from a patriarchal point of view, their "no" to sex is a pronouncement of "yes" in the absence of appropriately feminine deferrals. Women are described as sexually hysterical, jealous, spiteful, and characteristically deceptive in refusing to admit that they consented to something of which they are ashamed. Patriarchal myths that (1) women cannot be trusted, (2) women are the source of evil in the world, and (3) women have hidden agendas (so that they will lie and manipulate to get what they want) are disguised as objective facts about women's nature rather than understood as products of a socially constructed, culture-specific gender politics whose raison d'être is the degradation and exploitation of women. "Boys will be boys" and "You know how men are" are standard excuses for sexual harassment perceived as a normal and natural outgrowth of men's biologically based sexual aggression, for which men may be required to apologize but not be held responsible ("I was just trying to flatter her" "I thought she would like the attention"). Paradoxically, women are also made to believe that if they just don't provoke men sexually, then nothing will happen. Yet such beliefs run contrary to a world in which men's raging hormones supposedly prompt their spontaneous and unsolicited sexual advances.

It is also contended that emphasizing the sexual over the political reinvigorates the misleading claim that individual women have a "choice" as to whether or not to tolerate their harassment. Yet many feminists argue that when men dominate organizational hierarchies and define the terms and conditions of gender roles, women do not have the kinds of access to, or knowledge of, real alternatives to their harassment that would define their responses as unambiguous cases of genuine choice. As Clare Brant and Yun Lee Too assert, "An inability to give consent on equal terms lies at the heart of the theory which regards sexual harassment as an issue of power. Power is the capacity to disregard or override consent."[34] They would also agree that both species of harassment designated by EEOC guidelines—so-called quid pro quo harassment, where sex is made a condition of employment or employment-based decisions, and "hostile environment" harassment, in which sexual conduct creates an unreasonably intrusive or offensive working environment—make it difficult to identify cases of genuine consent. For example, a woman may consent unwillingly or grudgingly to sexual coercion or offense simply in order to keep her job or "not make waves," or because she is too humiliated or embarrassed to admit to its occurrence. Nervously laughing at crude jokes may thus be interpreted as willing participation in, even enjoyment of, what is in fact harassing, especially when curt retorts only increase the harasser's hostility. Indeed, E-mail and telephone harassment are particularly distressing precisely because the receiver cannot anticipate the harassment and so cannot choose not to receive it. From this view, the advice that students and faculty are often given that they should simply not read the offending mail is disingenuous at best.

Thus, many feminists would contend that it is a mistake to accept Edmund Wall's claim that sexual harassment is a form of wrongful communication in which failed attempts to gain consent to a certain kind of communication result in a violation of the victim's right to privacy.[35] Wall is concerned that without investigating the intent of the harasser, as opposed to the behavioral content of the harassment, the so-called innocent sexual remarks, stares, or gestures of an "ignorant but well-intentioned" offender will be taken as harassing. However, Wall's picture is premised on the assumption that women and men living under conditions of individual and institutionalized male dominance are nevertheless free and equal moral agents each of whose obligations to respect the other's rights will not be abridged without moral censure. If the terms and conditions of that censure are defined by those with the power and authority to advantage men and discredit women, then women will be blamed for misunderstanding men's "good intentions," which as men define them, are tied to those sexually aggressive tendencies that (oops!) sometimes just don't come out right. Wall dismisses an analysis of sexual harassment as sex discrimination because he does not believe that "sweeping social assumptions" about gender politics can be used to define sexual harassment, but from the feminist perspective outlined here, it is just as sweeping to assume a universal right to privacy among women and men all of whom have an equal capacity and opportunity for its exercise.

Moreover, it is contended that privatizing the power issue—the dominance and control issue, the use and abuse issue, the intimidation and coercion issue—obscures sexual harassment from public scrutiny and public censure. Sexual harassment becomes a "private matter" inappropriate for the law and made unnecessarily public by formal in-house sexual harassment procedures. Indeed, some legislators have predicted that the courts will become flooded with trivial sexual harassment suits, and employers and college administrators argue that monitoring, much less eliminating, every personal eccentricity in workplaces or campuses is impossible.[36]

However, a small percentage of all sexual harassment cases ever reach the courts, and an even smaller percentage of all sexual harassment claims are vindictive, conspiratorial, or manufactured; thus, some feminists have argued that men's fears of malicious or specious prosecution betray men's inability, if not unwillingness, to accept their own responsibility for the conduct in question. It is argued that such an attitude also displays men's projection of what *they* would do if denied a well-deserved promotion or excluded from work that would advance their careers. From this feminist perspective, plays like David Mamet's *Oleanna,* in which we watch a college professor suffer at the hands of a feminist student enraged by what she perceives as his sexual assault, and novels like Michael Crichton's *Disclosure,* about a lusting female executive's sexual harassment of her male employee, betray men's fears of the sexual power, audacity, and mendacity of women. Indeed, many feminists critical of the gendered analysis presented here contest that it is a sign of women's power that men have gone to such lengths to prevent women from exercising it.

Men's laments about both the end of easy office banter and women's sexual paranoia may themselves be designed to harass women into compliance with men's sexual standards. "She's after my job" and "She just can't take the competition" are common defenses against women's charges. Yet lawsuits are time consuming, costly, and extremely humiliating for the women who file them. Nevertheless, men continue to believe that women do so to get even or to get rich, when most simply want the harassment to stop. Indeed, a woman's fears of reprisal (including suspensions, transfers, formal reprimands, and exclusion from plum assignments by others who have been threatened by her harasser), her fears of not being believed, her distrust of any procedures designed to investigate the harassment, her own embarrassment at her predicament, and even her reluctance to hurt her harasser all militate against the sexual harassment ever being complained about at all. (Ironically, her lack of complaint is then used to show that "it was no big deal.") She may keep silent simply because she needs the money, class, or graduate work; she may believe that her harassment will not continue or may not believe that what is happening to her is harassment. If her tolerance cracks, rather than suffer with ineffective or insensitive in-house procedures or go to court, she simply leaves. Thus, a gendered analysis of sexual harassment is designed to reveal how women are oppressed by a form of sexual intimidation that is aimed at maintaining and reinforcing male power, status, and authority. From this view, patriarchy ascribes to women maximum credibility to do men harm on the witness stand at the very same time that it affords them minimum credibility to understand and assess their own harassment.[37]

Men also complain that since men can be harassed by women, "there just isn't anything to this patriarchal nonsense." Yet men filing claims against female harassers or filing for defamation of character and wrongful dismissal are apparently winning their cases.[38] Because men's masculinity is typically tied to work-oriented achievement ("bringing home the bacon") and male-dominated jobs are supposed to require traits that distinguish men as superior to women, women who would challenge men's exclusive right to those jobs pose a threat to men's self-esteem.[39] Indeed, from the feminist perspective outlined here, *any* sign of women's economic independence will be a threat to patriarchy. As Susan Faludi has pointed out, "If establishing masculinity depends most of all on succeeding as the prime breadwinner, then it is hard to imagine a force more directly threatening to fragile American manhood than the feminist drive for economic equality."[40] Thus, men privatize and personalize their sexual conduct in order to deny their positions of power and control in personal relationships, but they flaunt their power when it reinforces their gender identity and gender dominance.

Feminists who understand sexual harassment in terms of sexism and not sex also note that sexual harassment is part of a continuum of violence and victimization of women under patriarchy, a continuum that begins with sexual ogling and ends with rape.[41] Feminists have noted similarities in how myths about women's sexual provocation, manipulation, and vindictiveness pervade discussions of both sexual harassment and rape, including how the victim's own conduct appears to go on trial in ways that recreate the original victimization and deflate the case for the prosecution.[42] Women and girls from all walks of life and of different ages, physical abilities, races, classes, and sexual orientations are subjects of harassment along this continuum, although it is not surprising that youth and relative lowness on the economic ladder (both of which correlate with lower credibility and less comfort with confrontation) are good indices for potential harassment.

Teens harass other teens with bathroom graffiti, snapped bras, and vulgar language or gestures, often in a vicious cycle of revenge, since there is no clear institutional power differential to dissuade the harassed from attempting to return the abuse or abusing another. Moreover, despite written policies warning of suspensions or expulsions for harassment of fellow students, there is often no adult support for making harassment claims stick or for preventing repeated abuse, especially when some of the teachers harass students themselves. In such cases, girls will harass other girls by trashing their lockers or dropping lab specimens down their blouses in an attempt to recreate the hierarchies of power and authority that girls see their male classmates attaining with relative ease and impunity. Girls who continue to be sexually harassed by either other students or adults often betray a lack of self-esteem and self-confidence already made tenuous by well-socialized feminine cues to defer to men. For many such girls, their low self-image and the memories of their harassment will haunt them for life.[43]

Men who harass may be persistent suitors, hostile coworkers, competitive fellow classmates, or paternalistic employers, among others. Harassers can be unaware of their abuse or insensitive to women's rejections or fears of retaliation, or they can be hard-core victimizers determined to reaffirm their own masculinity by exhibiting displays of male dominance over women. Male harassers may be motivated by fear, envy, or hatred of women or may simply see women as available and accessible sexual objects whose attraction derives from their economic vulnerability within organizational hierarchies.[44]

The various types of harassment seem endless, with endless permutations. The harassment may be verbal, nonverbal, or physical. It may be sexual ("How about a little, hot lips?") or sex-based ("No woman is right for a man's job"). It can be sexual coercion, bribery, seductive behavior, imposition of a sexually offensive environment, or some combination of these. It may occur once or many times, in repeated or various guises, and in such disparate spheres as the military, the ministry, or marriage. It may be perpetrated by friends, lovers, acquaintances, or perfect strangers. And it may be a tolerable nuisance or something that devastates a career.[45] Disabled women, undocumented workers, and immigrants with limited English or limited knowledge of their civil rights are prime targets for a sexual harasser's manipulation and abuse. Supervisors have been known to threaten mandatory psychiatric evaluations of women to intimidate them into not complaining about their sexual harassment. New and creative forms of harassment follow cultural trends, particularly with the burst of activity across cyberspace. Internet harassers have been known to post on electronic bulletin boards insulting messages signed with the E-mail address of the person to be harassed. The victim is then bombarded with "flaming" responses from irate readers of the message. Persistent E-mail has replaced stalking as the sexual harassment of choice among many students facile with electronic communications.[46]

Although doctors, ministers, judges, therapists, professors, and coaches are typical of harassers in positions of authority within the professions, the strength for many feminists of a gendered analysis of sexual harassment is its perception that men do not require organizational dominance to dominate women successfully. The pervasiveness of men's sexual harassment of women inside and outside organizational contexts appears to be confirmed by statistics suggesting that anywhere from 30 percent to over 90 percent of women surveyed have been sexually harassed, depending upon the sample and the context. Indeed, feminists have argued that the normalization of sexual harassment, far from being a result of misreporting, misidentification, or misinterpretation by biased feminist researchers, contributes to its being *under*reported. Celia Kitzinger recognizes what she refers to as the "frequency double bind" of women's harassment when she notes that if sexual harassment is pervasive, then it is not treated seriously because it is simply "part of life." But if sexual harassment is not pervasive, then it is not taken seriously because it is not much of a problem.[47]

In summary, from this feminist perspective, sexual harassment is not merely an instance of moral impropriety best sorted out between private parties or an instance of isolated, unusual, or idiosyncratic sexual intimidation or abuse. It is an instance of a systemic and pervasive oppression of women, designed to reinforce male dominance over individual women and to maintain social control of the economic, political, and other cultural institutions of which both women and men are members. In a world where women are associated with the private sphere and men with the public one, bifurcating the personal from the political results in blaming women for their own sexual harassment, since by privatizing the harassment to find the impropriety, one finds the impropriety in women. This situates women as causally and morally responsible for the encounter by depoliticizing the gendered construction of the harassment. Instead of an aberrant and abusive manifestation of power, sexual harassment becomes a normal and natural expression of men's sexual desire whose unintentional misdirection can be nipped in the bud with a woman's simple and civil expression of displeasure. However, from the feminist perspective outlined here, failing a class or losing a job is not the result of either innocent flirtation or mild annoyance. Grabbing a girl's breasts in a crowded school hallway, yelling "Let me tune in Tokyo!" is not a private act meriting a good-humored response.[48] Since cultural institutions provide the context and legitimacy for sexual harassment, feminists who argue for a gendered reading of women's victimization assert that institutional, not just individual, remedies are required. Indeed, from this perspective, it is silence concerning the gender politics and organizational power that construct sexual harassment, not their publicity, that is the real victimizer of women. We can now turn to some of the criticisms of this conception of sexual harassment put forward by other feminists.

Fragile Flowers and Predatory Beasts:
Do Feminists Victimize Women?

What message are we sending if we say We can't work if you tell dirty jokes, it upsets us, it offends us?

—*Katie Roiphe*[49]

[S]exual harassment . . . is not a gender issue. It is our personal responsibility to define what we will and will not tolerate . . . . If Anita Hill was thrown for a loop by sexual banter, that's her problem.

—*Camille Paglia*[50]

ing, since it is not a show of power feminism to identify behavior as assault-ive where there is no obvious power imbalance. She would much rather encourage women to thrill over the "carnal recognition" of an attractive stranger's appreciative gaze than to shrink away at the possibility of his attack. In turn, Wolf advocates making finer distinctions between sexually inappropriate behavior and sexual harassment, since she is concerned that ambiguously worded definitions of sexual harassment blur the distinctions between real injury and bad manners. Wolf is a feminist who, unlike some who are critical of a gendered approach to sexual harassment, condemns any attempts to deny the existence of the patriarchal elements of individual men's sexual coercion and abuse of women in order to save women from a victim consciousness. She simply wants more women to see themselves as capable of thriving psychologically and sexually within a patriarchal mi-lieu.[55]

Rene Denfeld, on the other hand, criticizes gendered analyses of sexual assault precisely because she believes that they overstate the true severity and pervasiveness of men's violence and victimization of women.[56] In Denfeld's view, the wording of questions, the choices of respondents, and the interpretation of the data gathered in surveys of sexual assault can be designed by feminists to "reveal" precisely what they are looking for: a plague of intimidation and abuse that is "evidence" for the oppressive nature of patriarchy. According to Denfeld, such biased analyses contrib-ute to a debilitating "victim mythology" that paints a portrait of women as sexually naive and politically brainwashed creatures who believe that rape is good sex and that all heterosexual sex is assaultive. When women *say* they consent to sex, what this mythology interprets them to *mean* is that they were manipulated, cajoled, or coerced into having sex that they would not otherwise choose. As Denfeld wryly points out, "The blaring message is that women are too stupid to decide for themselves, just as in Victorian times when women were believed to be so pure they couldn't understand sexual relations."[57] Based on this mythology, women are doomed to be victims of physically and emotionally abusive men disguised as friends, lovers, husbands, and passing strangers, of whom women should live in a state of constant fear and trepidation, if not outright loath-ing. Denfeld points out that to define as sexual assault such behavior as leering, whistling, sexual jokes, and unexplained silent phone calls trivial-izes the real violation of rape and makes it virtually impossible to distinguish between rape, sexual harassment, inappropriate sexual behavior, and mere silliness.[58]

Denfeld laments that adopting a victim mythology means that "little discussion is paid to just what women can do to remedy the problem effectively."[59] When feminists say that sexual harassment is about power and not about sex, Denfeld hears feminism hearkening back to a Victorian era of social purity and sexual prudery when only the chastity of women could hope to stem the tide of male lust. This prudery is reinforced by date rape and sexual harassment prevention pamphlets, brochures, and educational programs, all designed, in Denfeld's opinion, to encourage a wariness of heterosexual sex and to embrace the identity of sexual victim. Like Wolf and Reardon, Denfeld would much rather encourage women to believe that they can really say "no" and mean it, particularly on college campuses where women's studies' emphasis on the gender politics of women's oppression appears to preach precisely the opposite. Indeed, according to Denfeld, we must begin teaching women that they can walk away from sexually undesirable circumstances in the knowledge that their "no" is respected. However, the Victorian daintiness, sexual naïveté, and social helplessness of women that a victim mythology advocates militates against such assertiveness, and the consequent stunting of women's heterosexual pleasure seeking, initiation, creativity, or exploration only insures women's continued sexual oppression.[60]

Denfeld is appalled that feminists would condemn women who participate in wet tee-shirt contests, beer guzzling, and alcohol-infused frat parties, since in Denfeld's mind, the feminist message is that bad girls cause rape by reinforcing a view of women as sexual objects. For Denfeld, this is simply more evidence that creative and responsible sex play is out and sexual prudery, purity, and passivity are in. She wants women to start telling leering men to "bug off," and to start admitting that they really do consent to sex despite sometimes regretting it the next day. Feminists should be telling women to watch their alcohol consumption and to take self-defense classes, instead of condemning consensual sex and diluting rape amid a sea of sexual misconduct that a self-consciously strong-willed and sexually confident woman can handle.[61]

Ellen Frankel Paul would agree with Denfeld, since Paul observes that putting rape in the same category as "offensive looks" or "witnessing unwelcome sexual overtures directed at others" only confuses the issue of sexual assault, reduces the value of statistical surveys, and makes us all into victims.[62] Paul feels it is absolutely necessary to make fine distinctions among cases because there is a lot of morally inappropriate behavior that may be considered "inconveniences of life" but is not the sort of conduct that should be a violation of the law. Like many feminists critical of a gendered analysis of sexual harassment, Paul believes that the feminist ideological commitment to expose male dominance in every nook and cranny encourages blurring the difference between being harmed by men and merely being offended by them. In Paul's opinion, encouraging the exercise of a right not to be offended, and giving this right equal moral and legal legitimacy with the right not to be harmed, will only result in a loss of liberty and privacy. With such a wide and ambiguous range of conduct considered harassing, people will no longer feel free to express themselves in the workplace or on campus overtly and unself-consciously, and courts will be overwhelmed with lawsuits designed to adjudicate people's private sexual lives.[63]

What Paul suggests is that women should suffer in silence, complain, or move on, but refrain from whining about the "envy, personal grudges, infatuation and jilted loves" that are part and parcel of ordinary workplaces. Since no workplace is stress free, Paul advises women to "develop a thick skin" and "dispense a few risqué barbs" now and then to male would-be provocateurs. This will insure that women are not perceived as weak kneed and unable to take the workplace churlishness that, as feminists, we ought to be trying to convince our coworkers we can handle. If women want equality in the workplace, then Paul suggests we should identify those specific behaviors worthy of in-house opprobrium and discipline and those that women are simply going to have to tolerate. Paul claims that tolerating sexual behavior in the workplace will be a whole lot easier once women "lighten up" in their attitudes about sexual offense. Indeed, according to Paul, once men recognize that women are not as vulnerable to harassment as men may think, the thrill of the intimidation (and, by implication, its practice) will cease.[64]

Daphne Patai and Noretta Koertge have worries similar to Paul's about feminists encouraging women to believe that they have a right not to be offended. By threatening an alleged harasser with loss of a job, academic post, or promotion or with costly fines and worse (not to mention lawsuits slapped on employers and universities for back pay and damages), those who would exercise this dubious right against an ambiguously defined practice are bound to promote censorship and self-censorship.[65] Like Denfeld and Wolf, Patai and Koertge find the feminist ideological agenda described in the previous section to suffer from an identity politics that seeks political advantage for women qua oppressed group. In adopting this identity, women's studies classes offer students an antimale and victimizing message that requires women's suffering from sexism, if not sexual assault, as the necessary condition of group affiliation with the class "women."

According to Patai and Koertge, the danger here is that women who have not suffered in the requisite ways will feel compelled to participate in some fashion in the sufferings and injustices of women. Such participation can become projective identification that then tempts the participants to invent grievances in order to qualify as sustaining members of that group.[66] The invented grievances then skew statistical surveys and inform the kinds of false charges that men who are keen to rationalize their sexual harassment can use to undermine women's credibility. Indeed, in the view of Patai and Koertge, if feminists are going to argue that given the debilitating process of accusation, women simply will not lie about their sexual harassment, the risk that a feminist identity politics will encourage many women to misrepresent men's sexual conduct is a serious one. From this critical perspective, the more outrage feminists encourage in women over sexual harassment, the more individual women will find it in their group-identified interests to make false or frivolous accusations, which will only weaken both the bona fide cases of sexual harassment and women's credibility as a class.[67]

Moreover, Patai and Koertge point out that balkanization of women's studies classes into special interest groups segregated by race, ethnicity, class, sexual orientation, or physical ability tends to create conflict when an individual with membership in more than one group seeks to cross ideological lines. According to this view, black feminists will inevitably clash with more traditional black women, and lesbian feminists will clash with lesbians who do not consider themselves feminists, even though the purpose of culture-specific interest groups is to gain solidarity and strength from within. Thus, Patai and Koertge are convinced that unless feminists can eliminate the dogma and intolerance from their political agenda, feminists will succeed in dividing the movement without any help from men.[68]

Christina Sommers would add to this warning her profound reservations about the increasingly totalitarian grip that women's studies faculty and students have on campus pedagogy and administrative policy. She notes that in women's studies classes, men can be made to feel responsible for all of the ills ever visited on women. Instead of women being silenced, men are interrupted, not listened to, patronized, insulted, and vilified— hardly, Sommers reminds us, the picture of feminist egalitarianism. Indeed, for Sommers, it is quite clearly a picture of the gender harassment of men.[69] Women's studies faculty respond that *they* are the harassed ones, treated to ever greater intimidation and verbal abuse by male students who write cruel evaluations, take exception to the professor's every generalization, dominate discussions, and never agree with anything the professor says. Sommers would contend that *not* to allow students to do these things would be to violate their own freedom of expression in the classroom, which, according to Sommers, seems to be precisely what women's studies faculty would prefer. Women's studies faculty argue that men's contentiousness in the classroom is simply an expression of deep-seated prejudice, resistance, or fear and, as such, should not be tolerated. However, Sommers would ask women's studies faculty to differentiate censorship from expressing concern over expression; this differentiation, Sommers believes, is too often lost when well-intentioned male students say something in class or on paper that offends the feminist sensibilities of their professors.[70]

For Sommers, women's studies academics on college campuses tend to be intolerant and dogmatic ideologues who are prejudiced and mean-spirited in the classroom and a powerful and organized lobby outside it. They take advantage of academic freedom to retain control over how women's studies courses and programs are managed. Instead of being interested in critical scholarship and careful scrutiny of their feminist platform, such feminists appear to Sommers to be interested solely in academic power and control, ironically echoing the alleged megalomania of their more traditional male colleagues. According to Sommers, the students that are graduated from women's studies programs are predictably ideologues themselves, who form "defense guard" groups to target alleged harassers on campus. Sommers finds their physical and psychological intimidation tactics the worst form of vigilantism, particularly when such students have been persuaded by doctrinaire feminists that men's sexual violation of women is pervasive and endemic to male power. In an environment where "offensive" conduct can mean so much and so little all at once, many male professors accused of harassment have no way of identifying, or defending against, their alleged wrongdoing and are compelled to pay high lawyers' fees simply to insure their own academic credibility. Women's studies faculty respond that feminist academics continue to be the victims of "intellectual harassment" by colleagues and students alike who dismiss feminist scholarship as "not rigorous enough" to warrant serious attention.[71]

Like Patai, Koertge, and Denfeld, Sommers believes that many feminists' intolerance of positions other than those confirming their own identity politics is exposed in the methodology and interpretation of their social research on sexual assault. Sommers contends that samples are often small, self-selected, and interpreted to suggest a prevalence of sexual victimization that is not borne out by the data collected.[72] When girls are discovered to sexually harass boys or other girls in large numbers, many feminists argue that girls suffer more from their harassment than boys do. But Sommers points out that girls may simply be better socialized than boys to express their discomfort, to be aware of their feelings, and to be accurate in reporting negative emotions. In one Harris survey of gradeschool students underwritten by the American Association of University Women Educational Foundation, many students thought that too many behaviors were being counted as harassing. Sommers notes that instead of reformulating the questions, the researchers saw this reaction as evidence of just how "normalized" sexual harassment had become in the students' lives. Instead of focusing on how patriarchy causes sexual violence against women, Sommers suggests that feminists look at whatever it is that causes all of the violent crime in the nation, since countries much more patriarchal than the United States seem to have much lower crime rates and since both gay and straight women can be brutally violent.[73]

Sommers also accuses so-called gender feminists of trying to have their cake and eat it too. That is, they use women's first-person experience to confirm sexual victimization and deny women's first-person experience when it does not fit the appropriate gender politics. According to Sommers, when feminists can twist any conduct they like to suit their political agenda, artistic creativity and freedom of expression are stifled by the fear of lawsuits in the very educational and cultural communities where such expression should be thriving in a liberal democracy. When Old Master paintings and family photos make their viewers uncomfortable, to claim to be harassed by such a display is itself harassing, Sommers believes, for there are much less hostile and confrontational ways of dealing with differences of aesthetic taste.[74] Sommers joins those critics mentioned above who claim that as long as feminists refuse to distinguish between offensiveness and real offense, their use of gender politics to identify the wrong of sexual harassment will continue to alienate and disempower the very women it is meant to serve.

Katie Roiphe is in much the same ideological camp as Christina Sommers and Rene Denfeld, especially when Roiphe criticizes sexual assault surveys in which the feminist researcher, not the respondent, characterizes the respondent's experience as harassing. According to Roiphe, when feminists think they know better than the rest of us about what "really" happens in our workplaces, on our dates, and in our classrooms, a sexual assault epidemic becomes a matter of ideological decision, not evidentiary proof. As rape and sexual harassment crisis rhetoric becomes increasingly vociferous, the flames of an oppressive patriarchy are fanned. Like Denfeld, Roiphe condemns rape and sexual harassment brochures for making women into victims by stereotyping men as predators and all women as their prey. Women are admonished to want only gentle, egalitarian, tender, and respectful sex (if they want any sex at all), while men are described as consumed by sexual desire that, at the very best, expresses men's ambivalence toward women.[75]

However, Roiphe contends that it is foolish to expect, or want, sex to be either unambiguous or egalitarian when its unpredictability and volatility are a part of its eroticism. Indeed, like Naomi Wolf, Roiphe believes that pressure, cajoling, and manipulation by both genders are a fact of life, so why make a special case against sex? From this perspective, sex without power, struggle, persuasion, or pursuit is "utopian."[76] Moreover, when we ask women to be "clear" with men about what their sexual needs are from the outset, it reinforces the very gatekeeper mentality that makes it easy to blame women for men's sexual irresponsibility. In such a scenario, women say "yes" only when they have to (like Denfeld's Victorian women) and men have only one purpose and goal in life, namely, to "get some." In addition to depicting women as unable to identify their own violation, despite being the perennial victims of it, feminism "peddles images of gender relations that deny female desire and infantilize women,"[77] a picture made additionally paradoxical by the characterization of women as the more sexually mature, albeit repressed, of the two genders. Roiphe contends that if feminists assumed women had basic competency, free will, and strength of character, there would not be the barrage of ground rules and political hype surrounding the issue of sexual assault. However, Roiphe argues that the messages women are being sent by feminist educators are that women cannot take care of themselves (they need sexual harassment policy administrators to do their dirty work); that women cannot make decisions with a clear head (women do not know assault when they feel it); and that women are vulnerable babes in a wood inhabited by rakish wolves ready to pounce at the first available opportunity. According to Roiphe, such messages institutionalize female weakness rather than combat it.[78]

In fact, Roiphe is convinced that a good share of young women's fears of sexual assault are actually fears about cultural mixing, about whether the "bad boys" from the other side of the tracks will try to get too close. According to Roiphe, if we continue to insist on the merits of a multicultural and increasingly diverse community, we should expect more sexual miscommunication, not less, as people of very different social backgrounds meet and wrestle with the "sex" question. Roiphe believes that much of the adolescent unease that many campus coeds experience over their relatively new sexual freedom gets transferred onto male students and professors, which may then account for some of the worries over sexual harassment voiced in dormitories. Moreover, if sexual assault is reduced to any kind of sex that a woman experiences as negative, even well after the fact, as Roiphe contends campus date rape brochures suggest, then rape itself is diluted, and unmannerly behavior is raised to the status of the legally actionable. Indeed, in Roiphe's opinion, to equate being raped by a stranger at knifepoint with being verbally coerced by a boyfriend with such taunts as "I'll break up with you if you don't" or "Everyone's doing it" is ludicrous.[79]

So too, if sexual harassment is merely equivalent to unwanted sexual behavior, then, Roiphe believes, we will all be sexually harassed, since "[t]o find wanted sexual attention, you have to give and receive a certain amount of unwanted attention."[80] With the swath of sexual harassment cut so wide, it is no wonder that the mere fact of being a man is enough to turn a woman into a quivering bowl of Jell-O. Roiphe clearly resents a gender politics that would give any man the de facto power to "plow through social hierarchies, grabbing what he wants, intimidating all the cowering female[s]" in his path.[81] For Roiphe, it is the ultimate in insult to presume that men have some sort of primal power that is greater than women's, so that any of our hard-won social authority can be instantaneously undermined with one good male stare. She thinks ogling, leering, and sexual innuendo are trivial affairs made intimidating by a feminist rhetoric that confuses being a jerk with being injurious. But once sexual harassment becomes a pervasive part of everyone's experience, it becomes impossible to make the distinction; indeed, sexual intimidation becomes a fact of life. Conversely, to remove all offensive conduct from campuses and workplaces would remove so much of contemporary sexual banter as to make work and campus life sterile. According to Roiphe, professors' fears of frivolous charges of sexual harassment have all but eliminated the intense personal exchanges of intellectual firepower that were once staples of office hours, tutorials, and late-night coffeehouse conversation between a male professor and his female students. If women's academic work suffers, Roiphe believes that it is feminists' destructive gender politics, not lecherous professors, that is to blame.[82]

Like the other critics discussed above, Roiphe would call for less vague and inclusive sexual harassment policies and would eliminate most hostile environment harassment from the behavior prohibited, since current conceptions give women too little credit for telling men where to shove it and too much room to prohibit the uncomfortable. Roiphe agrees with the theme of playwright David Mamet's *Oleanna,* which warns that feminists "will conjure up the sexist beast if they push far enough."[83] If we make campus women distraught over the least compliment, Roiphe wonders what they will do outside dormitory walls in the big, cruel world where sexist beasts lurk in much greater numbers. As Reardon, Paul, and Wolf have advocated, Roiphe wants feminists to train women to deal with "the difficult, the uncomfortable, and the even mildly distasteful" aspects of adult relationships, rather than try to expurgate those aspects by complaining to ethics review boards. Hysterical, sobbing victims are a far cry from the women of fortitude, conviction, and sexual savvy that Roiphe regards as her feminist role models.[84]

Sexual savvy is also right up Camille Paglia's alley—indeed, without it, according to Paglia, women will end up in beds they would rather not have slept in and will have no one to blame but themselves. For Paglia, personal responsibility and self-defense are keys to women's successful sexual liberation; otherwise, men will take full advantage of women's naïveté, if not stupidity, about sex and make the most of it. Indeed, according to Paglia, women live in a world of constant sexual danger because "[h]unt, pursuit, and capture are biologically programmed into male sexuality."[85] Paglia believes that we can still teach men that sexual assault and intimidation are wrong, so that we can hold them responsible for their violent sexual behavior. Nevertheless, women cannot expect to get drunk in men's apartments, have sex they wish they hadn't, and then blame men for it. As far as Paglia is concerned, flirting, drinking, and visiting a man's room alone constitute consent to "going all the way." Verbal forms of consent in the heat of passion are misguided, in her view, since sexual signals are often so subtle and subliminal that translating these signals into verbal language is a losing proposition. While Roiphe believes that verbal negotiations "from the first moment on" sterilize the sexual encounter, Paglia is convinced that women need to give clear, upfront messages as to what their sexual wishes are; they simply shouldn't wait until they are half-drunk to do it.[86]

From Paglia's point of view, feminists ought to be teaching women more than just prudence and caution; women must learn to own up to their own mistakes. Women who ignore men's "aggressive, unstable, combustible" sexuality and get caught in men's clutches ought to be blamed for their own obvious lack of self-awareness about men and sex.[87] Men are not going to change, in Paglia's opinion, so women must be ready for them. Even rape is not the end of the world, she admonishes, so pick yourself up and move on.

The important point is to recognize that women, after all, have the real power, a "cosmic sexual power" that men both envy and fear. Paglia is convinced that men carry with them into adulthood a sense of infantile dependency on women, such that any hint of returning to that state drives men crazy. Those hints turn blatant more often than not, according to Paglia, when women mercilessly tease, test, compare, flirt, and self-consciously hem and haw, quite often only to reject men, who can do nothing more than harass, show off, and brawl—or murder, as O. J. Simpson was alleged to have done. But feminists, according to Paglia, don't like to acknowledge women's power over men because it means acknowledging that not all women are benevolent, nurturing, and sexually forgiving; some women have "kinky tastes," and some women *like* being beaten up. The inevitable power plays in sex and the potential dangers accompanying them are real, but they are also part of the thrill of sex. For Paglia, sexual risk is where the "sizzle" is.[88]

In Paglia's view, much of the whimpering about men's apparent sexual insensitivity comes from middle-class, white girls whose antiseptic socialization and parental pampering make them totally unprepared for the onslaught of male lust. When they complain about sexual assault, they are simply working out their own neuroses about sex. (Recall Roiphe's complaint about campus coeds displacing their own sexual insecurities onto their professors.) According to Paglia, women of color or working-class women come from cultures that are much more open and realistic about sex, which accounts for the fact that the date rape furor is an overwhelmingly middle-class, white girl thing.[89] Paglia believes that the credibility of real sexual assault charges will inevitably erode when women refuse to acknowledge that they get themselves into messes when they should have known better. When women begin to see sex as driven by ego and a desire for dominance, they will be able to protect themselves more effectively.[90]

Paglia believes that sexual harassment guidelines are essential to put potential offenders on notice and to help women identify their harassers. She also believes that false charges are brought with enough regularity to warrant stiff and formal penalties for false accusations. To warrant sexual harassment charges, Paglia requires some sort of identifiable threat, pressure, or coercion associated with a blatant abuse of power. Thus, she regards Anita Hill's complaints of verbal harassment by Clarence Thomas as no more than moralizing whines for women's special treatment in the workplace, when, as feminists, we ought to be asking for *equal* treatment. According to Paglia, the real feminist heroines are the ones who sacrifice their jobs to make public their harassment. Because Hill waited years to tell the world about her run-ins with Thomas, until she was out of range of his retaliation, Paglia regards Hill's public humiliation of Thomas over some dirty language and crude invitations to be the height of feminist arrogance.[91]

In Paglia's view, campus grievance committees do not have the legal bite needed to handle assault charges. Paglia would much prefer that women who have been abused by sexually violent men go straight to the police or take men to court, since this keeps campus administrations out of the business of legislating private behavior. Consultants and specialists in the field of formulating campus policies on rape and sexual harassment are often poorly trained and "schoolmarmish" in their attitudes about sex. Indeed, sexual harassment that does not involve physical violence is, in Paglia's opinion, inappropriately legislated against precisely because it is a private affair that two responsible adults ought to be able to work out. Even terrorist-style sexual stalking is a matter for women to deal with outside the courts, since restraining orders, Paglia believes, only exacerbate the pursuit. In her estimation, legal systems that try to tell women and men how to negotiate their personal relationships smack of totalitarianism.[92]

Like Roiphe, Paglia is concerned that the feminist focus on sexual assault in the workplace and on campus portrays women as defenseless on their own, in need of special protection by those supposedly more powerful and authoritative than women are. Like Patai, Koertge, and Sommers, Paglia notes that feminists can be victimizers themselves when their own opportunism becomes wrapped up in a reactionary, repressive, puritanical political agenda. Like Reardon, Wolf, and Paul, Paglia wants more women to fight like men and take their hits like men, so that they can succeed like men. She asserts that there is little more than "primitive egotism and animality ever-simmering behind [the] social controls" of both women's and men's conduct. Yet Paglia bristles at making rape the paradigm of heterosexuality, since she believes that such a paradigm only succeeds in reducing women to helpless victims.[93]

According to Paglia, since men's egotism and animality will otherwise rule the day, women must set the tone for how they wish to be treated in any context. However, if women set the tone in the workplace with genteel standards of decorum, they will not succeed in climbing their way up the corporate ladder. Whereas Ellen Frankel Paul believes that no workplace is stress free, Paglia asserts that work engenders hostility because rank competition for scarce positions at the top of the corporate hierarchy engenders "head-on crashes." Indeed, in her view, workplaces that are pleasant and stress-free are not as productive, creative, or profitable as those driven by the anxiety of being only as good as your last performance, which is why women ought to get off their high horses (if they are on them) and get down and dirty with the rest of the guys. Decrying crude or rude language, even *Playboy* calendars or magazines, is not showing a world of cutthroat competition that women *can* cut it and *can* take care of themselves in the process. Paglia concludes that sexual harassment is a class issue, since professional women often disdain soft-porn centerfolds in men's sweaty locker rooms but sigh appreciatively over men's bourgeois collections of fine art prints depicting female nudes.[94]

Paglia joins Patai, Koertge, and Roiphe in their strong belief that words should not be policed, especially since forbidding the expression of social resentment is bound to push it underground or make it even more sexually exciting because taboo. Women's sensuality—their perfume, lacquered nails, silks, and high heels—is going to disrupt the workplace anyway, so

Paglia advises women to recognize the sexual power they have and use it. According to Paglia, some girls can and do sexually harass their male teachers precisely because such girls know how to use their power over men. If women in positions of organizational power are beginning to harass men, for Paglia this is only proof of her belief that power relations generate their own eroticism and that "hierarchy can never be desexed." With more public libido and less public whining about crude men, Paglia believes that women will thrive in a milieu that exposes men, not women, for their sexual vulnerability.[95] Paglia gives voice to all of the critics named above in challenging feminists to make women's sexuality a site of celebration and empowerment and to refrain from casting women into a mold of fragility and hypersensitivity conducive to their victimization by men.

Reconstructing a Feminist Dialogue: The Sexual Politics, Process, and Dialectic of Sexual Harassment

[W]hether you see sexual harassment, what you see, and how you interpret that view is a function of who you are and where you are in the organization.

—*Eleanor K. Bratton*[96]

We are well served by creating a new vocabulary for the relative nature of harm, a vocabulary that makes room for the fact that a woman's choice and vulnerability, a man's authority and power, are not always constants.

—*Naomi Wolf*[97]

Feminists responding to the critical claims described in the preceding section argue that such claims falsely attribute to a gendered analysis of sexual harassment an antisex, antimale bias that determines women to be the sexual victims of men's rapacious lust. It is argued that critics misreport the motives and misinterpret the findings of feminist researchers on sexual harassment and make false generalizations about women, men, and feminists, all of which recreate the very victimization that critics accuse other feminists of reinforcing. Feminists critical of the notion that sexual harassment is a paradigm of the patriarchal oppression of women are themselves criticized for being too quick to dismiss the economic and sexual vulnerability of women, investing in women a power to confront their harassers that many, if not most, women simply do not have. It is contended that the relatively few women who harass other women and men do so because they have adopted patriarchal values of status and privilege, which require the manipulation and control of others. From this perspective, without a continuum of sexual violence and victimization with which to conjoin sexual abuse, sexual harassment, and rape, women will not recognize sexual harassment as anything more than the isolated, spontaneous, and entirely natural expression of men's sexual desire. To ask women to take "personal responsibility" for a crime against women as a class whose members do not welcome or request their sexual violation strikes many feminists to be the height of insensitivity and arrogance.[98]

I agree that feminists who are skeptical of a gendered analysis of sexual harassment undervalue the important political exposure such an analysis gives to men's sexual oppression of women. But I also believe that the kinds of feminist responses enumerated in the immediately preceding paragraph have the unintended effect of stalling any discussion that would advance the dialogue among feminists of differing perspectives, since the critics discussed in the previous section continue to stand their ground in defiant repudiation of their own critics' contentions. The inevitable result has been the alienation of feminists from one another and the inability of many women who might otherwise call themselves feminists to feel they can identify with a movement advocating such apparently single-minded and irreconcilable views on either side. Therefore, in this section, I wish to offer a characterization of sexual harassment that embraces the tensions among competing feminist perspectives in order to further discussion concerning sexual harassment and inform future debate among feminists and nonfeminists. This tactic requires that I retain the political medium within which sexual harassment is understood in its larger cultural and organizational context but nuance the gendered message to negotiate the competing feminist perspectives enumerated in the previous sections.

Specifically, I wish to retain the power dynamic that underlies the institutionalization of sexual harassment but expand upon the sexual dynamic that informs the wide variety of motivations for, reactions to, and experiences of sexual harassment. I wish to replace a continuum of sexual violence and victimization with overlapping conceptual and normative frames of sexual violation, in order to flesh out the variety in sexual harassment, the incommensurability of its severity, and the phenomenological similarity of types. With this framework, I also wish to underscore the interpretive process by which assessments of sexual harassment, informed by race, class, gender, sexual orientation, age, physical ability, and other social locations, are generated and regenerated over time. I will also describe the phenomenon of women's sexual harassment as a dialectical process of sexual politics in which women can be both the sexual objects of an oppressive patriarchy and the self-identified subjects of their own sexual lives. In this way, the organizational hierarchies and cultural stereotypes that circumscribe women's sexual harassment can be understood as informing and facilitating, instead of essentializing and determining, men's sexual violation and victimization of women. My ultimate aim is to provide a characterization that is "messy" enough to accommodate the variety of experiences of, the ambivalence of reactions to, and the contradiction in assessments of sexual harassment, at the same time that it is "neat" enough to guide women and men in understanding what sexual harassment is and what is wrong with it for the purposes of legislating against harassing behavior and formulating social policy.

The Power of Sexual Stereotypes and the Sexiness of Power

When feminists say that sexual harassment is about power, and not about sex, feminists tend to underplay how the *sexualization of women* in the context of harassment informs and elucidates the dominance and control of women. In the absence of a discussion of the ways in which cultural beliefs shared by both women and men fuse gender, sexuality, and power, feminists make men the predators in the game of gender politics but fail to include gender in an assessment of sexual politics. When beliefs such as "Power is sexy" and "Sex is all about power" are understood as part of the social construction of sexual harassment, complaints that sexual harassment is invasive or violative are not the complaints of moralizing prudes who would remove all sex from public discussion. Such complaints become reflections of the ways in which the sexual stereotypes associated with women and men of various cultural backgrounds encourage the specifically *sexual* harassment of women by men. A *sexually* harassed woman does not find a rubber chicken on her computer keyboard; she finds a rubber dildo. A red painted voodoo doll, or even a Barbie doll, is not what a sexually harassed woman sees hanging from her overhead projector; she sees a red painted tampon. She might gladly lend her boss her new golf clubs for a first chance at a cover story but not lend him her body. These distinctions are important in a culture where men can use sex as an instrument of power over, and control of, women. This is accomplished by taking advantage of pervasive and often contradictory sexual stereotypes that circumscribe women's and men's behavioral expectations in contemporary Western culture: Men chase and women retreat; men dominate and women submit. Sex turns men into "studs" and women into "whores" (who cannot get enough). Women are the proper and unconditional sexual objects of men's use and abuse. Women who do not ultimately accept men's sexual advances are sexual neurotics (frigid, lesbian, paranoid). Sex is pleasurable, playful, and fun, but women have to be talked into "feeling okay" about liking it.

Boys' sexual objectification of girls is reinforced by such stereotypes and confirms in boys' minds their own sense of sexual dominance. Boys who grab at, stalk, tease, and pull down the pants of teenage girls just discovering a sexual identity are communicating to such girls that their sexuality is accessible to boys without regard to what the girls want. Such conduct reinforces girls' lack of entitlement in the classroom, where intellect is divorced from sex, and confirms their belief that girls' sexuality must be gate-guarded from men's uncontrollable urges.[99]

When a female aviator at the 1991 Tailhook Convention in Las Vegas voiced her support for women flying combat missions, Navy men accused the aviator of having sex with senior officers on carrier assignments. This type of accusation is specifically designed to humiliate and marginalize ambitious working women by painting them as salacious seductresses who cannot get to the top without sleeping their way up there. The ad feminam harassment by the Tailhook conventioneers thus served to delegitimize the aviator's position on women in combat. At the same time, the sexual "gauntlets" in which women's clothes were literally torn from their bodies before they could walk down a convention hotel hallway were regarded as "spontaneous" fun and "no big deal" by several of the men involved. Women deemed sexually unattractive were rated aloud with a "wave off" that would leave them untouched yet humiliated, a paradoxical form of the sexualization of women through their desexualization, with degrading effects no less painful than those suffered by their groped colleagues.[100]

Faculty women who have supported female students' sexual harassment claims have also become topics of sexual discussion as a way of dismissing their agendas. Like the Tailhook men's denunciations of the female flyer, questioning female faculty's sexual propriety is designed to delegitimize women's support of claims that men do not wish to acknowledge (Is she having a lesbian affair with her student? What are her relations with men? How provocatively does *she* dress?). I find it additionally frustrating that I have been dubbed "one of the guys" by several of my heterosexual male friends, who mean it as a compliment for being accessible, good-natured, and nonthreatening; yet this communicates to me that if they sexualized me, they could not treat me as one of them, that is, as a professional and moral equal.

Indeed, complaints of sexual harassment may arise simply from the introduction of sexuality into an otherwise asexual environment, as a graduate student does when he places a photo of his bikini-clad wife on a desk shared by other female graduate students.[101] I suggest that these women complain of being sexually harassed, because they feel their intellectual professionalism has been delegitimized in the service of their cultural image as sexual objects. A photo of the graduate student's wife playing with their children on the beach would not have this same effect; while women also suffer from a stereotype as domestic and reproductive subordinates, their domestic responsibilities may complicate, but do not eviscerate, their professional status the way their sexual stereotype does. These graduate women are no moralizing prudes, nor are they believers in the predatory "nature" of their male office mate. These are women who, like the women at Tailhook, live with a culture-specific, socially constructed gender identity the content of whose sexual stereotype assumes women's accessibility and subordination to men.

To say that women can "choose" to ignore such stereotypes by "choosing" not to believe their content is too facile, since it is not a matter of what these particular women believe. What matters here is that these stereotypes provide recognizable sexual standards by which other women and men will measure and formulate their own attitudes and behavior. The female aviator's position on women in combat was effectively delegitimized, not because she "allowed" herself to be humiliated by the other conventioneers, but because the cultural milieu in which their comments were addressed provided an ideological framework for her harassment. So too, the women who feel harassed by the bikini photo may not think of themselves as unconditionally sexually available to men, but they know that men other than the one who displayed the photo, particularly other male students who may come by for office hours, either believe this or would like to believe this, if given permission. Indeed, campus undergraduates may find the photo less harassing than their graduate or employed counterparts because they see their environment as legitimate grounds for "checking out" the sexually available "goods."[102]

Power can be sexy to those at the bottom looking up, as when social climbing women associate men's wealth and professional status with men's sexual attraction. Conversely, vulnerability may be sexy to those at the top looking down. John Bargh and Paula Raymond suggest that men's institutionalized authority automatically and nonconsciously triggers thinking in terms of sex toward those women whom they harass.[103] Indeed, feminists have argued that it is a woman's economic vulnerability that makes her easy prey for sexually harassing men who can threaten loss of her job for reporting or complaining about harassment. When she smiles in deference to his position in the organizational hierarchy, he may understand her friendliness as approval of his sexual flirtation or advances. This understanding is exacerbated by specifically sexual myths about women, which assert that women really do want men's sexual attentions but that feminine propriety (recall the "slut" stereotype) precludes women from being forthcoming about it. Such myths also make it easy for men accused of sexual harassment to turn the tables and say that women provoked their own harassment by dating several men at the office, telling dirty jokes, wearing "provocative" clothing (and woe be it to the woman who doesn't!), or simply flirting—which, as noted above, can translate into nothing more than acting with appropriate helpfulness and congeniality. Indeed, a male harasser's organizational power may make him think of himself as sexy, if only because he believes that women will find him attractive in virtue of it.

I would add to this analysis, however, that much of men's sexual harassment of female peers or coworkers is motivated not by women's vulnerability but by their apparent power to threaten men by their presence, as intellectual or workplace competitors. This does not always include a perception of the threatening and raw sexual power that Camille Paglia says women have at their disposal, although it does involve a sexualization of women. Many harassers, whether in positions of organizational power or not, harass particular women because men perceive them as *not* sexually desirable or available when men think they ought to be—this is the complaint of many elderly women, gay women, or women whom men unilaterally decide to "wave off," and smart young girls with no sexual maturity

at all are the objects of genital touching by boys who would rather com-
pete in ways that put them "on top."

I would further suggest that much harassment of women is based on
men's presumption of women's sexual accessibility to them, undergirded
by the sexual stereotype of women as "fair game," and not solely, or even
primarily, on the organizational authority to which Bargh and Raymond
refer. African American women may be particularly vulnerable to this presumption by white men whose stereotype of black women as voracious
sexual animals may make them eager to try sex out "with a black chick."[104]
Thus, when feminists say that sexual harassment is about power, not about
sex, they lose the complex *sexual* politics, played out in gender expectations across cultural lines, that organizational politics can hide. Indeed,
because sexualizing women in a public context can degrade women by
telling women what they are "really good for" and can humiliate women
by publicizing what so-called good girls are supposed to keep private, men
who wish to "put women in their place" will have an especially useful
tool in *sexual* harassment. This humiliation is particularly painful when a
woman's sexuality is reexposed in the courtroom or in front of a board of
policy administrators.

Moreover, men may threaten women by sexual harassment, because
women are vulnerable to sexual violence by men in ways that men as a
class are not; thus, women are disproportionately victims of sexual assault.
Women who have sex with men are "knocked up," "nailed," or
"strapped," and this is supposed to be when women are having fun! Men
in positions of power may also manipulate those whom they feel are their
own to do with as they wish. If they deem women to be sexual objects,
the manipulation will be in the form of sexual coercion, bribery, E-mail
stalking, or other forms of hostile environment sexual harassment against
which women may feel helpless once the incidents have occurred. In sexual harassment, to remind a woman of her sexuality is to remind her of
her vulnerability to whatever a man wants to "dish out."[105]

Starting from grade school, many boys see sexual harassment as a rite of
passage to manhood, which shows them to be sexually aggressive, provocative, daring, "macho." If masculinity is associated not simply with dominance but with heterosexual dominance, it will not be enough to trash a
girl's locker; a boy must lift up her skirt, make kissing noises at her, or
trash her locker with pinup photos. If men are more likely to *sexually* harass women than women are to harass men (remember the rubber dildo

and not the rubber chicken), it is because of the way many men are taught to think about their (hetero)sexuality, namely, as a vehicle for expressing power and authority over women. Even young women use female sexual epithets like "bitch" and "ho' " in an attempt to harass boys who irritate them, a sorry commentary on their own status as women.[106]

However, women are much less notorious and successful than men at peer harassment precisely because women are not well socialized to think of men, nor men to think of themselves, as women's sexual objects. Indeed, women's heterosexual initiative must be culturally repressed, if men are to define the terms and conditions of the encounter and so reap the rewards of their own sexual initiative. At the same time, this gender role-playing encourages women's view that "men only think with their dicks."[107] Catharine MacKinnon observes of this discrepancy, "[W]omen are defined as gender female by sexual accessibility to men . . . . Sexual harassment makes of women's sexuality a badge of female servitude." Indeed, for MacKinnon, unless we isolate the *sexual* in sexual harassment, thus locating the *sexism* of the sexual stereotype of women, we will not identify the *gender* inequality that is prohibited by law.[108] By contrast, gender stereotypes that associate masculinity with heterosexuality inform men's actions with the presumption of sexual access to women and of gender status when that access occurs. This presumption explains why some men will not identify women's leers, sexual gestures, crude jokes, *Playgirl* calendars, or persistent requests for dates as anything more than a reaffirmation of men's sexual desirability as men. It also explains the fact that when men do feel harassed, more men than women will see themselves as capable of fighting back with treatment in kind, direct confrontation, reports to authorities, or lawsuits, wondering why women will not do the same.

When a woman charges sexual harassment due to favoritism resulting from a coworker's sexual relationship with her boss, what is being charged is that a woman's sexual relationship has conferred an unfair power advantage to her. If feminists talk about examples of sexual harassment such as this one and those detailed above in terms of power and not sex, we lose the ways in which women's sexuality is invested with both the power of seduction and the powerlessness of sexual objectification. On the other hand, if we talk about sexual harassment in terms of sex but not power, women are blamed for men's sexual faux pas in that women are accused of being conniving seductresses who would delude others into thinking they are sexual innocents. My strategy is to talk in terms of the sexual stereotypes that inform the cultural context of sexual harassment, in order to understand the complex relations between gender, sexuality, and power that circumscribe harassing conduct. Submerging the sexual element for fear of "privatizing" and "normalizing" the harassment means that we lose these important relationships. Sexual harassment is about sex because it is about how sexuality can empower some and disempower others; the sexual harassment of women by men is the relegation of women as a class to an inferior status by sexualizing women.

However, this is not to say that sexualizing women always reduces them to subordinates of men. Clearly, women have as much to gain in pleasure and creativity by being sexual subjects as they have to lose by being sexual objects; and both women and men will measure themselves against sexual stereotypes that will affect individuals of different cultural backgrounds and personalities in different ways. To say that men participate in and maintain cultural institutions that oppress women as a class is not the same as saying that every man is a harasser, sexual abuser, or rapist, or even that all men dominate all women. Indeed, since a small minority of men, who repeatedly harass women, seem to constitute the majority of offenders, the sexual stereotypes described here must be understood as circumscribing social behavior under conditions that reinforce and facilitate, but do not dictate or determine, the sexual harassment of women. Thus, I am not, in Katie Roiphe's words, putting an "absolute value on the leer";[109] rather, I am talking about the various possibilities and the potentialities for sexual violation within a framework of socialized gender expectations, so that I may broaden and deepen the discourse on sexual harassment. Re-situating the *sex* in *sexual* harassment can then serve the purpose of negotiating the tensions between feminists who favor a gendered analysis and feminists concerned about an antimale, antisex, and victimizing bias in that analysis, while recognizing the legitimacy of gender politics in discussions of sexual harassment.

Overlapping Frames of Sexual Violation

Critics have contended that feminists who make gender politics the foundation for their analyses of sexual harassment trivialize rape and exaggerate sexual harassment by positing a continuum of sexual violence and victimization with sexual staring at one end and sexual assault at the other.

I wish to retain the phenomenological connections among various forms of sexual violation in order to identify their common patriarchal framework, but I wish to replace a linear continuum that presumes a static and objective measure of the severity of forms of victimization with overlapping conceptual and normative frames of sexual violation. As I have noted thus far, sexual harassment is experienced differently by different women and men and can be experienced differently by the same person over the course of a single life. Women of color have to contend with a variety of sexual stereotypes and gender role expectations specific to their race or ethnicity, and lesbians have to contend with the straight male presumption of heterosexual access to women in addition to men's intrusion into their personal space. As I mentioned in the overview, a woman's economic vulnerability or her experience with sexual abuse may profoundly influence what she finds harassing. Factors such as her age, her belief in traditional gender roles, and even her church attendance all combine to inform her assessment of the harassment, which is further complicated by the details of the context, perpetrator(s), and circumstances. Naomi Wolf's sparkle of "carnal recognition" from an attractive stranger could inspire unmitigated fear in a woman recently raped. The who, what, when, where, how, how often, and to what extent of any one case of sexual harassment will thus profoundly affect where the offending conduct should "sit" on the continuum, but the continuum's mapping of severity solely by type of conduct precludes this.

On the other hand, overlapping frames of violation allow for flexibility and instability in conceptual placement and normative assessments of the conduct. Indeed, when a sexual gesture or joke is not a sexual *offense* that constitutes sexual harassment, then the conduct simply drops from the frame. "Offensive" conduct that is discomfiting, disconcerting, even anxiety-producing becomes something that may or may not be an *offense* worthy of moral disapprobation and legal censure. I suggest that conduct such as sexual ogling, gestures, jokes, innuendo, touching, coercion, and bribery, persistent requests for dates, and exposure to sexual imagery cannot and should not be formally quantified as more or less severe for any and all women who are harassed by such conduct; nor does a continuum that grades such types of harassment by the severity of single violations account for the severity that is due to a repetition or combination of violations. "More and less serious" does not capture patterns of "less serious" conduct that, over time, becomes severe. Indeed, persistent "milder" forms of sexual harassment can be just as disturbing to many women as the quid pro quo variety.[110]

Even if all other variables remain constant, which is "worse" overall: One pinch on the buttocks or one breast squeeze? Three hard stares or two crude jokes? A continuum of sexual violence and victimization implies a normative commensurability between instances of sexual harassment that many such events simply do not have. Moreover, by putting ogling and sexual assault on the same objective and commensurable spectrum of severity, ogling becomes offensive to anyone, at any time, anywhere, while sexual assault becomes a simple, if egregious, case of bad manners. Thus, what was once a breach of etiquette becomes innately abusive, and the seriously injurious is trivialized. The continuum model also encourages complaints that sexual harassment charges violate freedom of speech, since "merely offensive" language or pictures at one end of the spectrum, although apparently innocuous (because "mild"), are equated with "strong" cases of coercion or assault at the other end of the spectrum.

A model of overlapping frames of violation can avoid these problems, yet still identify some of the phenomenological similarities between rape and sexual harassment, such as the privatizing and normalizing of the conduct to hide its political ramifications under patriarchy; the emotional and physical reactions of the victim; the myths about women that rationalize the conduct because women ask for it, want it, and lie when they do not get what they want; and the re-creation of a woman's victimization when she reports her violation or files suit in a court of law. Such an overlap is actually reflected in critics' complaints about a gendered continuum. In lamenting the profusion of sexual assault charges against spouses or lovers, Camille Paglia writes that "real rape" should be confined to rape by a stranger or "the intrusion of overt sex into a nonsexual situation."[111] Yet the latter disjunct is a description that also handily fits cases of sexual harassment. Using a model of overlapping frames of violation, I can argue that rape is a form of sexual violence against women, whose physical penetration differentiates it from other forms of sexual victimization. Yet this model also accounts for a woman's claim that sexual harassment is a "little rape." Indeed, it allows me to say that rape is a form of sexual harassment but that sexual harassment may or may not include rape. Overlapping frames also allow me to talk about several different kinds of rape, as well as several different kinds of sexual harassment; some of these violations will be more or less assaultive, traumatic, pervasive, or severe for some victims than others, but not in virtue of their place on a spectrum of violation whose commensurability is objectively and noncontextually assessed.[112]

I also wish to use the model of overlapping frames of violation to characterize each woman's experience of sexual harassment as unique to her own culture and history and, at the same time, as a form of discrimination against women, who are imposed and intruded upon because they are women. Race, class, and sexual orientation combine with gender to complicate the sexism of sexual harassment. Is it racism or sexism (or both) when a black woman with braided hair is asked by her white boss if her "other hair" is done to match? Judy Ellis believes there should be a classification for "combination discrimination" when both racism and sexism (among other biases) inform harassing conduct.[113] Beverly Grier argues that when black women say that racial solidarity should take precedence over more "personal" or "family" matters like the sexism of African American men, black women fail to take stock of how gender and class inform their lives. When black women are labeled by black men as promiscuous, sexually insatiable, opportunistic, and disloyal to their men, then a black woman who wishes to expose her sexual harassment by another black man will be especially hard pressed to do so. She may be called "uppity" or accused of "thinking white" for apparently denigrating someone already beaten down by white racism and reinforcing the white stereotype of the sexually aggressive black male. For many feminist women of color, the culturally imposed code of silence under which African American, Latina, American Indian, and Asian women live is a ready excuse for sexism within their own communities, despite these feminists' concerns over racial or ethnic fragmentation by whites.[114]

On the other hand, many African Americans believe that education, housing, drugs, crime, police harassment, racism, and poverty, not sexual harassment of black women by black men, are the more pressing issues that black (and white) feminists should be worried about. Many working-class black women could not understand why a career professional like Anita Hill would publicly condemn Clarence Thomas for his verbal abuse, since she appeared to be trying to deprive a fellow black of a chance at the Supreme Court over a sexual slight; after all, as some would contend, he didn't rape her. Angela Davis and Elsa Brown join other black feminists in pointing out that Anita Hill virtually lost her status as an African American when Clarence Thomas played "the race card" by calling his appearance

before the Senate Judiciary Committee in 1991 a "high-tech lynching."
Successfully characterizing himself as a victim of white racism, Thomas
became an African American falsely accused of sexual aggression, while
Hill, his accuser, came to be regarded by many blacks as a pawn of a white
power elite, a member of an "extremist" white, middle-class feminist
movement eager to support a victim of sexual harassment, and a villainess
who would lie, as white women historically have done about their sexual
treatment by black men. Brown points out that while black women have
had to underplay their public sexuality in response to a stereotype of sexual
insatiability, white women have had to fight a Victorian stereotype of asex-
uality and moral prudery.[115] It should come as no surprise then, that white
feminists critical of a gendered analysis of sexual harassment accuse other
white feminists of "a new Victorianism."

Lesbians remain double outsiders, in virtue of their gender and their
sexual orientation, especially if they work in settings not traditionally open
to women. Lesbians are not typically dependent upon men for either financial support or sex, and thus they threaten men's masculinity both as
primary wage earners and as active heterosexuals. Celia Kitzinger points
out that the beatings, shootings, burnings, property damage, and verbal
abuse that gay men and lesbians experience in their lives constitute an
entire heterosexist culture's sexual harassment of gays. Indeed, research
on teenage sexual harassment indicates that being called gay would be
more upsetting to most boys than actual physical abuse, a sad commentary
on the homophobia in contemporary American culture. Kitzinger also
notes that interlocking social oppressions like racism, sexism, and hetero-
sexism make sexual harassment difficult to identify. She argues that individual oppressions structure one another by being "not additive, but interactive," and should not be parsed out, even if this makes sexual harassment
less amenable to ready identification.[116]

When lesbianism is seen primarily in terms of sex, an "out" lesbian is
perceived not only as "coming out" sexually, by identifying herself as erotically attracted to women, but she may also be perceived as "coming
onto" men by being openly identified as a sexualized woman, which is just
the excuse many men need to make their sexual moves. Closeted lesbians
often do not know how to respond to sexual harassment, not wanting to
reveal their sexual status. Thus, they may betray a sexual vulnerability that
only encourages their sexual harassment by men. Lesbians are harassed

whether they are regarded as straight women, as challenging "turn-ons," or as women with disgusting sexual tastes.[117]

My point in providing these examples is to note how variable and overlapping the conceptual and normative frames of sexual violation may be. As the above cases demonstrate, many instances of sexual harassment simply cannot be parsed out by single type, nor is it easy to identify how cultural conditions individually or in combination affect the perception and experience of sexual harassment. Moreover, the quid pro quo of sexual bribery can create a hostile environment for a woman persistently pressed by her harasser to make a decision, a further example of a merging of two types. Indeed, when does sexual coercion not produce a hostile environment for the harassed? Refusing to tolerate further humiliation by a coworker determined to oust her, an employee quits: sexual coercion or hostile environment? A coworker on a corporate project threatens another with undermining her professional credibility unless she sleeps with him: sex as a condition of employment or "unreasonable" interference with her work? Witnessing a supervisor's quid pro quo harassment of a coworker can create a hostile environment for another. Acquaintance rape may involve both the verbal abuse typical of hostile environment sexual harassment and the sexual coercion typical of quid pro quo sexual harassment. Sex as a condition of employment is forced sex, sex without consent, sex under duress. Such sex has been referred to as "aggravated" sexual harassment, but how is this any different from acquaintance rape?[118] Pinups of Pets of the Year at the corporate offices of *Penthouse* magazine may be intimidating to a new advertising manager trying to make a budget presentation; is Penthouse corporation guilty of sexual harassment? When a student complains about a feminist's guest lecture and slide presentation on empowering women to masturbate in order to overcome the "hardship" of heterosexual sex, is the student complaining about an exercise of academic freedom or sexual harassment?[119]

The EEOC guidelines on sexual harassment currently offer separate categories for harassment, one that is both "gender-based but non-sexual in nature" and "motivated by animus against women" and another that is "sex-based discrimination" of a "sexual nature" such as inappropriate expressions of affection or sexual pursuit.[120] While both forms of harassment in workplaces and on campuses are illegal under federal law, differentiating between these categories raises some fascinating philosophical questions relevant to my thesis: are teasing and crude references to a woman's ample bustline a form of gender harassment or sexual harassment? What about the display of degrading pornography cited at the beginning of this essay? In a feminist psychology class, is consistently interrupting female students with anecdotes about what women enjoy in bed a form of sexism, hetero-sexism, or sexual harassment, a forgivable manifestation of male insecurity, or all of these at once? There may be or may not be animus in the expression, "A woman's place is in the home," but is it not still sexist? And is there no hostility in "A woman's place is on her back" when used in sexual pursuit?

Women typically have a more liberal, broad, and inclusive definition of sexual harassment than men do. But surveys are mixed, and many women virtually equate sexual harassment with sexual assault (recall "He didn't rape her"). Indeed, when the harassment is considered mild or the event is ambiguously described, neither sex exhibits consensus. Men may under-report their experience of being harassed if they believe they should welcome women's sexual advances, and younger women as well as women who have "steeled" themselves to the psychological hazards of their work-places may not report harassment that they believe is a "fact of life." Single incidents may not be considered harassing, but if repeated over time, they would be. Many respondents will not consider an experience to be harass-ing until they have actually experienced it. When researchers ask, "What behaviors do you find harassing?" they cannot know what the respondent means by "harassing," even if the respondent's examples match what re-searchers consider sexual harassment. And when they ask, "Have you ever experienced X behavior?" researchers must interpret for themselves whether what was experienced was harassment. Even if EEOC guidelines are offered to respondents to guide their assessments, what researchers can discover from their data is whether the respondents believe their experi-ence matches the guidelines, not whether the respondents thought their treatment was harassing. Indeed, the guidelines themselves have been found to be much too vague in their use of "unwelcome," "offensive," "unreasonably interferes," or even "sex as a condition of employment" for many raters to associate such terms with sexual harassment.[121]

In short, I am arguing for a way of thinking and talking about sexual harassment in terms of dynamic, unstable, and overlapping conceptual and normative frames of sexual violation. As such, the phenomenon of sexual harassment can be understood as an interpretive and regenerating *process* of interaction, particularized and politicized by the persons and cultural contexts involved. This model embraces the incommensurability of many types of sexual violation and does not attempt to reduce the ambivalence, the contradiction, or the lack of consensus about what sexual harassment is. Thus, the relevant question, according to this model, is not a definitional one but a political one, namely, who defines the terms and conditions of the discourse by which judgments of sexual harassment are made? Such a model accommodates, rather than hides, the facts that not all women (or men) are sexually harassed in the same ways, to the same extent, by the same types of people, and in the same contexts, and yet that each victim may call her treatment "sexual harassment." This model also reflects how the process of coping with sexual harassment is as important, if not more important, to an understanding of a victim's reactions to her sexual harassment, as is the mastery of stopping it.[122]

Understood in this way, the concept of sexual harassment is a "sensitizing concept," an expression I borrow from Kathryn Pyne Addelson, who adapts her sense of such concepts from Herbert Blumer. According to Addelson, "Sensitizing concepts are developed to investigate a world in which participants are continually creating and changing and reinterpreting the meanings of their activities. Sensitizing concepts are developed to trace the processes of human interaction, not capture its products."[123] Thus, sexual harassment is not a "capturable" phenomenon amenable to guidelines designed to encompass all appropriate cases. Rather, it is a dynamic and dialectical phenomenon whose meaning is interpreted and reinterpreted, generated and regenerated, depending upon the power of those who can appropriate its terms and conditions. As a professional feminist philosopher, I am in the kind of status-conferring position of authority to offer my own culturally located characterization of sexual harassment, one that I believe must be both flexible enough to accommodate the phenomenon of sexual harassment as an interpretive process, and definitive enough to identify a terrain of practice that is useful in assessing cases. In my view, a strategy with more closure and a stronger emphasis on "objective assessment" would be rationalized by perpetrators as either too narrow ("But I didn't do that!") or too broad ("How am I supposed to know what to do?"), and victims would either not think their own sexual harassment fits the requisite conditions or misidentify conduct to the detriment of their legitimate claims. I find it fascinating that the object of the board game called Harassment is not to state whether the scenario involves harassment but to guess the majority opinion of the other players, replacing the question "Did it happen?" with the postmodern alternative "What do others think happened?" If, as Camille Paglia contends, "[p]assion disorders" and "emotion is a maelstrom" for the players of the real-life game of sexual harassment, then we should expect sexual harassment to be as quixotic a phenomenon as the sexual politics and gender expectations that circumscribe it.[124]

The Dialectical Relationship between Sexual Object and Sexual Subject

I mentioned above that the process of sexual harassment is a dialectical one, given the ways in which sexual harassment shifts in meaning and interpretation. In addition, it is importantly dialectical in virtue of the experience of the sexually harassed victim herself. Because many harassed women who live under patriarchal constraints are resisting those constraints, I believe it is useful to understand the metaphysics of men's sexual harassment of women in terms of a dialectic between the gender politics of women's sexual objectification and the political liberation of women's sexuality. In short, women are both the objects and the subjects of their experience of sexual harassment.[125]

I have presented much of this dialectic already, in the contradiction between women's experience of sexual harassment and the ambivalence of many women's reactions to it. Men impute to women maximum credibility to convince judges and juries of the truth of women's purportedly false accusations but give them minimum credibility to know their own sexual needs or to express them with authority. Individual women initiate sexual harassment lawsuits in response to their victimization, only to see their own conduct go on trial as if they welcomed their victimization. Women are made out to be powerful sexual seductresses who actively provoke men's sexual advances at the same time as women are regarded as exploitable sexual objects of male desire, to be manipulated at men's discretion. Women can be perceived by men as simultaneously vulnerable, defenseless, and overwhelmingly irresistible ("She cast her spell over me"). A new generation of feminists are telling young women that they should feel a sense of entitlement to their physical expression and cultural space, only to watch those same women be bombarded with verbal, visual, and physical harassment. Women clearly threaten many men's sense of priority in the workplace, so women are sexually harassed to remind them that they have no legitimacy there from these men's point of view. Indeed, the fact that the sexual harassment of women is about *de*legitimizing and *de*grading women from self-identified subject to sexual object reveals the subjectivity necessary for women's successful objectification; sexual harassment would not be about power were there not something perceived as a real asset to be corralled or a real threat to be repressed.

Individual women act out this object-subject dialectic when they ambitiously want to get ahead in their chosen fields but see that the only way up is through an objectifying sexual compliance. A woman's direct refusal to a subtly coercive invitation could spell dismissal ("Do you *really* want to know how to stay on this assignment?"), but direct acquiescence could label her a "slut." In any case, her acquiescence is no assurance that the manipulation of her will cease. As Catharine MacKinnon observes, "Women learn early to be afraid that men will not be attracted to them, for they will then have no future; they also learn early to be afraid that men will be attracted to them, for they may then also have no future."[126] The woman who wants to be regarded as a "team player" and who grudgingly tolerates what she considers to be objectifying sexist jokes often finds herself being told she was not harassed, since she never complained. Indeed, the fusion of coercion and mutuality in much of women's sexual harassment is one reason why "proof" of unwelcomeness can be so difficult to come by. One of the many ironies here is that a woman's "no" reinforces her image as men's sexual gatekeeper, responsible for not letting men go too far, but her not saying "no" means men will go as far they want to, presuming her silence to be assent.

Moreover, joining in on "the fun" of sexual gestures, jokes, and innuendo may only earn a woman a "bad reputation" among men for crossing a male-identified line between virgin and whore, whose labile boundaries women cannot confidently predict. Women who believe that being friendly and helpful will earn them brownie points with their bosses find out all too soon that their bosses want to be more than "just friendly." The woman who "dresses for success" by dressing to please men (at least, the ones with the keys to her promotion) may do herself a disservice by prompting the very objectification her appearance is designed to eliminate; yet women who do not wear heterosexually attractive clothing may (literally) not attract the attention they need to get a leg up. Women who feel determined to report their harassment are often promptly returned to the degraded status of their original predicament with retaliatory dismissals or blatant disbelief. A woman's reporting her sexual harassment in a public forum has been interpreted by some men as the action of a "loose woman" sending sexual signals of her availability. Small wonder, then, that many women feel profoundly *un*ambivalent about whether or not they have been harassed and profoundly ambivalent about what to do about it or how to feel about it.

However, it is the dialectical nature of sexual harassment that precludes feminists who actively identify its pervasive and systemic character from being reduced to the objects of their own identity politics. Feminist support groups and counseling services, designed to help women live with, and through, women's experience of sexual harassment, allow grieving to occur and reempower women to go on with their lives.[127] There is no logically necessary connection between the existence or the documentation of the pervasive sexual violation of women by men and the "fact" of women's helplessness. Even if heterosexual men are genetically programmed to play sexual power games with women, this is still no reason for thinking that women would not, and could not, fight back. As Patai and Koertge point out, being oppressed and responding to being oppressed are two distinct sides of the same feminist coin.[128] Moreover, an important part of that response is feminist defiance of male-identified norms that disadvantage women. Many feminists, from Catharine MacKinnon to Camille Paglia, would like women to be more outraged and indignant than they are because such indignation replaces self-blame, nameless anxiety, and consistently suffered discomfort with emotions that can galvanize women to action. Indeed, I would argue that women need to take back their ability to "provoke" sexual responses in men and other women as positive expressions of their sexual exploration, pleasure, and agency.

Thus, I argue that a characterization of sexual harassment that dialectically identifies both women's objectification and women's subjectivity under patriarchy negotiates the tensions between those feminists who urge a gendered analysis of sexual harassment and those feminist critics who see in such an analysis nothing more than the revictimization of women. A dialectical understanding of sexual harassment that recognizes women's subjectivity through political confrontation belies the notion of woman as helpless victim, and the exercise of sexual agency or pursuit of sexual integrity that can motivate such confrontation precludes criticisms that a gendered analysis must be antisex. Moreover, the fact that women are ready and willing to educate men about women's lived experience of harassment cannot credibly be interpreted as antimale. In this way, an understanding of sexual harassment as a dynamic and dialectical process of sexual politics may serve to unite, rather than to divide, competing feminist constituencies.

Practical Guidelines and Interpretive Frameworks

In light of the above discussion, I offer the following characterization of sexual harassment, which is designed to give some identifying parameters to the offending conduct: Sexual harassment is a dynamic, dialectical, and interpretive process of sexual politics in which the harasser's conduct, words, images, or other icons are regarded as a violation of the sexual integrity of the harassed. This violation constitutes a sexual imposition or intrusion upon the harassed, which is facilitated by organizational hierarchies or informed by cultural stereotypes or both, in ways that delegitimize, manipulate, or threaten the harassed or presume sexual access to her. As such, sexual harassment constitutes an abrogation of the responsibility of the harasser to treat the harassed as a moral equal whose sense of herself as a sexual subject in the world is as worthy of empathy and respect as any other person's.

According to this characterization, either harassed or harasser may be a woman or a man, a boy or a girl, a person of any cultural background or belief. Harassment may be of the quid pro quo variety or create a hostile environment or both; the characterization allows these categories to be nonexclusive and overlapping. Gender (sex-based) harassment may be differentiated from sexual harassment only when gender harassment does not also involve a violation of the sexual integrity of the harassed, although gender harassment may still delegitimize, manipulate, or threaten in unacceptable ways. Moreover, according to my characterization, sexual harassment is a form of discrimination against the harassed in virtue of the harasser's failure to treat the harassed as the moral equal of other persons in similarly situated circumstances. This discrimination may itself be sexist or heterosexist and may combine elements of other forms of discriminatory oppression. Differences in cultural stereotypes and gender expectations held by women and men and differences in their positions within organizational hierarchies help explain the asymmetries in their experience of, and reactions to, sexual harassment, where these asymmetries exist. Not all men harass and not all sexual conduct is harassing, because not all men are disposed to violate the sexual integrity of women in the ways specified above. According to this view, sexual conduct such as adultery, promiscuity, sexual deviance, unprotected sex, or paid sex would not be considered sexual harassment unless it also violated the sexual integrity of the harassed in the ways specified above.

Whatever rudeness, offensiveness, or insensitivity (among other things) is involved in sexual harassment, these are moral wrongs, not just breaches of etiquette to be apologized for and promptly forgotten. The violation of sexual integrity I describe above is crucial to identifying the harm of sexual harassment, since the harm to the harassed, namely, being delegitimized, manipulated, threatened, or sexually presumed upon, results from the failure of the harasser to make any attempt either to respect the autonomy of the harassed or to empathize with her worldview. Recognizing the boundaries of another's "personal space" and caring for and about the particular needs of that person are not incompatible. What I shall refer to as "care respect," an expression I borrow from Robin Dillon,[129] requires that we treat all persons with the kind of Kantian respect that would prohibit coercion, exploitation, intimidation, or abuse. But it also requires that we treat each person with the kind of particularized care and consideration that asks us to treat each individual as special. This does not require that we delve into every person's sexual history or try to intuit exactly what people want or need out of their sexual lives, but it does require more than simply recognizing a woman's wish to work confidently, competently, and unmolested. Care respect requires that we make some attempt to look at the world through the eyes of the other, without rationalizing the attempt as an excuse to intrude upon another's personal space.

María Lugones refers to this attempt to understand another's social and psychological location as " 'world'-traveling."[130] A sexual harasser does not "world"-travel. He may be too full of his own self-importance, too competitive, or too eager to dominate the discourse to inquire after others' perspectives on their own "worlds." He may also simply be too narrowly focused on *his* world and *his* way of doing things to give a caring and respectful regard to those around him. In any case, a sexual harasser's violation of the sexual integrity of the harassed means that the harasser has either arrogantly or insensitively made another's "world" accommodate his own. A sexual harasser is someone who has failed to "world"-travel, because he has failed to ask of himself, "What is it like to be her?" and "What is it like to be me in her eyes?"

I suggest that these are questions of profound political importance to feminists, since such questions ask of the harasser that he situate his conduct within the organizational hierarchies and cultural stereotypes that circumscribe his relationship to the harassed. In the absence of doing so, he will not see her, nor will he see himself, as situated within a social context of institutional power; moreover, he will neither see his actions nor her reactions as circumscribed by the cultural expectations that flow from that power. When the alternative is to presume that women are legitimate sexual targets, a woman will welcome respectful inquiries from "world"-travelers concerning her sense of how she would like to be treated in this context by this person. Respectfully asking a woman for information about the kind of environment within which *she* likes to work is not equivalent to harassing her about it, precisely because, in the former case, her sexual subjectivity and moral equality may remain intact.

I am not suggesting that there will be consensus on what counts as a violation of sexual integrity or what may best be deemed delegitimizing, manipulative, or sexually presumptuous. I have been arguing that it is a mistake to look for such agreement, since the phenomenology of sexual harassment as a regenerating and interpretive process precludes it. But consensus has never been necessary for moral or legal prohibition. "Pervasive" and "severe" are themselves highly contested terms, yet they have been crucial to determining legal violations of Title VII and Title IX. What I am interested in offering is a way of thinking and talking about sexual harassment that speaks to the sexual politics, the contextual variety, and the dialectical process hidden by expressions like "unwelcome," "unwanted," "offensive," and "unreasonable," which have become standard fare for describing harassing conduct in legislative and social policy guidelines. Indeed, I will argue that in order to insure an "equal opportunity courtroom" in which both the claimant and the alleged perpetrator are assumed credible until proven otherwise, any normative assessments of sexual harassment must be based on identifying the conduct in question as a violation of sexual integrity, not on how the harassed responds to the conduct. The extent to which my own characterization of sexual harassment may inform current legal and social policy is the subject of the next section.

Sexual Harassment Legislation, Policies, and Procedures: A Feminist Perspective

Although it cannot hold an employer liable for the evils of society, so to speak, a court does have the power to consider how the cultural norms of our society impact the dynamics of the working environment and the harm resulting from sexually harassing incidents that take place within that cultural context.

—*Jolynn Childers*[131]

If societal views about concepts like discrimination, reasonableness, etc., are the product of a discriminatory status quo, then the private sphere cannot provide a neutral, external definition of those concepts to guide judicial decisions . . . . [D]octrinal constructs like consensus are merely vehicles for articulating value choices, not determinants of results.

—*Nancy Ehrenreich*[132]

Sexual harassment legislation and social policy can be politicized in ways that not only recognize the influence of cultural stereotypes and organizational hierarchies in formulating perceptions of sexual harassment but also speak to the wide variety of concerns that women and men have about it. In this section, I argue that the application of sexual harassment law and the implementation of social policy will be more successful if legislators and policy makers appreciate and promote the dialectical and interpretive framework I have outlined thus far.

Legal Issues

The EEOC is responsible for investigating, negotiating, and filing federal charges of sexual harassment for claimants whose cases are brought to the EEOC's attention for possible violations of Title VII of the Civil Rights Act of 1964, which prohibits sex discrimination in the workplace. The EEOC enforces antidiscrimination law either on behalf of claimants directly or it issues them a "right to sue" letter that authorizes claimants to file suit themselves. The EEOC can sue for claimant restitution such as job reinstatement, back pay, and court fees, as well as for compensatory and punitive monetary damages capped according to the number of employees in the company sued.[133] Victims of sexual harassment may sue employers for discriminatory practices under some states' fair employment practices (FEP) laws, sue employers under some states' workers' compensation laws, or sue the harasser (or anyone else) privately for personal injury, such as assault and battery or emotional distress, through common-law torts. Criminal complaints of assault or rape involved in cases of sexual harassment are the province of the criminal law.

FEP agency policies for handling sexual harassment claims vary widely from state to state, often with severe limitations on what, if any, restitution or damages can be recovered. While tort claimants suing privately can ask for compensatory and punitive damages far exceeding what the EEOC or relevant FEP agency allows, the purpose of common-law tort claims is not to provide reinstatement or make structural reforms in the campus or workplace. Also, tort claims can be more difficult for the claimant to prove than EEOC and FEP charges because she may be required to show the defendant's intent to inflict injury. Moreover, tort charges brought privately provide fewer protections against retaliation or publicity than those provided by the EEOC.

In a manner similar to that of the EEOC, the U.S. Office of Civil Rights (OCR) is in charge of handling complaints of violations of Title IX of the Education Amendments of 1972, which prohibit sex discrimination in educational institutions receiving federal funds. However, the impact of sexual harassment case law has been primarily in the area of workplace harassment.[134]

The EEOC's definitions and standards for sexual harassment remain the most influential and generally accepted guidelines throughout the United States for judges, juries, campus administrators, and social policy specialists who wish to assess sexual harassment claims. Under current EEOC guidelines, sexual harassment violates federal law if the conduct (1) constitutes unwelcome sexual or sex-based conduct that is made a condition of employment or of employment-based decisions or (2) "has the purpose or effect of unreasonably interfering with an individual's work performance or creating an intimidating, hostile or offensive working environment." The severity or pervasiveness of the unwelcome conduct has been interpreted by the Supreme Court to be the benchmark for what is to count as creating a "hostile environment" in employment, while quid pro quo sexual harassment is thought by the courts to be sufficiently severe (because inherently coercive) to be "unreasonable" on its own account. Consistent with EEOC guidelines, the courts have ruled that employers may be held strictly liable for the quid pro quo harassment perpetrated by their supervisors or managers and that employers are liable for hostile environment sexual harassment by one employee against another if it can be shown that the employer knew or should have known about the harassment but failed to take appropriate corrective action. The EEOC guidelines recommend looking at all the facts in context and on a case-by-case basis.[135]

The reason traditionally offered for requiring the claimant to prove that the conduct in question is unwelcome is that some sexual conduct in the workplace or in academia is, in fact, welcomed by those who reside there. As Katie Roiphe and others have pointed out, to preclude sexual conduct from these environments would be to take much of the enjoyment and stress relief out of an appropriate venue for sexual repartee and rendezvous. Indeed, there may be occasions when the claimant herself has solicited, encouraged, or desired sexual advances, gestures, or jokes or other sexual conduct from others. In addition, some standard of reasonableness in determining the offensiveness of sexual harassment has been recommended, in order to defend against accusations by the hypersensitive, the paranoid, the idiosyncratic, or the vindictive, whose sense of what constitutes a hostile environment lies well outside normal and "reasonable" boundaries of social impropriety.

However, feminists like Susan Estrich and Melinda Roberts have pointed out that having to prove the unwelcomeness of the sexual conduct in question assumes that sexual conduct in the workplace or academia is welcomed by the person toward whom the conduct is directed unless shown otherwise.[136] This assumption allows the defense, who represents the employer or institution sued, to argue that the claimant did nothing to communicate to the alleged harasser that his conduct was unwelcome. The issue of whether or not the claimant was sexually harassed then becomes one of whether or not the claimant successfully communicated her lack of consent to be treated in the way that she was. Thus, an unwelcomeness criterion requires that the claimant prove in court that she neither requested, provoked, nor desired the conduct in question, by showing tangible behavioral evidence of her unwillingness to engage in the conduct and her abhorrence of it.

There are several problems with this way of giving evidence for sexual harassment: First, the case immediately becomes one of questioning the conduct and the credibility of the claimant, not the alleged harasser, whose conduct is not evaluated for its injuriousness on its own account. If the claimant is a woman, her credibility regarding her own sexual conduct may be suspect from the beginning. Second, an unwelcomeness criterion reinforces the stereotype of women as the sexual gatekeepers against men's uncontrollable sexual urges, such that women are responsible for stopping men before things "get out of hand." From this view, unless women conduct themselves in appropriately off-putting ways, women are to blame for their own harassment. Third, women's fears of retaliation or of not being believed often mean that they remain silent with regard to their harassment. Some may acquiesce out of fear of reprisal or in the belief that they must tolerate their abuse in order to get ahead. Indeed, to retain her job or research appointment, a woman may do everything she can at the time *not* to show her harasser that his conduct was unwelcome. Other women may have tolerated sexual harassment for so many years that they simply do nothing about its continuance. Some may be too embarrassed to discuss their abuse with anyone and may hope that it will just go away. Still other women may not recognize their harassment for what it is until years afterward, if at all. Louise Fitzgerald and others have astutely pointed out that the courts continue to equate women's coping with women's consent to their harassment.[137] Those women who fail to confront their harassers, actively, on record, and in front of credible witnesses will thus be hard pressed by an unwelcomeness criterion to convince the courts of their harassment.

As I have already noted, what constitutes free and informed consent in cases of sexual harassment is complicated by the organizational hierarchies, gender politics, economic pressures, and sexual stereotypes that circumscribe the social environment in which the sexual harassment takes place.[138] Since judges and juries are a part of the culture that frames the politics of sexual harassment, their sense of whether a female claimant provoked her own harassment (by her conduct, dress, or manner) may be influenced by those politics, which the defense may exploit to depict the victim as a sly seductress (slut), as a sexual fantasizer or vindictive bitch (nut), or as sexually prudish (so what?). If the claimant has had a prior sexual relationship with the alleged harasser, the defense may try to show that the suit is the result of her anger at his rejection or her dissatisfaction with the current state of their relationship, even if she has openly demanded that the conduct stop. Without the incentive or the desire to "world"-travel to the claimant's social space, those in positions of social power who have the authority to define the terms and conditions of the unwelcomeness standard will do so according to their own favored ways of seeing the claimant's predicament. Claims of gender neutrality and impartialty, in such cases, may be nothing more than the claims of persons whose culturally located perspectives frame their own political worldviews. According to Drucilla Cornell, if women are divided into "good" girls and "bad" girls, then an unwelcomeness standard means that women will never be harassed, since "good" girls never tempt men beyond their bounds and "bad" girls always "ask for it."[139] In short, not only does an unwelcomeness criterion put the victim's conduct on trial in place of the alleged harasser's conduct, but it also does so within a cultural milieu that will tend to bias the case against the female complainant.

The standard of reasonableness delineated by EEOC guidelines is even more problematic for the female complainant than is the unwelcomeness criterion because the courts have appeared to take steps to insure that the law is *not* biased against the female victim. In *Ellison v. Brady*, for example, the court recognized that a "reasonable person" standard encourages judges and juries to assess sexual harassment cases by measures of severity and pervasiveness that may not be what a reasonable *woman* would find severe and pervasive sexual conduct. The adoption of a "reasonable woman" standard for recognizing and evaluating sexual harassment has been based on surveys that suggest that women as a class versus men as a class tend to have different ideas about what constitutes sexual harassment. Moreover, the reasonable woman standard is designed to point out that gender-neutral standards must be suspect in a society hierarchically structured along gender lines.[140]

However, Barbara Gutek, Maureen O'Connor, Jolynn Childers, and others have pointed out that there is no single type of woman to which a standard of reasonableness can be applied across the board.[141] Differences of race, ethnicity, class, sexual orientation and experience, age, and ability, among many other differences, mean that what is offensive sexual conduct to one woman may be inoffensive to another. Differences in power and authority among women mean that reaching consensus even among women themselves will be a matter of whose voices dominate the discourse. By invoking a reasonable woman standard, judges and juries are required to construct a projective stereotype of whatever they believe any reasonable woman would find offensive, not what this particular woman in this particular situation found offensive. Adjudicators are then required to agree as to the content of this stereotype. But a reasonable woman standard is developed within a patriarchal cultural framework whose "community standards" of what any reasonable woman would find offensive may still be defined from a male-identified perspective of "natural" differences between the sexes. Indeed, how can a woman be "reasonably" offended by sexual conduct within this milieu, when not expressing her displeasure is interpreted as no big deal and expressing her displeasure betrays no sense of humor? Thus, a reasonable woman standard offers no incentive for the court to "world"-travel in ways that would sensitize it to the context and circumstances of individual cases.

It has also been suggested that such a standard reinvigorates the image of women as fragile flowers who need to be singled out for special protection in virtue of their sex. This apparent need for differential treatment, then, has the effect of diminishing a woman's legal claim that her sexual harassment *wrongly* treats her differently than others in virtue of her sex. Along similar lines, Sarah Burns notes that emphasis on a reasonable woman standard results in opposing policy positions that defeat the purpose of the standard to delineate offensiveness: (1) Women should not suffer for men's insensitivity, and (2) men should not be required to adhere to a perceptual standard that they do not share.[142]

In light of these problems, Barbara Gutek and Maureen O'Connor have recently argued for a "reasonable victim" standard that would place the emphasis on the unequal power component, and not on the unequal gender component, of a reasonableness standard. They point out that several surveys are mixed in their evaluations of exactly how gender figures in women's and men's assessments of sexual harassment; most cases that go to court are cases of unambiguous or pervasive sexual harassment about which women and men tend to agree. (The important legal questions then become whether the harassment occurred and, in cases of hostile environment harassment, whether employers or academic institutions were sufficiently diligent in taking action to eliminate the harassment.)[143]

However, I contend that judges and juries would still have to make their assessments of victim reasonableness according to their own projective stereotypes of victimization, while failing to particularize *this victim's* victimization. The fact that the vast majority of sexual harassment victims are women means that female complainants judged by a victim reasonableness standard in the courtroom will still bear the burden of proving that *as women*, they were not overly sensitive, mean spirited, or crazy in thinking that they were injured by the conduct. Jane Dolkart has argued for an

entirely individualized standard for offensiveness, since she believes that
there are few, if any, true predictors of what particular women or men will
find offensive.[144] Yet I agree with Drucilla Cornell that any standard that
measures the claimant's perception of offensiveness still places the burden
too squarely on the claimant to prove how she responded to the conduct
in question, instead of how the alleged harasser conducted himself; judg-
ing sexual harassment in terms of its offensiveness to this individual still
means that this woman must convince a court that her experience of the
conduct in question proves the conduct was harassing. As Cornell points
out, "No matter how carefully tailored these standards are to the individual woman's experience, it is her experience that will still be on trial."[145]

On the contrary, the strength of my characterization of sexual harassment is that assessments of harassing conduct are based on the unaccept-
ability of the conduct of the alleged perpetrator, not on the victim's encouragement of the conduct or on the offended-ness of the victim. As
such, problematic standards of unwelcomeness and reasonableness, which
require evaluations based on the victim's conduct or state of mind, become unnecessary. A violation of sexual integrity is an injury to the person
violated and, as such, is prima facie not welcome and not something a
"reasonable" woman/man/victim would tolerate. Therefore, according
to my characterization, evidentiary proof of sexual harassment requires an
assessment of whether the alleged harasser's conduct constitutes a violation of sexual integrity, not whether the victim welcomed the conduct or
whether the victim was "reasonable" in her perception of the offensiveness
of the conduct. As such, the courts are not encouraged to put the claimant's conduct on trial in place of the conduct of the alleged perpetrator.
At the same time, the courts can still assume that not every sexual advance
is an unwelcome one, since not every sexual advance is a violation of sexual
integrity.

This does not mean that the victim's conduct should be excluded from
a determination of the case, since judges and juries will still need to place
"the totality of circumstances" in context. I am simply arguing that the
initial presumption of credibility should be balanced as between claimant
and alleged harasser. The claimant should be required to show that the
alleged harasser violated her sexual integrity, by showing how he delegitimized, threatened, or manipulated her or presumed sexual access to her
in ways that affected the terms, conditions, or privileges of her employment as per Title VII. The defense should be expected to answer those

charges by arguing that the alleged harasser's conduct did not constitute such a violation or that the employer was sufficiently diligent in taking action to eliminate it. Each side will then be assessed according to the explanatory power, plausibility, coherence, and consistency of its story without the presumption of the implausibility of the claimant's failure of consent. The emphasis of the assessment thus remains squarely on how the alleged perpetrator acted, not on how the claimant responded.[146] It should be pointed out, however, that whatever explanatory power each narrative has will still be circumscribed by the cultural background of those applying the explanatory standards. One of the advantages of my characterization, as I will explain below, is that judges and juries will have more incentive to "world"-travel, so as not to presume that their own epistemologies are absolute. As Helen Watson notes, "Credibility is itself dictated by narratives invoking the familiar, i.e. the stereotypical norms and values."[147]

Notice that if the alleged harasser is (appropriately) assumed innocent until proven guilty, then, according to my characterization, he is assumed not to have harassed the claimant until she can prove otherwise. However, assuming an alleged harasser's innocence in a case of sexual harassment is not equivalent to presuming that the claimant is guilty of lying until she can prove otherwise. What it presumes is that she must provide evidence to show, and cannot assume, that the alleged perpetrator's conduct was injurious. However, if she must prove, as evidence of injury, that her state of mind was in accordance with a standard of reasonableness, the court is presuming her unreasonable until she can prove otherwise. As such, her credibility is in question from the beginning in ways that bias the case in favor of the alleged harasser. Add to this bias the bias of the gender stereotype claiming that a woman will lie to save her sexual respectability, even though she asked for and wanted the sexual attention she received, and the deck is stacked unfairly against female complainants. Within such a cultural milieu, if the claimant must also prove unwelcomeness by defending her own conduct as entirely unprovocative and appropriately off-putting, she will have little chance of convincing the court.

On the other hand, if both the reasonableness and the unwelcomeness standards are dropped, courts can assume a credible claimant and a respectfully empathetic alleged harasser between whom the burden of persuasion as to the merits of the case is balanced. This is particularly important so that as the EEOC guidelines recommend, judges and juries will assess each claim on a context-specific, case-by-case basis, without making invisible the ideological gender boundaries that a depoliticized assessment of the "totality of circumstances" can hide. This type of specificity will also help preclude the presumption that the victim's conduct will always and inevitably go on trial. Indeed, the Violence against Women Act of 1994 extends rape shield laws to sexual harassment cases, so that publicly detailing a woman's sexual history, gynecological or psychological records, habits of dress, and so on may be done only if the defense can convince the judge of the relevance of such details to the credibility of the prosecution's case.[148]

Moreover, according to my characterization, by being required to investigate the nature of the conduct of the alleged harasser, judges and juries will be required to understand the concept of "world"-traveling and its importance in the caring and respectful treatment of persons. As a result, judges and juries will have some basis and incentive to begin testing their own judgments against this moral standard. By asking of both claimant and alleged harasser, "What is it like to be them?" and "What is it like to be me in their eyes?" judges and juries can begin to take stock of their own interpretive biases, as well as of the organizational hierarchies, gender politics, and sexual stereotypes that complicate the picture of sexual harassment.

I am arguing that depicting a simpler picture of sexual harassment will result in less considered judgments and judgments less likely to reflect the dynamic and interpretive process of sexual harassment itself. I am unconvinced that what is needed is a less messy way of adjudicating cases, since EEOC guidelines are already highly interpretive and any simpler picture will not reflect the social and political realities of the cases being adjudicated. The strength of my characterization is not that it allows for more efficient or effective consensus but that it encourages what I call an "equal opportunity courtroom" that is particularized, relational, and politicized in ways that give clarity and credibility to the voices of both women and men. Indeed, with women's experience given a stronger voice in the courtroom, we will have a much better chance of influencing what is legally recognized as discriminatory, so that in Catharine MacKinnon's words, "what *really* happens to women, not some male vision of what happens to women, is at the core of the legal prohibition."[149]

However, MacKinnon has argued against a tort approach to sexual harassment, since she believes tort law privatizes and personalizes what is, in fact, a social and discriminatory injury. Kathryn Abrams has also critiqued incorporating fault-based tort schemes into findings of sex discrimination, since she believes that such an approach requires the court to find the most legally credible voice in a cultural context already biased against women.[150] I agree that a tort approach alone takes the gender politics out of the injury of sexual harassment; trying to prove the "intentional infliction of emotional distress" can require detailed and culturally loaded reviews of a plaintiff's psychiatric history.[151] But I also believe that criticisms of tort approaches to legal findings of sexual harassment minimize the importance of the personal and moral violation of sexual integrity in legal assessments of sexual harassment. Downplaying the violation in those assessments discourages an emphasis on the injurious conduct of the harasser and encourages the courts to look for outward signs of consent.

On the other hand, if both unwelcomeness and reasonableness standards are dropped in favor of a more particularized, relational, and politicized understanding of the injury of sexual harassment, the bias that would make faultfinding disadvantageous to women is minimized. By treating a violation of sexual integrity as both a personal injury and as a failure to treat persons as moral equals, my characterization of sexual harassment claims combines the advantages of tort law's emphasis on personal injury and antidiscrimination law's emphasis on social injustice. Indeed, Title VII and Title IX reflect this combination by allowing claimants to seek compensatory and punitive damages as well as mandatory reforms in workplace policy. Moreover, conceptualizing sexual harassment as a failure to treat persons as moral equals establishes unequal treatment as the link between sexual harassment and other forms of discrimination, such as discrimination on the basis of race or sexual orientation; thus, sexual harassment case law that does not use a reasonableness standard to generalize about women can be extended to other forms of discrimination and so can provide for a more culturally complex legal reading of the harm.

What makes the moral violation of sexual integrity actionable is described in section 703(a) of Title VII as that conduct which would "discriminate against any individual with respect to his [or her] compensation, terms, conditions, or privileges of employment" because of that individual's sex. What counts as sex discrimination within this framework then becomes the subject of judicial debate "on a case-by-case basis." Indeed, my characterization implies that whatever legal consensus may be reached in each courtroom will be a matter of engaging in a dynamic and dialectical process of interpretation, generated and regenerated by the judges and juries who hear sexual harassment cases. But given my characterization, that process will more likely be in a courtroom that recognizes the confluence of personal injury, sexual politics, and gender expectations than in one whose less socially complex standards for sexual harassment bias the case against the "reasonable woman."

Social Policy Issues

A particularized, relational, and politicized approach to adjudicating sexual harassment cases also applies to the policies and procedures for handling sexual harassment complaints in educational institutions and workplaces. Such policies and procedures serve the vital function of allowing sexual harassment complaints to be handled in-house without the necessity of what can often be time-consuming, expensive, emotionally exhausting, and very public legal suits. In-house sexual harassment policies and procedures typically include formal policy statements and definitional guidelines for determining sexual harassment, examples of the conduct proscribed, a description of how procedures for receiving, investigating, and evaluating sexual harassment complaints will be implemented, and a plan for the public education or training of all concerned regarding the identification and prevention of sexual harassment. Institutional policies can have not only practical but also strategic advantages over legal procedures; such policies stress the importance of intervention, prevention, and change and can be tailored to suit the specific needs of, and modifications in, the institutions in question. These qualities are essential if in-house grievance procedures of both an informal and a formal variety are to provide successful resolutions for those whom they are designed to serve.

Adopting my characterization of sexual harassment for the formulation and implementation of workplace and campus sexual harassment policies will mean several things. Educational institutions and workplaces should make an unequivocal and public policy statement that sexual harassment will not be tolerated and that breaches of policy will be dealt with efficiently and effectively. Potential complainants must be assured publicly and in writing that their complaints will be taken seriously. Confidentiality must be guaranteed to those filing initial complaints, so that fears of reprisals or of "troublemaker" stigmas do not inhibit students, professors, or other employees from reporting their harassment. Alleged harassers must be allowed to know their accusers, but only after procedures have been set up to insure that such exposure does not subject the complainant to further injury. Due process may be assured when both claimant and alleged harasser understand that evaluations of, and consequences for, the conduct in question will be based on specific, consistent, and well-publicized procedures that are evaluated independently of the review boards that implement them. Such assurances should also include the clear statement that review boards will hear testimony that balances the burden of persuasion between accuser and accused in the ways specified above for court cases. Disclosure of the types of penalties imposed and the number and types of grievances heard, without disclosing the identities of the parties involved, still sends a clear message to the community that the institution is aware of the gravity of the problem and acts on the complaints it receives. Students and employees have complained that they have a right to know who are the harassers in their midst, but I believe that in-house policies will fail miserably if alleged harassers cannot be guaranteed the same confidentiality as their accusers.

The characterization of sexual harassment accompanying a formal policy statement should focus on the injuriousness of the harassing conduct, not on the offended-ness of the victim, and give examples. If such a characterization is to reflect the dialectical and interpretive process of sexual harassment, yet allow women and men to identify what counts as harassing conduct, then the characterization must be sufficiently specific to make useful comparisons between what is characterized and the conduct suspected of being harassing. At the same time, the characterization must be open-ended enough to allow for a wide variety of cases. I argued in the section "Reconstructing a Feminist Dialogue" that the characterization I have offered satisfies this condition. Narrower definitions can still be ambiguously worded in ways that cannot guarantee due process, confidentiality, or timeliness of investigation. Thus, consistency of application of my characterization, conscientious "world"-traveling to cultural backgrounds otherwise foreign to the assessors' own, and the equitable presumption of the credibility of both claimant and alleged harasser will go far to offset any of the advantages of a more closed or definitive characterization. Also helpful are detailed directives of how to document instances of pervasive sexual harassment, including the keeping of journals and photocopies of one's personnel files, and tips on how to politely but firmly tell a harasser that his behavior should cease. Comments such as "You must stop winking at me endlessly during board meetings—your actions interfere with my work," versus "I really find your conduct offensive," let the harasser know that his conduct, not the woman's hurt feelings, is at issue.

Because "world"-traveling is so conspicuously absent from instances of sexual harassment, it should be encouraged in sexual harassment awareness programs as a means of identifying the sort of caring and respectful conduct that is to be promoted in the workplace and as a means of helping to prevent harassment from occurring. "World"-traveling by administrators means that sexual harassment policies will be more sensitive to the particular work culture, management philosophy, and organizational boundaries of the environment for which the policies are designed. Managers or administrators who may have never experienced harassment or have forgotten harassment in their distant past should be encouraged to ask concerning their employees, faculty, or students, "What is it like to be them?" and "What is it like to be me in their eyes?" In this way, administrators may begin to see sexual harassment as more of a problem than they often do, given their different life experience, and so be quicker to respond to reports of problems. More "world"-traveling among coworkers will encourage them to feel they can support the complaints of their peers who have been harassed, instead of unreflectively trivializing, denying, or ignoring those complaints. A clear policy statement encouraging collaboration and cooperation among peers as well as senior staff can help "world"-traveling women and men understand the value of each other's work, and keep them from feeling that sexual harassment policies require teamwork only "at a safe distance." Discussions of "world"-traveling in terms of balancing freedom of speech with social responsibility for the well-being of others can assure those suspicious of possible censorship engendered by overzealous policy makers that women and men may take part in a workplace with the freedom to express their opinions within a moral framework of care respect.

Grievance procedures must be of both an informal and a formal sort. In this way, claimants who do not wish to impose on their alleged harassers sanctions that are as public and adversarial as those available under formal procedures may nevertheless have a safe, reliable, and effective means of reporting, investigating, and (ideally) eliminating the harassing conduct. For truly hostile or persistent harassment, however, informal mediation, letter writing, or third-party communication, in the absence of a formal body to punish wrongdoing and enforce compliance by the harasser, may not be the answer, yet a formal lawsuit may be out of the question for a variety of emotional and practical reasons. Thus, formal in-house grievance procedures may serve as an appropriate nonlegal venue, particularly for identifying one person's repeated harassment of more than one victim, documenting the sexual harassment in institutional records, and meting out punishment to the harasser. As Stephanie Riger wryly points out, "A victim of a mugging is not required to solve the problem with the mugger through mediation."[152]

However, like the gender-sensitive legal courtroom I described above, such formal procedures must still be sensitive to the political context and social circumstances of each case, so that public proceedings do not become as humiliating or intrusive as the original incident. Otherwise, an alleged harasser with the benefit of organizational authority and political connections may easily outmatch a younger or less experienced claimant perceived by a review board as having no long-term ties to the institution, even if both have advocates in formal proceedings, and this may be precisely the harasser against whom informal reprimands have proved useless. Thus, it is imperative that review boards "world"-travel to the claimant's perspective on events as well as to the alleged harasser's, in order to insure that board members' own institutional biases do not disadvantage one party over another. Members of review boards must also have the administrative power and authority to put potential harassers on notice that formal charges will be taken seriously, even when board members are colleagues or coworkers. Institutional follow-up must assure complainants that possible retaliation or backsliding will not be tolerated. For example, in California, grade-school principals may legally suspend or expel students in the fourth through twelfth grades who are found guilty of sexual harassment. In California schools, formal sexual harassment policies are required by law.[153]

A variety of both external and internal resources for investigating and evaluating complaints is vital, so that complainants do not fear that the only boards to which they can report have members who are themselves a part of the problem. Thus, I disagree with Alan Kors, who believes that normal grievance procedures for handling such incidents as extortion and abuses of authority can do as well as formal sexual harassment policies and procedures for resolving cases of harassment. I contend that such all-purpose forums are not designed to accommodate what individual female complainants of sexual harassment may want or need out of the claims

process. Moreover, such venues disguise the pervasiveness and the prevalence of sexual harassment, marginalize the gender politics of the injury,
and make it impossible for authorities to underscore its special seriousness.[154]

Public awareness and education programs must be implemented to encourage the prevention, as well as the identification and reporting, of sexual harassment. In-house or extramural sexual harassment support groups
can provide emotional solace and legal advice for those uncertain about
their predicament. Feminist nonprofit organizations can make their
money talk by contributing only to those academic or workplace institutions with a strong record of antidiscrimination efforts on behalf of
women. These same feminist resources can provide databases, financial
support, and legal counsel for women considering filing sexual harassment
claims. In turn, awareness programs must educate both women and men
to be sensitive to their own gender expectations, as well as to the sexual
politics, cultural stereotypes, and organizational hierarchies that both inform and motivate sexual harassment. Explaining how sexual harassment
qua sex discrimination may also include racial discrimination, age discrimination, classism, or heterosexism may help program members become
aware of some of their own social biases without pointing any accusatory
fingers that might alienate members from sexual harassment discussions.
Learning about alternatives to sexist verbal and nonverbal communication,
as well as perceptual differences in this communication, can be an important part of such programs.

Women must be given more visibility and authority at all institutional
levels, in order to have the opportunity to provide the kinds of leadership
and role modeling that can improve performance and help erode sexist
attitudes. Such authority will also greatly reduce the kind of sexual harassment whose success is based on women's depressed economic status.
Women can also militate against the incidence of sexual harassment by
demonstrating care respect for colleagues and employees, openly addressing the common fear that women will take advantage of sexual harassment
policies simply to gain power over men. Men must be given the opportunity to air their concerns about their own sexual harassment by women
and must be afforded participation in the formulation and implementation
of gender-sensitive harassment policies. Training programs designed to
teach assertiveness and self-confidence in reporting harassment must go
hand in hand with organizational protection from retaliation and stigma,

the incidence of which should be openly discussed in terms of the gender politics of sexual harassment. School newspapers, student brochures, classroom visits, campus speak-outs, student or employee orientation programs, employee newsletters, faculty workshops, management retreats, academic course or project evaluations, and community activism through a variety of campus or employee organizations are all vehicles for the dissemination of information on identifying sexual harassment and on filing both in-house and legal complaints.

Everyone in the workplace or on campus—students, staff, faculty, administration, employees, management—should be given responsibility for preventing and addressing sexual harassment. This can be accomplished by including all members in the formulation and implementation of policy statements, educational awareness programs, and policy or procedural evaluations. Such cooperative participation by both employees and management, students and faculty, workers and coworkers, can inspire the kind of mutuality that is more likely to keep environments free of sexual harassment than if only some members have a stake in excising it. However, "task forces," "periodic surveys," and "investigative follow-ups" of the most participatory kind will be useless without the kind of "world"-traveling to both harassed's and harasser's social spaces that can help those outside the harassment context understand the particular cultural backgrounds and gendered perspectives of the participants.

The costs of failing to implement practical and effective sexual harassment policies are very real. Millions of dollars a year are lost to individual companies nationwide in low productivity, employee turnover, and absenteeism, in addition to any costs that may accrue from lawsuits.[155] Women who have been the victims of sexual harassment at work report lower job satisfaction, less confidence in management, and absenteeism due to job-related stress; they have a greater likelihood than those who have not been harassed of leaving, transferring, or losing their jobs. At universities, sexual harassment can cause student retention rates to drop, overall morale to remain low, and teaching and learning to be far less successful. Universities can lose federal monies if they are not in compliance with requirements for sexual harassment policies and procedures. While private businesses may not fear loss of federal funding, employers with fifteen or more employees are subject to sexual harassment law and thus, under certain conditions, are legally liable for the sexual harassment perpetrated by their employees; indeed, as I noted earlier, employers may be held strictly liable for quid pro quo harassment by supervisors or managers. Therefore, it greatly behooves businesses to obtain management's full support of formal, written policies for dealing with sexual harassment.[156] Wrongful dismissal suits by alleged sexual harassers are always a possibility, but their incidence can be greatly reduced by forward-thinking employers who make sure that employee concerns about due process and academic freedom are met in the ways specified above.

The benefits of in-house sexual harassment policies are equally real. Accessible and effective sexual harassment policies are thought to greatly reduce lawsuits by resolving problems before in-house negotiations break down over irreconcilable differences. Persons whose institutions can assure them that sexual harassment will be taken seriously and handled fairly can feel more confident in their own work and the work of others. If social policy can be formulated in the particularized, relational, and politicized way I have been advocating, institutions will have a much better chance of creating an individually meaningful, mutually cooperative, and increasingly productive workplace for all.[157]

Beyond Sexual Harassment to a Feminist Sexual Ethic

I don't have much sympathy for men who say they "don't get it." They may not know what it's like to be a woman, just as one individual doesn't know what it's like to be a member of another race. But society requires us to develop a sensitivity to racial issues anyway.

—*Kim Masters*[158]

Plainly, the wooden dichotomy between "real love," which is supposed to be a matter of free choice, and coercion, which implies some form of the gun at the head, is revealed as inadequate to explain the social construction of women's sexuality and conditions of its expression, including the economic ones.

—*Catharine MacKinnon*[159]

Sexual harassment is illegal outside of institutional contexts only if the harassment counts as a personal injury actionable under common-law torts or if the harassment is a type of criminal assault subject to criminal charges. But a public harasser on the street, in a movie theater, or at the beach is often anonymous, quick to blend into a crowd, and so not readily answerable in the same ways employers, staff, or faculty can be for the purposes of filing a civil suit. A harassing friend, husband, or lover may be in precisely the kind of relationship with the harassed for which criminal law suits are the least desirable option. Yet, as I discussed earlier in this essay, men's sexual harassment of women can exist almost anywhere, at any time, in any place women and men congregate, where the dynamics of gender, sexuality, and power converge to constitute a violation of sexual integrity. Thus, it is particularly important to advocate a particularizing, relational, and politicized sexual ethic in order to encourage women and men to treat each other with care respect even when they are not motivated by any legal prohibition.

Part of what this means is inculcating the desire *not* to treat others only as *we* would like to treat them. "World"-traveling in personal relationships means being sensitive to how this person with this cultural background in this situation would want to be treated. It is framed by moral parameters of respectful treatment of the kind that is not exploitative, coercive, or abusive. We cannot know the personal histories of many of our acquaintances, much less of strangers, but the sort of "world"-traveling I have been advocating does not encourage women and men to try to find out all they can about each other. To "world"-travel is, in part, to make ourselves more accessible to others from whom we may be very different, so that they may be encouraged to tell us more about themselves; it is also to ask others to make their own social spaces accessible to the kind of imaginative identification that can facilitate our care respect for them. "World"-traveling thus requires a kind of collaborative and cooperative social responsibility to one another to learn about difference and to respect it, in the recognition that ours is only one of many "worlds" worth knowing.[160]

The sexual ethic that flows from this perspective means tolerance for cultural diversity and respect for gender difference within a society whose sexual ideology confers de facto authority, priority, and credibility to white, educated, affluent, heterosexual men. A sexual ethic of care respect requires both a personal sensitivity to the individual sexual needs and interests of others and a social responsibility to situate those interests within the context of the organizational hierarchies, sexual politics, and gender expectations of the relationship. From this perspective, men may be better able to understand many women's fears of male violence, shame at being publicly or degradingly sexualized, and reluctance to offend, while women may learn more about men's fears of being falsely accused of sexual misconduct and of being overcome by the seductive powers of devouring women. If men can begin to hear women's complaints about men's sexual conduct without hearing them as threats to their masculinity, women can begin to communicate their complaints without attacking men's egos. This requires that both women and men understand prevailing ideological connections between masculinity, heterosexuality, and male dominance that can provide the subtext for such exchanges.

From this ethical perspective, women and men may also understand the value of requesting women's opinions on projects and praising women's team efforts, thoroughness, and overall work performance without simultaneously delegitimizing women with sexual comments. Many men want to know how *not* to violate women's sexual integrity, but do not know how to read the behavioral cues women give them or how to act in the absence of such cues. Some men will not ask what the parameters of others' sexual integrity are, since their masculinity hinges on authorizing other persons' parameters and knowing where to draw them. Women must shed their sexual gatekeeper status by actively discussing with men, in protected formal meetings and informal discussion, how to anticipate the particulars of what women, as individuals, want from their workplaces or their academic or social lives. If women wish to show a patriarchal world that their own ideas are worth listening to, they must provide men with the opportunity to listen to them. Such discussions should be ongoing as a way of maintaining the flexibility of a dynamic process of personal and sexual interaction. The men who participate in these discussions can then act as role models for those men "on the street" whom women have not actively sought out. This means that women and men must examine their own social and sexual needs so that those needs can be communicated with clarity and confidence. Neither women nor men can simply expect others to "get" the particulars of what each person wants out of every hour of social or sexual life, but both women and men are entitled to the kind of care respect that does not unreflectively and injuriously impose another's "world" onto their own.

In sexual relationships, this will mean offering my sexual partner the opportunity to tell me his sense of what kind of sex he would like, not simply making sure that I get what I want or that I give my partner what I *think* he might want without asking myself, "What is it like to be him?" and "What is it like to be me in his eyes?" This also means more than just listening to what my partner may tell me. It means actively supporting and pursuing his sexual interests within the parameters of the care respect of others. Such "world"-traveling by no means eviscerates the power of the erotic in sexual relationships. If Catharine MacKinnon is right, manipulation and affection can be part of the same erotic package. However, in the feminist sexual ethic put forward here, erotic power in sexual relationships is transformed from the "power over" that violates a partner's sexual integrity, to the "power with" of relationships that share the power to seduce and satisfy each other.

On the other hand, as long as (1) sexual conquest, gender dominance, and organizational control are essential components of the masculine persona, (2) masculinity is an essential component of men's sense of self, and (3) society rewards men for "being men" and punishes them for acting "like women," then men will continue to sexually harass women to confirm the social status and gender identity that define men's sense of self. Therefore, instead of threatening men's masculinity and selfhood with the potential loss of men's power base, feminists must encourage women and men to transform current hierarchically structured power relations in ways that challenge prevailing ideological connections between identity and dominance. I believe that trying to eliminate power altogether in personal relationships is unrealistic and is oblivious to the role of power in eroticism and in the formation of gender identity. However, trying to take power away from men in order to give it to women only replaces one partial and culturally located regime with another. Instead, women and men must begin to see power as qualitatively, not quantitatively, assessed. In this way, power can be shared using a power-with model, without the threat to self that can accompany "losing" one's power when one uses a power-over model.

Capitalism seems far from conducive to the application of a power-with model, since the profits that provide the capitalist's power base are measured in terms of quantitative capital assets that give the capitalist power over his workers. Yet the conversion to a more socialist state appears too distant a goal for any practical or immediate application of the feminist politics advocated here. With capitalism's current lock on an industrialized liberal democracy, women must therefore demonstrate, despite a power-over economic model, that women and men can be more creative, productive, and satisfied with their lives when both genders share the benefits and the burdens of power. From this view, both women and men have authority and credibility, but neither has the kind of dominating priority that presumes that one gender, but not the other, should have the last word "when it counts." When no one is left feeling vulnerable, fearful, paranoid, or anxious by another's quest for power and all persons experience the joys of giving and receiving care without being consumed by that care, the equation of identity with dominance appears less attractive. I see no reason why women should begin acting more "like men," when this means constantly jockeying for power-over positions in a dog-eat-dog world of cutthroat competition. Violations of sexual integrity will ultimately disappear in an environment where women and men perceive their own identities enhanced by the power of others, not by the weakness of others.

Women and men can be highly ambivalent and quixotic about their own sexual needs, and this is exacerbated by conflicting cultural messages from family, media, education, and peers. Men may want their wives to be virgins but their girlfriends to be sexually available to them. Some women are sexually attracted only to the "love 'em and leave 'em" type, even though these same women say they would much prefer a steady relationship. What else can you expect from a culture in which rock 'n' roller John Cougar Mellencamp laments, "Sometimes love don't feel like it should, you make it hurt so good"?[161]

Women's clothing is a particularly complex case of the personal and the political. Many women wear clothes that accentuate their most sexually desirable features, because such clothes reinforce a personally and culturally valued image of themselves as sexually desirable women. For working women, this desirability can be both a blessing and a curse. On the one hand, they are expected to dress desirably, but on the other, they may "attract the wrong kind of attention." Deborah Tannen suggests that working women are still bound by courtship rituals originating outside the workplace that require women to attract and seduce men.[162] Moreover, one of the important ways for women to measure their heterosexual attractiveness is by the way male friends and colleagues react to the way they dress. Even perfect strangers can be given this power of sexual commentary.

Yet many women take offense at these same men for making sexual comments, noises, or gestures in response to the very thing for which these women are dressing—heterosexual attraction and allure. Some women simply want both the power to attract men and the power to say how, when, where, how often, and to what extent that attraction should occur, even if they do not know exactly how to articulate this. Such ambivalence is bound to make even the keenest of "world"-travelers frustrated. Men often respond to this ambivalence by boldly going where many men have gone before, namely, as far as women will let them. Many men assume that a woman's sexual ambivalence, if she has any, is due to a repressed sexuality, supposedly revealed in her dress or manner, that can be unearthed once a woman's sense of feminine propriety has been effectively removed, often with various "mood enhancers" like alcohol. Other men, unfortunately, simply take what they want.

My characterization of sexual harassment as a dialectical and interpretive process of sexual politics is designed to reflect the ambivalence, instability, and contradiction in much of our sexual lives. However, unlike Camille Paglia, I have argued that such instability allows for the kind of care respect that can transform the "war" between the sexes into a power-sharing relationship. I am less interested in resolving this instability than I am in promoting a feminist sexual ethic that interprets consensus as itself an ongoing process of the appreciation and negotiation of difference through political dialogue. My belief is that within that dialogue may arise programs for change in the ways that women and men think about gender, sexuality, and power—programs that may provide a framework for protecting and promoting the sexual integrity of us all.

Notes

1. Bob Packwood, quoted in "Voices," *Los Angeles Times*, 8 September 1995.

2. U.S. Senate Ethics Committee affidavits as reported in "The Complaints," *Los Angeles Times*, 8 September 1995.

3. Examples taken from William Petrocelli's and Barbara Kate Repa's discussion of *Robinson v. Jacksonville Shipyards, Inc.*, 760 F. Supp. 1486 (M.D. Fla. 1991), in their *Sexual Harassment on the Job: What It Is and How to Stop It* (Berkeley: Nolo Press, 1992), 3/14 (authors' pagination: chap. 3/p. 14).

4. Quoted in Helen Watson, "Red Herrings and Mystifications: Conflicting Perceptions of Sexual Harassment," in *Rethinking Sexual Harassment*, ed. Clare Brant and Yun Lee Too (London: Pluto Press, 1994), 75.

5. For some current statistics, see American Association of University Women, *Hostile Hallways: The AAUW Survey on Sexual Harassment in America's Schools* (Washington, D.C.: American Association of University Women Educational Foundation, 1993); Billie Wright Dziech and Linda Weiner, "Sexual Harassment

on Campus: The State of the Art," chap. 1 in *The Lecherous Professor: Sexual Harassment on Campus*, 2d ed. (Urbana: University of Illinois Press, 1990); Louise F. Fitzgerald, Sandra L. Shullman, Nancy Bailey, Margaret Richards, Janice Swecker, Yael Gold, Mimi Ormerod, and Lauren Weitzman, "The Incidence and Dimensions of Sexual Harassment in Academia and the Workplace," *Journal of Vocational Behavior* 32 (1988): 152–75; Amy L. Culbertson, Paul Rosenfeld, and Carol E. Newell, *Sexual Harassment in the Active-Duty Navy: Findings from the 1991 Navy-Wide Survey* (San Diego: Navy Personnel Research and Development Center, 1993); U.S. Merit Systems Protection Board, *Sexual Harassment of Federal Workers: An Update* (Washington, D.C.: U.S. Government Printing Office, Office of Merit Systems Review and Studies, 1988).

6. The issue of whether sexual harassment violates Title VII of the 1964 Civil Rights Act reached the Supreme Court only as recently as 1986 in *Meritor Savings Bank v. Vinson*, 477 U.S. 57 (1986). For a brief history of sexual harassment case law and its various applications of EEOC guidelines, see Susan L. Webb, *Step Forward: Sexual Harassment in the Workplace: What You Need to Know!* (New York: MasterMedia, 1991), 3–21; Martin Eskenazi and David Gallen, eds., *Sexual Harassment: Know Your Rights* (New York: Carroll & Graf, 1992), 160–89; Petrocelli and Repa, *Sexual Harassment on the Job*, 1/19–24.

7. See Patricia Frazier, Caroline C. Cochran, and Andrea M. Olson, "Social Science Research on Lay Definitions of Sexual Harassment," *Journal of Social Issues* 51 (1995): 21–38; Richard Arvey and Marcie A. Cavanaugh, "Using Surveys to Assess the Prevalence of Sexual Harassment: Some Methodological Problems," *Journal of Social Issues* 51 (1995): 39–52; Louise H. Kidder, Rebecca A. Lafleur, and Carole V. Wells, "Recalling Harassment, Reconstructing Experience," *Journal of Social Issues* 51 (1995): 53–68.

8. For a variety of commentary by both women and men on the U.S. Senate Judiciary Committee's 1991 Anita Hill–Clarence Thomas sexual harassment hearings, see Geneva Smitherman, *African American Women Speak Out on Anita Hill–Clarence Thomas* (Detroit: Wayne State University Press, 1995); Toni Morrison, ed., *Race-ing Justice, En-gendering Power: Essays on Anita Hill, Clarence Thomas, and the Construction of Social Reality* (New York: Pantheon, 1992); Anita Faye Hill and Emma Coleman Jordan, eds., *Race, Gender, and Power in America: The Legacy of the Hill-Thomas Hearings* (New York: Oxford University Press, 1995).

9. Quoted in Petrocelli and Repa, *Sexual Harassment on the Job*, 3/3; also see Barbara A. Gutek, "How Subjective Is Sexual Harassment? An Examination of Rater Effects," *Basic and Applied Social Psychology* 17 (1995): 447–67.

10. See Associated Press, "Man Harassed by Female Boss Gets $237,000," *Los Angeles Times*, 23 November 1995; Anna Cekola, "Orange County Student, 13, Files Sexual Harassment Suit," *Los Angeles Times*, 23 November 1995; Amy Harmon, "Caltech Student's Expulsion over Contents of E-Mail Raises Concerns," *Los Angeles Times*, 15 November 1995; Ellen Goodman, "Packwood Takes His Tongue on the Road," *Los Angeles Times*, 20 August 1995; Stuart Silverstein,

"U.S. Charges Sex Harassment at Mitsubishi Plant," *Los Angeles Times*, 10 April 1995.

11. Fitzgerald, et al., "The Incidence and Dimensions of Sexual Harassment in Academia and the Workplace," 173.

12. Quoted in Watson, "Red Herrings and Mystifications," 66.

13. Dziech and Weiner, *The Lecherous Professor*, xxv.

14. See Associated Press, "Women's Choices, Not Bias, Blamed for Lower Earnings," *Los Angeles Times*, 15 December 1995. Many women also claim that they would not dare to leave their children in the care of potentially volatile or violent male partners, and the dubious expression "house husband" still rings a false note among many women and men (compare "henpecked").

15. Thus, Jolynn Childers, Michele Paludi, Richard Barickman, and others recommend combining organizational and socio-cultural models of sexual harassment for a more expansive understanding of the problem. See Jolynn Childers, "Is There a Place for a Reasonable Woman in the Law? A Discussion of Recent Developments in Hostile Environment Sexual Harassment," *Duke Law Journal* 42 (February 1993): 858; Michele Paludi and Richard Barickman, "Sexual Harassment of Students: Victims of the College Experience," in *Academic and Workplace Sexual Harassment: A Resource Manual*, ed. Michele A. Paludi and Richard B. Barickman (Albany: State University of New York Press, 1991), 150–51; also see Webb, *Step Forward*, 104–5; U.S. Merit Systems Protection Board, *Sexual Harassment of Federal Workers*.

16. See Larry May and John C. Hughes, "Is Sexual Harassment Coercive?" in *Sexual Harassment: Confrontations and Decisions*, ed. Edmund Wall (Buffalo, N.Y.: Prometheus Books, 1992), 61–68; also see Webb, *Step Forward*, 63–64; Peggy Crull, "Are Sexual Harassment in Nontraditional and Traditional Workplaces the Same Thing? Lessons from the Construction Industry" (paper presented at "Sex and Power Issues in the Workplace: A National Conference to Promote Men and Women Working Productively Together," Bellevue, New York, March 1992); Beth E. Schneider, "Consciousness about Sexual Harassment among Heterosexual and Lesbian Women Workers," *Journal of Social Issues* 38 (1982): 75–98; Celia Kitzinger, "Anti-Lesbian Harassment," in *Rethinking Sexual Harassment*, ed. Brant and Too, 125–47.

17. See Office of the Inspector General, *The Tailhook Report: The Official Inquiry into the Events of Tailhook '91* (New York: St. Martin's Press, 1993); also see Stanford Medical School Professor Frances Conley's account of being sexually harassed by her male colleagues, reported in *Sexual Harassment: Research and Resources*, Deborah L. Siegel, revised by Marina Budhos, 3d ed. (New York: National Council for Research on Women, 1995), 16; Petrocelli and Repa, *Sexual Harassment on the Job*, 1/15. For statistics on academic peer harassment, see American Association of University Women, *Hostile Hallways*; Dziech and Weiner, *The Lecherous Professor*.

18. See Siegel, *Sexual Harassment: Research and Resources*, 12, 34–35; Jim Conway and Sally Conway, *Sexual Harassment No More* (Downer's Grove, Ill.:

InterVarsity Press, 1993), 89–98; Fitzgerald, et al., "The Incidence and Dimensions of Sexual Harassment in Academia and the Workplace"; Amber Coverdale Sumrall and Dena Taylor, eds., *Sexual Harassment: Women Speak Out* (Freedom, Calif.: Crossing Press, 1992); Celia Morris, *Bearing Witness: Sexual Harassment and Beyond: Everywoman's Story* (Boston: Little, Brown, 1994).

19. See Dziech and Weiner, *The Lecherous Professor*, 15; Richard Barickman, Sam Korn, Bernice Sandler, Yael Gold, Alayne Ormerod, and Lauren M. Weitzman, "An Ecological Perspective to Understanding Sexual Harassment," in *Ivory Power: Sexual Harassment on Campus*, ed. Michele A. Paludi (Albany: State University of New York Press: 1990), xvi–xvii.

20. See Sue Rosenberg Zalk, Judy Dederich, and Michele Paludi, "Women Students' Assessment of Consensual Relationships with Their Professors: Ivory Power Reconsidered," in *Academic and Workplace Sexual Harassment,* ed. Paludi and Barickman, 109; Paludi and Barickman, "Sexual Harassment of Students," 153.

21. See Dziech and Weiner, *The Lecherous Professor*, xx, 23–24; Eskenazi and Gallen, eds., *Sexual Harassment: Know Your Rights*, 111–12, 114–16, 118; American Association of University Professors, "Consensual Relations between Faculty and Students," *Academe* (July/August 1995): 64; J. Gross, "Love or Harassment? Campuses Bar (and Debate) Faculty-Student Sex," *New York Times*, 14 April 1993.

22. Dziech and Weiner, *The Lecherous Professor*, 36, 126–46, 175; Catharine R. Stimpson, "Overreaching: Sexual Harassment and Education," in *Academic and Workplace Sexual Harassment,* ed. Paludi and Barickman, 117; Stephanie Riger, "Gender Dilemmas in Sexual Harassment: Policies and Procedures," in *Sexual Harassment: Confrontations and Decisions*, ed. Wall, 208–9. For sociological and psychological data regarding who harasses and why, see Louise F. Fitzgerald and Lauren M. Weitzman, "Men Who Harass: Speculation and Data," in *Ivory Power*, ed. Paludi, 125–40; Sue Rosenberg Zalk, "Men in the Academy: A Psychological Profile of Harassment," in *Ivory Power*, ed. Paludi, 141–75.

23. See Dziech and Weiner, *The Lecherous Professor*, 147–62.

24. Frazier, et al., "Social Science Research on Lay Definitions of Sexual Harassment," 33; also see Barbara A. Gutek and Maureen O'Connor, "The Empirical Basis for the Reasonable Woman Standard," *Journal of Social Issues* 51 (1995): 154–55, 160; Gutek, "How Subjective Is Sexual Harassment?" 455–56, 461.

25. Quoted in Peggy Orenstein, *SchoolGirls: Young Women, Self-Esteem, and the Confidence Gap* (New York: Doubleday, 1994), 129.

26. See Deborah Tannen, *Talking from 9 to 5: Women and Men in the Workplace: Language, Sex and Power* (New York: Avon Books, 1994), 250–51.

27. Riger, "Gender Dilemmas in Sexual Harassment," 201; also see Nancy S. Ehrenreich, "Pluralist Myths and Powerless Men: The Ideology of Reasonableness in Sexual Harassment Law," in *Sexual Harassment: Confrontations and Decisions*, ed. Wall, 229–60. Since top, and not middle, management must ultimately approve sexual harassment policies and procedures, it is worth noting that 95 percent

of senior management at the nation's largest corporations are men. See Rochelle Sharpe, "Women Make Strides, but Men Stay Firmly in Top Company Jobs," *Wall Street Journal,* 29 March 1994. As Kathryn Pyne Addelson notes, "[L]abeling is not simply a matter of words. It is a matter of actions, authority, and dominance." *Moral Passages* (New York: Routledge, 1994), 123.

28. For some examples of these laments, as well as other complaints about political and cultural liberalism, see William A. Henry III, *In Defense of Elitism* (New York: Doubleday, Anchor Books, 1994); Dinesh D'Souza, *Illiberal Education: The Politics of Race and Sex on Campus* (New York: Vintage, 1992); Editorial, "Talking Dirty," *New Republic,* reprinted in *Sexual Harassment: Confrontations and Decisions,* ed. Wall, 225–28.

29. Paradigm (and ground-breaking) expressions of this view can be found in Catharine A. MacKinnon, *Sexual Harassment of Working Women: A Case of Sex Discrimination* (New Haven: Yale University Press, 1979); Catharine A. MacKinnon, *Feminism Unmodified: Discourses on Life and Law* (Cambridge: Harvard University Press, 1987), 103–16; also see Lin Farley, *Sexual Shakedown: The Sexual Harassment of Women on the Job* (New York: MacGraw-Hill, Warner Books, 1978); Center for Women Policy Studies, *Harassment and Discrimination of Women in Employment* (Washington, D.C.: Center for Women Policy Studies, 1981).

30. See Naomi Wolf, *Fire with Fire: The New Female Power and How to Use It* (New York: Fawcett Columbine, 1993), 193. Barbara Gutek and Barbara Morash refer to "sex-role spillover," where gender role expectations carry over into the workplace. See Barbara Gutek and Barbara Morash, "Sex-Ratios, Sex-Role Spillover, and Sexual Harassment of Women at Work," *Journal of Social Issues* 38 (1982): 55–74.

31. See Gwendolyn Ettes-Lewis, "High-Tech Lynching on Capitol Hill: Oral Narratives from African American Women," and Beverly Grier, "Making Sense of Our Differences," in *African American Women Speak Out on Anita Hill–Clarence Thomas,* ed. Smitherman, 80–99, 150–58.

32. See Rosemarie Tong, *Women, Sex, and the Law* (Savage, Md.: Rowman & Littlefield, 1984), 66; Suzanne Gibson, "Loose Rules and Likely Stories," in *Rethinking Sexual Harassment,* ed. Brant and Too, 74–75; Stimpson, "Overreaching," 121 n. 6; Childers, "Is There a Place for a Reasonable Woman in the Law?" 873–74; Webb, *Step Forward,* 29; Petrocelli and Repa, *Sexual Harassment on the Job,* 3/28.

33. Susan Estrich, "Sex at Work," *Stanford Law Review* 43 (1991): 813–61. Unable to credibly characterize Anita Hill as promiscuous, some U.S. senators accused her of being a psychotic woman with sexual fantasies. See Andrea Dworkin, "Introduction," in *Sexual Harassment: Women Speak Out,* ed. Sumrall and Taylor, 8–9.

34. Clare Brant and Yun Lee Too, "Introduction," in *Rethinking Sexual Harassment,* ed. Brant and Too, 17.

35. Edmund Wall, "The Definition of Sexual Harassment," in *Sexual Harassment: Confrontations and Decisions,* ed. Wall, especially 74–77.

36. See Tong, *Women, Sex, and the Law*, 77–79.
37. See Louise F. Fitzgerald, Suzanne Swan, and Karla Fischer, "Why Didn't She Just Report Him? The Psychological and Legal Implications of Women's Responses to Sexual Harassment," *Journal of Social Issues* 51 (1995): 117–38. Indeed, many women admit that, in hindsight, reporting their harassment was *worse* than just tolerating it. See Helen Watson, "Red Herrings and Mystifications," in *Rethinking Sexual Harassment*, ed. Brant and Too, 80 n. 9.
38. See Associated Press, "Man Harassed by Female Boss Gets $237,000," which reports that a manager of a Domino's Pizza outlet successfully sued his regional manager for sexual harassment. Professor J. Donald Silva from the University of New Hampshire was found guilty of sexual harassment by the university and was dismissed in 1993 but was reinstated in 1994 after filing suit against the university for wrongful dismissal. See Siegel, *Sexual Harassment: Research and Resources*, 50; also see Eskenazi and Gallen, eds., *Sexual Harassment: Know Your Rights*, 14; Petrocelli and Repa, *Sexual Harassment on the Job*, 3/2, 3/9; Kitzinger, "Anti-Lesbian Harassment," 129–30; Stimpson, "Overreaching," 117.
39. Susan T. Fiske and Peter Glick, "Ambivalence and Stereotypes Cause Sexual Harassment," in *Journal of Social Issues* 51 (1995): 105.
40. Susan Faludi, *Backlash: The Undeclared War against American Women* (New York: Crown, 1991), 65.
41. See Lois Copeland and Leslie R. Wolfe, *Violence against Women as Bias Motivated Hate Crime: Defining the Issues* (Washington, D.C.: Center for Women Policy Studies, 1991); Charlotte Bunch and Roxanna Carrillo, *Gender Violence: A Development and Human Rights Issue* (New Brunswick, N.J.: Center for Women's Global Leadership, Rutgers University, 1991); MacKinnon, *Sexual Harassment of Working Women*, 2; Webb, *Step Forward*, 26; National Organization for Women (NOW) Legal Resource Kit, "Overview of Federal Sexual Harassment Law," in *Sexual Harassment: Know Your Rights*, ed. Eskenazi and Gallen, 128; Petrocelli and Repa, *Sexual Harassment on the Job*, 1/2.
42. See Estrich, "Sex at Work," 815; Siegel, *Sexual Harassment: Research and Resources*, 11–12; MacKinnon, *Sexual Harassment of Working Women*, 218–21.
43. See Siegel, *Sexual Harassment: Research and Resources*, 24; "Teen-on-Teen: Sexual Harassment," *Issues Quarterly* 1, no. 1 (1994): 1–11; Myra Sadker and David Sadker, *Failing at Fairness: How Our Schools Cheat Girls* (New York: Simon & Schuster, Touchstone, 1995), 110–15; Orenstein, *SchoolGirls*, 111–54; also see Cekola, "Orange County Student, 13, Files Sexual Harassment Suit."
44. See Fiske and Glick, "Ambivalence and Stereotypes Cause Sexual Harassment"; Webb, *Step Forward*, 66–67; Petrocelli and Repa, *Sexual Harassment on the Job*, 1/2; John Bargh and Paula Raymond, "The Naive Misuse of Power: Nonconscious Sources of Sexual Harassment," *Journal of Social Issues* 51 (1995): 85–96; Dziech and Weiner, *The Lecherous Professor*, 115–46; Fitzgerald and Weitzman, "Men Who Harass"; Zalk, "Men in the Academy."
45. For a fascinating look at harassment beyond the workplace and educational institutions, where antidiscrimination legal sanctions against sexual harassment do

not apply, see Carol Brooks Gardner, *Passing By: Gender and Public Harassment* (Berkeley: University of California Press, 1995).

46. See Harmon, "Caltech Student's Expulsion." For more examples of Internet sexual harassment, see Cheris Kramarae and Jana Kramer, "Net Gains, Net Losses," *Women's Review of Books* (February 1995); also see Mark Dery, ed., *Flame Wars: The Discourse of Cyberculture* (Durham, N.C.: Duke University Press, 1994). For testimonials to the variety and debility of sexual harassment, see Sumrall and Taylor, *Sexual Harassment: Women Speak Out*; Morris, *Bearing Witness*; Office of the Inspector General, *The Tailhook Report*, 37–57; M. Komaromy, A. B. Bindman, R. J. Haber, and M. A. Sande, "Sexual Harassment in Medical Training," *New England Journal of Medicine* 328 (1993): 322–26; Greta Foff Paules, *Dishing It Out: Power and Resistance among Waitresses in a New Jersey Restaurant* (Philadelphia: Temple University Press, 1991); Siegel, *Sexual Harassment: Research and Resources*, 23–32, 47, 51.

47. Kitzinger, "Anti-Lesbian Harassment," 129. For ways in which surveys may fail to identify women's sexual harassment, see Fitzgerald, et al., "The Incidence and Dimensions of Sexual Harassment in Academia and the Workplace," 170; Gutek, "How Subjective Is Sexual Harassment?" 461–62; Riger, "Gender Dilemmas in Sexual Harassment," 207; also see Karen Bursik, "Perceptions of Sexual Harassment in an Academic Context," *Sex Roles* 27 (1992): 401–12.

48. Quoted in Orenstein, *SchoolGirls*, 120.

49. Katie Roiphe, *The Morning After: Sex, Fear, and Feminism on Campus* (Boston: Little, Brown, 1993), 100.

50. Camille Paglia, "The Strange Case of Clarence Thomas and Anita Hill," in *Sex, Art, and American Culture* (New York: Vintage Books, 1992), 47.

51. See Kathleen Kelley Reardon, *They Don't Get It, Do They? Communication in the Workplace—Closing the Gap between Men and Women* (Boston: Little, Brown, 1995); also see Meg Sullivan, "Some Hard Facts about Soft-Spoken Women," review of *They Don't Get It, Do They?* by Reardon, *University of Southern California Chronicle*, 17 April 1995.

52. Wolf, *Fire with Fire*, 192.

53. Ibid., 142. For Wolf's explication of the meaning and mythology of "victim feminism" versus "power feminism," see ibid., 135–51.

54. Ibid., 139.

55. Ibid., 135–42; 191–97.

56. Rene Denfeld, *The New Victorians: A Young Woman's Challenge to the Old Feminist Order* (New York: Warner Books, 1995), 62–76.

57. Ibid., 73.

58. Ibid., 58–62.

59. Ibid., 61.

60. Ibid., 76–83.

61. Ibid., 84–89.

62. Ellen Frankel Paul, "Bared Buttocks and Federal Cases," in *Sexual Harassment: Confrontations and Decisions*, ed. Wall, 153.

63. Ibid., 153–56.

64. Ibid., 156–57.

65. Daphne Patai and Noretta Koertge, *Professing Feminism: Cautionary Tales from the Strange World of Women's Studies* (New York: Basic Books, 1994), 62–66.

66. Ibid., 80.

67. Ibid., 50–52, 77–78.

68. Ibid., 59–76.

69. Christina Hoff Sommers, *Who Stole Feminism? How Women Have Betrayed Women* (New York: Simon & Schuster, 1994), 92–93.

70. Ibid., 93–94.

71. Ibid., 105–6, 112–16.

72. Ibid., 181–87.

73. Ibid., 181–87, 209–26.

74. Ibid., 270–72.

75. Roiphe, *The Morning After*, 52–55, 59–60.

76. Ibid., 79–80.

77. Ibid., 65.

78. Ibid., 62–65, 69, 71–72, 74.

79. Ibid., 67, 75–76, 79, 81–82, 92.

80. Ibid., 87.

81. Ibid., 89.

82. Ibid., 89–90, 94–99.

83. Ibid., 107.

84. Ibid., 111–12.

85. Paglia, "Rape and Modern Sex War," in *Sex, Art, and American Culture*, 51.

86. Ibid., 49–52; Paglia, "The Rape Debate, Continued," in *Sex, Art, and American Culture*, 64, 67, 69–70; Camille Paglia, "No Law in the Arena: A Pagan Theory of Sexuality," in *Vamps and Tramps* (New York: Vintage Books, 1994), 35.

87. Paglia, "Rape and Modern Sex War," in *Sex, Art, and American Culture*, 53.

88. Paglia, "The Rape Debate, Continued," in *Sex, Art, and American Culture*, 56–60, 63–66, 68; Paglia, "No Law in the Arena," in *Vamps and Tramps*, 31–32, 35, 45–47.

89. Paglia, "The Rape Debate, Continued," in *Sex, Art, and American Culture*, 57, 60–61, 66, 73; Paglia, "No Law in the Arena," in *Vamps and Tramps*, 27, 30, 32.

90. Paglia, "The Rape Debate, Continued," and "The M.I.T Lecture: Crisis in the American Universities," in *Sex, Art, and American Culture*, 59, 268–69; Paglia, "No Law in the Arena," in *Vamps and Tramps*, 25–26.

91. Paglia, "The Strange Case of Clarence Thomas and Anita Hill," in *Sex, Art, and American Culture*, 46–48; Paglia, "No Law in the Arena," in *Vamps and Tramps*, 48.

92. Paglia, "The Rape Debate, Continued," in *Sex, Art, and American Culture*, 58–59, 68; Paglia, "Introduction," and "No Law in the Arena," in *Vamps and Tramps*, xii, xiv, 23, 47, 49, 53.

93. Paglia, "The Rape Debate, Continued," and "The M.I.T. Lecture," in *Sex, Art, and American Culture*, 64, 269; Paglia, "No Law in the Arena," in *Vamps and Tramps*, 23–25, 54–55.

94. Paglia, "No Law in the Arena," in *Vamps and Tramps*, 49–51, 53–56.

95. Paglia, "No Law in the Arena," "Woody Allen Agonistes," and "Satires and Short Takes," in *Vamps and Tramps*, 50, 52, 132, 400.

96. Eleanor K. Bratton, "The Eye of the Beholder: An Interdisciplinary Examination of Law and Social Research on Sexual Harassment," *New Mexico Law Review* 17 (1987): 99, quoted in Childers, "Is There a Place for a Reasonable Woman in the Law?" 867 n. 42.

97. Wolf, *Fire with Fire*, 196–97.

98. For reviews and criticisms of some of the feminist perspectives expressed in the third section of this essay, see Leora Tanenbaum, "Divide and Conquer?" review of *The New Victorians*, by Denfeld, in *Women's Review of Books* (June 1995); Carol Sternhell, "The Proper Study of Womankind," reviews of *Who Stole Feminism?* by Sommers, and *Professing Feminism*, by Patai and Koertge, *Women's Review of Books* (December 1994); Leora Tanenbaum, "Fear of Feminism," review of *Professing Feminism*, by Patai and Koertge, *In These Times*, 28 November 1994, 36–38; also see Katha Pollitt, "Not Just Bad Sex," review of *The Morning After*, by Roiphe, *New Yorker* (4 October 1993), 220–24; Ruth Picardi, "Culture of Complaint," review of *The Morning After*, by Roiphe, *New Statesman and Society* (January 1994): 37. For feminist critiques of Camille Paglia's views of men, women, and feminism, see Molly Ivins, "I Am the Cosmos," *Mother Jones*, September/October 1991; B. Ruby Rich, "Top Girl," *Village Voice*, 8 October 1991; Teresa L. Ebert, "The Politics of the Outrageous," *Women's Review of Books* (October 1991).

99. See Orenstein, *SchoolGirls*, 117.

100. Office of the Inspector General, *The Tailhook Report*, 17, 45, 50.

101. For critical commentary on this case, see Sommers, *Who Stole Feminism?* 271; Paglia, "No Law in the Arena," in *Vamps and Tramps*, 50.

102. Gutek, "How Subjective Is Sexual Harassment?" 459.

103. Bargh and Raymond, "The Naive Misuse of Power."

104. For court cases in which white men's sexual harassment of black women complicates the issue of discrimination, see Judy Trent Ellis, "Sexual Harassment and Race: A Legal Analysis of Discrimination," *Journal of Legislation* 8, no. 1 (1981): 41–44.

105. See Tannen, *Talking from 9 to 5*, 257–60; also see Linda LeMoncheck, *Dehumanizing Women: Treating Women as Sex Objects* (Lanham, Md.: Rowman & Littlefield, 1985), 87–89.

106. See Orenstein, *SchoolGirls*, 150.

107. See LeMoncheck, *Dehumanizing Women*, 89–90, 92–94. For further dis-

cussion of the relationship between sexual self-image and identity, see E. Person, "Sexuality as the Mainstay of Identity," in *Women: Sex and Sexuality*, ed. Catherine R. Stimpson and Elaine S. Person (Chicago: University of Chicago Press, 1980).

108. MacKinnon, *Sexual Harassment of Working Women*, 182, 189, also see 178–92, 219–20.

109. Roiphe, *The Morning After*, 102.

110. Fitzgerald, et al., "Why Didn't She Just Report Him?" 124–25.

111. Paglia, "The Rape Debate, Continued," in *Sex, Art, and American Culture*, 69; Paglia, "No Law in the Arena," in *Vamps and Tramps*, 25.

112. For a discussion of how philosophical analyses of rape, sexual harassment, sexual battering, and the sexual abuse of women and girls can benefit from identifying the conceptual and normative overlap among types of intimidation, see Linda LeMoncheck, "Appropriating Women's Bodies: The Form and Function of Men's Sexual Intimidation of Women," chap. 5 in *Loose Women, Lecherous Men: A Feminist Philosophy of Sex* (New York: Oxford University Press, 1997).

113. Ellis, "Sexual Harassment and Race," 39–45. I borrow the braiding example from Ettes-Lewis, "High-Tech Lynching on Capitol Hill," 86.

114. Grier, "Making Sense of Our Differences."

115. Elsa Barkley Brown, "Imaging Lynching: African American Women, Communities of Struggle, and Collective Memory," and Angela Y. Davis, "Clarence Thomas as Lynching Victim: Reflections on Anita Hill's Role in the Thomas Confirmation Hearings," in *African American Women Speak Out on Anita Hill–Clarence Thomas*, ed. Smitherman, 100–124, 178–81; also see Grier, "Making Sense of Our Differences"; Margaret Randall, "Doublespeak and Doublehear, Anita Hill in Our Lives," in *Sexual Harassment: Women Speak Out*, ed. Sumrall and Taylor, 19; Tong, *Women, Sex, and the Law*, 162–66.

116. Kitzinger, "Anti-Lesbian Harassment," 133, also see 131–33; American Association of University Women, *Hostile Hallways*, 23.

117. Kitzinger, "Anti-Lesbian Harassment," 134–36; also see Tong, *Women, Sex, and the Law*, 186–89.

118. See Tong, *Women, Sex, and the Law*, 71; also see Brant and Too, "Introduction," 8.

119. See Asra Q. Nomani, "Was Prof's Lecture Academic Freedom or Sexual Harassment?" *Wall Street Journal*, 7 March 1995.

120. See EEOC, "Notice of Proposed Rulemaking," *Federal Register* 58 (1 October 1993): 51266.

121. See note 7 above; Gutek and O'Connor, "The Empirical Basis for the Reasonable Woman Standard," 154–60; Gutek, "How Subjective Is Sexual Harassment?"; Fitzgerald, et al., "Why Didn't She Just Report Him?" Identifying sexual harassment as "sex as a condition of employment" makes it especially difficult for prostitutes and other sex workers to allege sexual coercion or bribery, since the "condition" already defines the terms of their work; so too, prostitutes' apparent consent to sex makes any charges of rape by customers or pimps almost

impossible to legitimize. Of course, making many sex workers' work illegal only exacerbates this problem. See LeMoncheck, " 'I Only Do It for the Money': Pornography, Prostitution, and the Business of Sex," chap. 4 in *Loose Women, Lecherous Men*.

122. Fitzgerald, et al., "Why Didn't She Just Report Him?" 126–29.

123. Addelson, *Moral Passages*, 171; also see Addelson's incisive critique of the ways in which professionals disguise the collective process of their expertise as individually and objectively knowable in her "The Knowers and the Known," chap. 7, *Moral Passages*, 160–82.

124. See Paglia, "No Law in the Arena," in *Vamps and Tramps*, 45. A description of the board game "Harassment" can be found in Brant and Too, "Introduction," 13.

125. I flesh out the thesis that women are both the objects and the subjects of our sexual experience as women in my *Loose Women, Lecherous Men*. For an overview of the epistemology required to think and talk about women's sexuality in this way, see my "What Is a Feminist Philosophy of Sex?" chap. 1 in *Loose Women, Lecherous Men*.

126. MacKinnon, *Sexual Harassment of Working Women*, 217.

127. See Kathryn Quina, "The Victimizations of Women," in *Ivory Power*, ed. Paludi, 99–100.

128. Patai and Koertge, *Professing Feminism*, 78–79.

129. See Robin S. Dillon, "Care and Respect" in *Explorations in Feminist Ethics: Theory and Practice*, ed. Eve Browning Cole and Susan Coultrap-McQuin (Bloomington: Indiana University Press, 1992), 69–81; also see my analysis of a sexual ethic of care respect in "Challenging the Normal and the Perverse: Feminist Speculations on Sexual Preference," chap. 3 in *Loose Women, Lecherous Men*.

130. María Lugones, "Playfulness, 'World'-Traveling, and Loving Perception," in *Women, Knowledge, and Reality: Explorations in Feminist Philosophy*, ed. Ann Garry and Marilyn Pearsall (Boston: Unwin Hyman, 1989), 275–90. For the importance of both respect and empathy in discussions of treating women as sex objects, see Linda LeMoncheck, "What Is Wrong with Treating a Woman as a Sex Object?" in *Sex, Love, and Friendship*, ed. Alan Soble and Barbara Kirschner (Atlanta and Amsterdam: Rodopi, 1996); Linda LeMoncheck, "Feminist Politics and Feminist Ethics: Treating Women as Sex Objects," in *Philosophical Perspectives on Sex and Love*, ed. Robert M. Stewart (New York: Oxford University Press, 1995), 29-38.

131. Childers, "Is There a Place for a Reasonable Woman in the Law?" 871–72 n. 55.

132. Ehrenreich, "Pluralist Myths and Powerless Men," 246–47.

133. However, Judy Ellis advocates "front pay" as well, since back pay may not adequately recompense the plaintiff or deter the harasser and reinstatement is often impossible when the harasser is the boss. See her "Sexual Harassment and Race," 38.

134. See Petrocelli and Repa, *Sexual Harassment on the Job*, chaps. 5–8; NOW

Legal Resource Kit, "Overview of Federal Sexual Harassment Law," 120–50; Michele A. Paludi, Marc Grossman, Carole Ann Scott, Joni Kindermann, Susan Matula, Julie Ostwald, Judi Dovan, and Donna Mulcahy, "Myths and Realities: Sexual Harassment on Campus," in *Ivory Power*, ed. Paludi, 4–5; Sandra Shullman and Barbara Watts, "Legal Issues," in *Ivory Power*, ed. Paludi, 255–60. For a discussion of recent federal court decisions in which school districts were found liable for the sexual harassment of their students by other students, see David G. Savage, "School Officials Face Lawsuits if They Ignore Sex Harassment of Students," *Los Angeles Times*, 2 September 1996.

135. EEOC, "Guidelines on Discrimination Because of Sex," *Code of Federal Regulations* 29, sec.1604.11(a)–(c) (1996); Title VII of the *Civil Rights Act of 1964*, as amended, secs. 703(a)–(c); EEOC, *Theories of Discrimination* (Washington, D.C.: U.S. Government Printing Office, Office of the EEOC, 1995), 22; also see Webb, *Step Forward*, 7–21, 25–29, 31–36; Petrocelli and Repa, *Sexual Harassment on the Job*, 2/4–27, 4/5; Eskenazi and Gallen, eds., *Sexual Harassment: Know Your Rights*, 160–89; Dziech and Weiner, *The Lecherous Professor*, 19–21; *Meritor Savings Bank v. Vinson* 477 U.S. 57 (1986). Jolynn Childers points out that the Supreme Court in *Meritor* interpreted the guidelines as requiring severe or pervasive conduct *and* the creation of an abusive environment for sexual harassment that is not of the quid pro quo type. See Childers, "Is There a Place for a Reasonable Woman in the Law?" 860 n. 18, also see 879.

136. See Estrich, "Sex at Work," 830, 833; Melinda A. Roberts, "Sexual Harassment, the Acquiescent Plaintiff, and the 'Unwelcomeness' Requirement," in *"Nagging" Questions: Feminist Ethics in Everyday Life*, ed. Dana E. Bushnell (Lanham, Md.: Rowman & Littlefield, 1995), 105–22; also see A. C. Juliano, "Did She Ask for It? The 'Unwelcome' Requirement in Sexual Harassment Cases," *Cornell Law Review* 77 (1992): 1558–92.

137. See Fitzgerald, et al., "Why Didn't She Just Report Him?" 130–34.

138. Mitsubishi reportedly shut down its two assembly lines for the day and offered a free lunch and full day's pay to anyone who joined a 15 April 1996 march to downtown Chicago's EEOC offices to protest the EEOC's filing of sexual harassment charges on behalf of five hundred female Mitsubishi employees. Mitsubishi also warned its workers that negative publicity about the suit could result in layoffs due to lower sales. Workers were then asked to counter EEOC allegations with letters to politicians and local newspapers. In light of all this, plus an extra paid day off to lobby against the EEOC by using specially installed telephone banks at the plant, an assembly line worker's assertion that male and female workers organized the march of their own free will appears suspect. So too, given the litany of reports of coerced oral sex, pervasive and pornographic bathroom graffiti, monkey noises, and air guns blown up women's dresses on the assembly line (to name but a few examples), it is a fascinating testimonial to the interpretive process of sexual harassment to hear A'nna Rogers, a Mitsubishi technical coordinator, assert, "Sure, there's some sexual harassment at Mitsubishi, just like there is in any factory in America. But it's no worse than anywhere else, not like the government

says. And this company doesn't tolerate it at all." See Stephen Braun, "Workers Protest Harassment Suit against Mitsubishi," *Los Angeles Times*, 16 April 1996.

139. Drucilla Cornell, *The Imaginary Domain: Abortion, Pornography and Sexual Harassment* (New York: Routledge, 1995): 191–93.

140. Ellison v. Brady, 924 F. 2d 872 (9th Cir. 1991); also see Childers, "Is There a Place for a Reasonable Woman in the Law?" 883–88.

141. See Gutek and O'Connor, "The Empirical Basis for the Reasonable Woman Standard," 151–54; Childers, "Is There a Place for a Reasonable Woman in the Law?" 888–902 (Childers also points out that a "reasonable man" criterion has similar problems with overgeneralization); Cornell, *The Imaginary Domain*, 174–78, 201–5; Ehrenreich, "Pluralist Myths and Powerless Men," 244–53; Kathryn Abrams, "Gender Discrimination and Transformation of Workplace Norms," *Vanderbilt Law Review* 42 (1989): 1183–248; M. Chamallas, "Feminist Constructions of Objectivity: Multiple Perspectives in Sexual and Racial Harassment Litigation," *Texas Journal of Women and Law* 1 (1992): 95–142.

142. Sarah E. Burns, "Issues in Workplace Sexual Harassment Law and Related Social Science Research," *Journal of Social Issues* 51 (1995): 203.

143. Gutek and O'Connor, "The Empirical Basis for the Reasonable Woman Standard," 154–63.

144. Jane L. Dolkart, "Hostile Environment Harassment: Equality, Objectivity, and the Shaping of Legal Standards," *Emory Law Journal* 43 (winter 1994): 151–244.

145. Cornell, *The Imaginary Domain*, 205.

146. Roberts, "Sexual Harassment, the Acquiescent Plaintiff, and the 'Unwelcomeness' Requirement," 113–15.

147. Watson, "Red Herrings and Mystifications," 67. For a discussion of how sexual fantasies inform judgments of credibility, see Patricia Williams, "A Rare Case Study of Muleheadedness and Men," in *Race-ing Justice, En-gendering Power*, ed. Morrison, 159-71.

148. Siegel, *Sexual Harassment: Research and Resources*, 45; however, on the biases at work in assessing a woman's "provocative dress," see Childers, "Is There a Place for a Reasonable Woman in the Law?" 872 and n. 57.

149. MacKinnon, *Sexual Harassment of Working Women*, 26 (emphasis in original).

150. Ibid., 164–74; Kathryn Abrams, "Gender Discrimination and the Transformation of Workplace Norms."

151. See Tong, *Women, Sex, and the Law*, 74–77.

152. Riger, "Gender Dilemmas in Sexual Harassment," 207.

153. See Orenstein, *SchoolGirls*, 113.

154. Alan Charles Kors, "Harassment Policies at the University," in *Sexual Harassment: Confrontations and Decisions*, ed. Wall, 41–47.

155. William Petrocelli and Barbara Repa report that the average company can lose up to $6.7 million a year in productivity-related costs through lack of sexual harassment policies. The National Council for Research on Women reports that in

1993 over fifteen hundred complainants filing with the EEOC won a total of $25.2 million from their employers, up 98.3 percent from 1992. Many feminists attribute the increase in large part to the publicity surrounding the 1991 Anita Hill–Clarence Thomas congressional hearings, which in turn prompted passage of a bill allowing tort damage claims to be filed with the EEOC under Title VII. This bill was a compromise for many feminists, since damages are capped according to the number of employees. In fact, the 1993 statistic does not reflect Title IX nonemployee restitution and damages that have not yet been capped by Congress, awards under state FEP laws, or awards won through private tort claims. See Siegel, *Sexual Harassment: Research and Resources*, 44; Petrocelli and Repa, *Sexual Harassment on the Job*, 1/24, 4/4, 6/6–7.

156. As Susan Webb points out, "The sooner we realize that it [sexual harassment] affects us all and that we all must play a part in solving this problem, the sooner we will be rid of it." Webb, *Step Forward*, xx; also see Petrocelli and Repa, *Sexual Harassment on the Job*, 6/4–13; Dziech and Weiner, *The Lecherous Professor*, 20–21.

157. In my discussion of sexual harassment social policy, I have benefited from the following references: Petrocelli and Repa, "Workplace Policies and Programs," chap. 4 in *Sexual Harassment on the Job*; "Handling Complaints of Sexual Harassment on Campus," sec. IV in *Ivory Power*, ed. Paludi, 191–250; Fitzgerald, et al., "Why Didn't She Just Report Him?" 135; Dziech and Weiner, *The Lecherous Professor*, 163–202; Gutek, "How Subjective Is Sexual Harassment?" 460–62; Riger, "Gender Dilemmas in Sexual Harassment," 203–8; Siegel, *Sexual Harassment: Research and Resources*, 13, 36, 39–44.

158. Quoted in Conway and Conway, *Sexual Harassment No More*, 29.

159. MacKinnon, *Sexual Harassment of Working Women*, 55.

160. Lugones, "Playfulness, 'World'-Traveling, and Loving Perception," 276–80.

161. John Cougar Mellencamp and G. M. Green, *Hurts So Good*, Riva Records, Inc., 1982.

162. Tannen, *Talking from 9 to 5*, 245.

2

Why the Fight against Sexual Harassment Is Misguided

Mane Hajdin

Much of the conduct that is currently classified as sexual harassment is morally wrong by almost any reasonable standard. It is conduct that no decent person would wish to condone, or even leave the appearance of condoning. That, however, does not mean that there are no questions regarding sexual harassment that are worthy of serious debate.

First, even with respect to conduct that is uncontroversially wrong, whether the nature of its wrongness is illuminated by classifying it as sexual harassment may be questionable. Second, people can agree that particular conduct, classified as sexual harassment, is morally wrong and still disagree in good faith over what the best way of dealing with it is. Specifically, decent and reasonable people may disagree over how much of such conduct should be handled by legal means and how much of it should be left to less formal mechanisms. When it is agreed that a particular form of such conduct should be handled by legal means, disagreements are still possible over the precise form that the laws on the matter should take. Finally, although it is easy to agree that much of the conduct currently classified as sexual harassment is morally wrong, it is by no means obvious that all of it is. Disagreements are possible over whether the net that the concept of sexual harassment casts over human sexual conduct is too wide, so that some innocuous acts get caught in it together with clearly wrong acts.

The character of these issues is bound to make any debate about sexual harassment less straightforward and more difficult than are the debates about most other contemporary moral issues. The debates about abortion, for example, focus on the far more straightforward issue of whether abortion is morally wrong or not. Typically, one of the two sides to such a debate regards abortion as very seriously wrong and thus as something that needs to be prohibited by law, while the other regards it as morally neutral and thus its legal availability as good. The contrast between these two positions is so stark that it is almost impossible to misunderstand what the conflict is about. Similarly, in the debates about affirmative action, one side typically argues that such policies are required by justice, while the other argues that they are manifestly unjust. Again, the starkness of the contrast makes such a debate easy to follow. The fact that the different viewpoints in a debate about sexual harassment are unlikely to be in such straightforward opposition means that there is a higher risk of their being misunderstood. Thus, if one argues that the current legal approach to sexual harassment is problematic, one can be all too easily misinterpreted as condoning the conduct that is so classified and thus as putting oneself on the side of various scoundrels that one does not really want to be associated with. The possibility of such misunderstandings is probably one of the reasons why some of the people who are, in fact, critical of different aspects of the present sexual harassment law have been reluctant to enter into debates about it publicly. I am well aware that some people will probably misinterpret my writing the "counterpoint" part of this volume in the same way. I do, however, hope that most of the readers will be careful enough to assess the arguments that follow on the basis of what they actually say.

Another way in which the debates about sexual harassment differ from debates about other moral problems is that one of the things at issue in the case of sexual harassment is the concept itself. The debates about abortion, for example, do not need to raise the question whether the concept of abortion is useful or well formed. It is normally taken for granted that the concept is useful and that we all know what it stands for; the interesting questions regarding abortion are not about the concept itself but about whether what the concept stands for is wrong or not. The usefulness and clarity of the concept of abortion would indeed be difficult to deny, given that it has been a part of our everyday conceptual framework for a fairly long time.

This is not so with the concept of sexual harassment. It is not a concept that came into being spontaneously, in some distant past. Rather, it is a concept that was created by feminist activists in the mid-seventies and was put in circulation by their deliberate efforts. Their main aim in creating the concept was to prompt the appearance of a body of law that would regulate the phenomena to which they applied it, and in that aim they have largely been successful. Only after the phrase "sexual harassment" had acquired currency in legal and theoretical contexts did it begin to percolate into everyday parlance. The phrase thus does not have an independently established everyday meaning; whatever meaning it does have in everyday communication is dependent on its meaning in legal and theoretical contexts, which is where its original "home" is. It is important not to be misled here by the fact that the word "sexual" and the word "harassment" do have well-established everyday meanings, because the meaning of "sexual harassment" is not a result of simply "adding up" the meanings of its two constituent words.

In this essay, I shall raise some doubts as to whether the concept of sexual harassment is useful or even well formed. So that my own use of the phrase is not regarded as preempting the challenges that I want to make to the concept, I need to make it clear at the beginning that I shall be using it in a noncommittal way. Whenever the phrase "sexual harassment" appears on the pages that follow, it should be read as an abbreviation for "the conduct that is currently labeled 'sexual harassment,' " without any suggestion that labeling the conduct in that way is, in fact, illuminating, useful, or unproblematic.

I shall use the phrase "the sexual harassment law" or "the law about sexual harassment" to refer only to the body of law in which the concept of sexual harassment plays a crucial role. This needs to be emphasized because the conduct to which the concept applies is often capable of being subsumed under other legal categories and thus often can be, and sometimes actually is, dealt with through other legal mechanisms. Thus, for example, the more drastic forms of sexual harassment may fit legal definitions of rape or assault, and can be prosecuted as such, under criminal law. Many cases of sexual harassment, to take another example, can be litigated as cases of intentional infliction of emotional distress under the general principles of the law of torts. The phrases "the sexual harassment law" and "the law about sexual harassment," as I use them in this essay, do not cover such legal mechanisms that can be used for dealing with sexual harassment but are not specifically aimed at it.

Having made these preliminary remarks, let me now acquaint the reader with my plan for this essay. The essay will consist of two main sections. The first section will be, so to speak, defensive. In that section, I shall consider several possible reasons for thinking that sexual harassment is morally wrong and conclude that none of them provides support for the fight against sexual harassment in anything like its present form. In the second half of the essay, I shall launch several more direct attacks on the law about sexual harassment, as well as on the nonlegal activities aimed at eradicating it: I shall be arguing that the law and these other activities are, in fact, pernicious.

Throughout most of the essay, my aim will be to criticize the way in which sexual harassment has actually been dealt with over the last two decades, and its theoretical background. I shall not attempt to produce a detailed positive account of what approach to sexual harassment should replace the present one, but I shall, at the end of the essay, offer a few hints in that direction.

The Wrong Reasons for Supporting the Fight against Sexual Harassment

In this section, I shall argue that the reasons that lead people to think that sexual harassment is morally wrong do not prove it to be wrong in the way that justifies special organized measures aimed at fighting it. In the course of that discussion, I shall acknowledge that these reasons may show that many instances of sexual harassment are morally wrong, but I shall argue that they fail to establish that sexual harassment *as a type of conduct* is morally wrong. In other words, the aim of this section is to show that the concept of sexual harassment is not a morally significant concept. The distinctions between sexual harassment and other similar kinds of conduct are not morally significant distinctions. Moreover, there are morally significant distinctions that the concept of sexual harassment hides: even when it is granted that much of the conduct that is classified as sexual harassment is morally wrong, it is difficult to escape the conclusion that different instances of that conduct are wrong on very different grounds. The thesis defended here is thus that classifying an act as an act of sexual harassment, even when it is granted that the act is morally wrong, does not reveal, but obscures, the ground of its wrongness. Our moral thinking about these matters is thus not assisted but confused by bringing into it the concept of sexual harassment.

The arguments of this section will present the claim that sexual harassment is morally wrong as similar to the claim that the acts that take place in dark alleys in the middle of the night are morally wrong. The latter claim is not entirely implausible. There are indeed quite a few acts taking place in dark alleys in the middle of the night that are morally wrong. But classifying those acts as acts taking place in dark alleys in the middle of the night does not illuminate but endarkens the grounds of their wrongness. An act of theft taking place in a dark alley in the middle of the night is, everyone would agree, morally wrong, but it is wrong in virtue of being an act of theft, not in virtue of taking place in a dark alley in the middle of the night. An act of rape taking place in a dark alley in the middle of the night is morally wrong in virtue of being an act of rape, not in virtue of occurring at such a place and time. An act of rape taking place in a dark alley in the middle of the night is morally wrong for the same reasons for which acts of rape at other times of the day and other locations are morally wrong. Different acts taking place in dark alleys in the middle of the night are wrong for different reasons: some because they are acts of theft, others because they are acts of rape, and so on. The concept of "an act taking place in a dark alley in the middle of the night" draws morally irrelevant distinctions, such as that between rapes that take place in dark alleys in the middle of the night and rapes that take place at other times and locations, and hides some morally significant distinctions, such as the one between thefts and rapes that take place in dark alleys in the middle of the night. "An act taking place in a dark alley in the middle of the night" is, therefore, not a morally significant concept. Although much of the conduct taking place in dark alleys in the middle of the night may well be morally wrong, that *type* of conduct is not morally wrong as such. What makes the claim that such conduct is wrong plausible is the fact that there happens to be considerable overlap between it and the types of conduct that are wrong as types, such as theft or rape.

Because the concept of "an act taking place in a dark alley in the middle of the night" is not a morally significant concept, we would find it bizarre, if not downright worrisome, if someone were to propose that a special rule for dealing with such acts be introduced into the legal system, a rule that would make these acts punishable as such. Even if we accept, for the sake of argument, that not many morally acceptable acts are, in fact, performed in dark alleys in the middle of the night, it still remains true that it is possible for such acts to be performed. If such acts were to be performed, they would be punishable under the rule, and that would strike us as unjust. Moreover, the rule would jumble together, under the same legal category, conduct that intuitively strikes us as morally wrong in very different ways, such as thefts and rapes. It seems far better to legally handle the wrongful conduct that occurs in dark alleys in the middle of the night by subsuming it under the concepts that reveal the real grounds of its wrongness, such as the concepts of theft or rape. We would also find it ludicrous if people insisted that those who suffered thefts in dark alleys in the middle of the night ought to think of themselves not simply as victims of theft, but that they should rather focus on thinking of themselves as victims of acts that occurred in dark alleys in the middle of the night. The arguments of this section will show that, analogously to "an act taking place in a dark alley in the middle of the night," "sexual harassment" is not a morally significant concept, and will thus lead to the conclusion that there is no good reason for having special laws and other institutions specifically devoted to eradicating sexual harassment. The arguments will, however, go even beyond that, in that they will show that some of the reasons that lead people to think that sexual harassment is wrong, when their implications are thought through, put sexual harassment morally on a par with actions most people think ought not to be legally regulated.

For the purposes of the first section of this essay, it will not be necessary to enter into detailed analysis of the concept of sexual harassment. The general knowledge of what the concept is applied to, that the readers have acquired through everyday experience, will be sufficient for following the arguments of this section. There is, however, one feature of the concept of sexual harassment that it may be useful to make explicit at this point because it will play an important role in the arguments that follow. The concept of sex al harassment can be applied to certain conduct only if that conduct occurs within a formal framework of a kind that is specified by the law. Employment and formal education are such kinds of frameworks, and it is within these two that the concept is applied most often. In recent years, some jurisdictions have enacted laws that make the concept applicable within some other kinds of formal frameworks, such as those of providing housing or professional services. But the concept simply cannot be applied outside a designated framework; otherwise similar conduct that occurs outside a workplace, educational institution, or other designated framework does not constitute sexual harassment. Any attempt to morally justify the law, or other special ways of dealing with sexual harassment, therefore has to explain why the fact that conduct takes place within a designated framework is supposed to be relevant. In other words, no argument in favor of the sexual harassment law and of the movement aimed at its eradication can be successful if it does not make any use of the character of the relevant formal frameworks.

With all these preliminaries in mind, let us now embark on a discussion of specific reasons that people may have for believing that sexual harassment is wrong.

Sexual Harassment Involves Adultery, Promiscuity, and Insensitivity

Much of sexual harassment involves conduct aimed at establishing sexual relationships that would be adulterous. Also, acts of sexual harassment often belong to a pattern of conduct that involves many short-term sexual relationships that are largely devoid of serious emotional involvement; in other words, it often involves promiscuity.

Most people believe that adultery and promiscuity are, in general, morally wrong (although the details of people's views on these matters differ considerably). It can be a matter of debate whether adultery and promiscuity are really wrong and what precisely it is that makes them wrong,[1] but I do not intend to enter into such debates here. I shall simply assume, for the sake of argument, that the prevailing view that adultery and promiscuity are morally wrong can be justified, in some way or other. If that view can be justified, then it follows that all cases of sexual harassment that involve (attempted) adultery or promiscuity (and there are quite a few of them) are also morally wrong. However, there are also quite a few cases of sexual harassment that involve neither adultery nor promiscuity and, therefore, cannot be wrong on that ground; if they are wrong at all, they are so on some other ground. Thus, although the wrongness of very many cases of sexual harassment can be established by pointing out that they involve adultery or promiscuity, it contributes nothing to proving that sexual harassment as a type of conduct is morally wrong. While there is considerable overlap between sexual harassment and these two types of sexual immorality, there is nothing more than an overlap: in addition to there being quite a few cases of sexual harassment that do not involve either adultery or promiscuity, there are many instances of adulterous and promiscuous conduct that do not constitute sexual harassment. Moreover, the existence and size of the overlap are contingent matters.

Therefore, if what one is bothered by in sexual harassment is the fact that it often involves adultery and promiscuity, then one should focus on the adulterous and promiscuous character of the relevant conduct and dispense with the notion of sexual harassment in thinking about it. One does not need the notion of sexual harassment to express one's moral concerns about adultery and promiscuity, because there already are other notions far better suited for *that* job, namely the notions of adultery and promiscuity.

If one believes that the wrongness of adulterous and promiscuous conduct warrants legal intervention, then one should advocate (re)introduction, or retention and revival, of legal prohibitions of adultery and promiscuity as such. Legal prohibitions of adultery and even of any kind of sex between people who are not married to each other existed in many jurisdictions until the not very distant past, and in some they are still "on the books," although they are practically never enforced. The idea that adultery and promiscuity should be legally prohibited as such may not have a very wide appeal nowadays, but it is a coherent idea. It is, however, incoherent to support the prohibition of sexual harassment on this ground, because that prohibition covers only *some* adulterous and promiscuous conduct, and even that is only contingent. Of course, if one does not believe that the wrongness of adultery and promiscuity is a reason for legal intervention, then it follows straightforwardly that the adulterous and promiscuous character of many instances of sexual harassment cannot be a reason for supporting the law about sexual harassment. Thus, regardless of what one thinks about whether adultery and promiscuity should be legally prohibited, one cannot rationally support the sexual harassment law on the ground of the adulterous and promiscuous character of the conduct involved.

Another way of understanding that point is to remind ourselves that sexual harassment is essentially conduct that occurs within a certain kind of formal framework, such as that of employment. But it is obviously irrelevant to the moral wrongness of, say, adultery, whether it occurs within or outside such a framework. An act of adultery taking place outside any such framework, viewed *as* adultery, is just as wrong as an otherwise similar act taking place within such a framework. The adulterous character of the latter act cannot provide a moral reason for its legal prohibition (or for legal prohibition of attempts at it) without also providing a moral reason for a legal prohibition of the former (and attempts at it).

Now, it is in principle possible for someone to agree that although the adulterous and promiscuous character of sexual harassment does not prove that sexual harassment as such is morally wrong, it may still justify the legal prohibition of sexual harassment, because the prohibition of sexual harassment is likely to be more effective in curtailing such sexual immorality than a straightforward prohibition of promiscuity and adultery. The old-fashioned legal prohibitions of sexual immorality were enforced by the legal system directly, and that, it could be argued, made them cumbersome to operate. The sexual harassment law, on the other hand, curtails such behavior through the employers of the individuals concerned, and the employers are arguably in a much better position to curtail the behavior effectively. Relying on such an argument would, however, be doubly unpopular: not only is support for the idea that sexual immorality such as adultery and promiscuity warrants formal intervention nowadays rather limited, but the argument also runs counter to the idea (which has become widely accepted in recent decades) that employees should enjoy a significant measure of privacy relative to their employers and that employers are allowed to intrude on that privacy only when there is a significant business-related reason for doing so.

Some of my more sophisticated readers will undoubtedly be tempted to say that I am here, in many ways, knocking at an open door because the literature that supports the sexual harassment law and the movement aimed at the eradication of such conduct normally does not rely on the adulterous and promiscuous character of the conduct involved as the ground of its wrongness. It is indeed true that the core of the feminist theorizing about sexual harassment does not use such arguments, but the literature about sexual harassment still often exploits the readers' preexisting attitudes about better-known forms of sexual immorality.

An influential report of early research on sexual harassment, carried out by the Working Women's Institute, for example, took the opportunity to mention that 79 percent of the harassers were married, in a manner that suggested that the fact was relevant to appreciating the seriousness of the problem.[2] A more recent article on sexual harassment quotes "a consultant . . . who specializes in sexual harassment issues," who offers what she calls the "Simple Test" of whether one's behavior is harassing.[3] The first question on that test is "Would you engage in this behavior if your partner or spouse were in the room?" Presenting the prohibition of sexual harassment in this way makes the connection between sexual harassment and adultery crucial, as most people would, of course, not engage in any behavior that is even suggestive of adulterous interests if their regular romantic partners were in the same room. Another question on the "Simple Test" is "Would you be comfortable reading about your behavior in the newspaper?" which presents the notion of sexual harassment as if it were a blanket notion for adultery, promiscuity, and practically every other form of sexual immorality: a person who engages in any such behavior typically would not be comfortable reading about it in the newspaper (not to mention that most people would not be too comfortable reading about their sexual behavior in a newspaper even when there is nothing immoral about it).

In other literature on sexual harassment, one reads that "most of the sex at work . . . does not grow out of a person's interest in establishing a long-term relationship with another employee"[4] and that "faculty Casanovas usually forget to inform the woman that she is only one in a long procession."[5] When interviewed about sexual harassment, a philosophy professor who chaired a committee dealing with such matters at her university said, "Graduate women don't realize, 'You're probably the umpteenth woman this professor had had.' "[6] Such remarks seem to be clearly intended to make people's views about sexual harassment influenced by their views about promiscuity.

Thus, although the connection between sexual harassment and such forms of sexual immorality as promiscuity and adultery is rarely presented as an explicit argument in favor of the sexual harassment law, it may easily, in the minds of many people, end up playing the role of such an argument. This is particularly important in light of the fact that the other arguments in favor of the law may not be fully understood by many people. Many ordinary people may thus be thinking something like the following:

> Some people believe very strongly that the sexual harassment law should exist. I do not quite understand all the reasons that they have for that belief, but I know that the law prohibits conduct, such as adultery and promiscuity, that is bad anyway. Therefore, I see no reason to oppose the law.

The existence of the sexual harassment law is probably as much a result of such quiet nonopposition as it is of direct militant support. Explicitly setting aside the argument that sexual harassment is wrong because it involves adultery and promiscuity is therefore an important first step in thinking about the law critically.

An argument similar to the one discussed above is sometimes made. It relies not on adultery and promiscuity but rather on more subtle forms of sexual immorality that do not have such well-established labels but that one might generally refer to as insensitivity in sexual interactions. Thus, Jan Crosthwaite and Christine Swanton say that

> the central aspect of the wrongness of sexual harassment is this. Behaviour of a sexual nature or motivation in the workplace counts as sexual harassment if and only if there is inadequate consideration of the interests of the person subjected to it.[7]

Now, it is easy to agree that sexual behavior in which "there is inadequate consideration of the interests of the person subjected to it" is morally wrong. But such insensitive conduct seems to be wrong in exactly the same way when it occurs outside a workplace, or any other designated formal framework, as it is when it occurs within it. It is, in the absence of some further argument, unclear why one should be *specially* concerned with insensitivity in sexual matters when it manifests itself within a designated formal framework, as opposed to simply being concerned with such insensitivity in general, regardless of where it manifests itself. It is unclear why insensitivity in sexual interactions should be treated differently depending on the surroundings in which it manifests itself. It is also unclear why insensitivity in sexual matters should receive more attention and be treated differently from insensitivity in other, nonsexual matters. Surely, "inadequate consideration of the interests of the person subjected to" some conduct is a morally bad thing regardless of whether the conduct is of a sexual nature or not. The incidents of nonsexual interaction in which people are insensitive to others, alas, occur every minute, and some of them are quite hurtful. If insensitivity is what one is concerned about, then it seems that one should be equally concerned with insensitivity in all social interactions, regardless of whether they are sexual or nonsexual. Bringing the notion of sexual harassment, with its focus on sexual matters, into one's thinking on these topics, only causes unnecessary confusion.

It is tempting to try to respond to the argument I have just made by saying that although insensitivity is always a bad thing, there is, in fact, a reason for being specially concerned about insensitivity within workplaces, educational institutions, and similar frameworks. It could be said that at such places people are more vulnerable to insensitive conduct of others, more likely to be adversely affected by it, than they are at other places. Being at work, for example, the argument could go, requires people to concentrate on whatever tasks they are expected to accomplish, which makes them feel tense and thus specially sensitive to the insensitive conduct of others.

However, even if thinking about sexual harassment as a form of insensitivity is supplemented in this way, it still does not show that sexual harassment as a type of conduct is wrong. First, the question of why insensitivity in sexual matters should be treated differently from insensitivity in nonsexual matters still remains unanswered. Second, while it is probably true that people are, on the average, significantly more tense and irritable while they are at work or at school than they are elsewhere, that is so only on the average. People often do find themselves under considerable stress and very tense while they are outside any such formal framework. On the other hand, workers in many occupations often enjoy considerable stretches of working time that are relatively free of tension. The difference between the average level of tension within designated formal frameworks and the average level of tension outside them does not justify drawing the *sharp* distinction that thinking in terms of sexual harassment makes between what happens within such frameworks and what happens outside them.

Furthermore, if the wrongness of sexual harassment is to be understood in terms of the insensitivity of its perpetrators, then the argument for its legal regulation becomes exceedingly weak. We do not normally think that the law should be preoccupied with insensitivity in social interactions.[8] The tools of the law are generally thought to be far too blunt for dealing with insensitivities as such, without causing more damage than benefit.

Sexual Harassment Involves Relationships of Unequal Power

A feature of many of the examples of sexual harassment that tend to be perceived as paradigmatic is a difference in age and general social status between the person engaging in the relevant conduct and the person to whom the conduct is directed. If one is asked to imagine a typical case of sexual harassment, chances are that what will first come to one's mind will be a case involving a balding, middle-aged executive and a subordinate employee in her twenties.[9] A considerable age difference is an even more obvious feature of sexual harassment in academic settings.

Many people seem to have a negative attitude toward sexual liaisons between persons of markedly different ages and social positions, although that attitude is by no means as widespread as negative attitudes toward adultery or promiscuity. The precise character of that attitude is not always clear, and it may vary from one person to another. In some people, this attitude may, upon analysis, turn out to be purely aesthetic and not at all moral. When it is moral, the grounds for it seem to involve the differences in life experiences, interests, and outlooks that typically accompany the differences in age and social status. One may, for example, believe that it is impossible for two people whose life experiences are as different as those of, say, a fifty-five-year-old executive and a twenty-two-year-old secretary are bound to be, to establish the kind of complete understanding and intimacy that one regards as necessary for a worthwhile romantic relationship. If one holds such a belief, one is led to regard all such liaisons as emotionally superficial, and if one also believes that all emotionally superficial sexual relationships are wrong, one is led to believe that all sexual liaisons between people of radically different ages or backgrounds are wrong. One may also believe that such a relationship is bound to be inegalitarian because the partner with more experience is bound to dominate it.

The factual premises of such reasoning are contestable, but what is relevant for our purposes is that even if the reasoning were sound, it would not in any way contribute to the justification of the law about sexual harassment. This line of thinking, again, does not support the claim that sexual harassment as a type of conduct is wrong. First, there are quite a few cases of conduct that is currently classified as sexual harassment to which the argument simply does not apply, because they involve people of similar age, social status, and so on. Second, the world is full of romantic relationships between people of vastly different ages and social positions, to which the concept of sexual harassment does not apply, because these relationships have been established and go on outside the framework of employment or education or any other formal framework within which the concept could be applied.

Even if it is, for the sake of argument, granted that such relationships are, in some way, less than ideal, it is generally thought that their less than ideal character does not provide a reason for legal intervention. It is, in general, legally permitted for men in their fifties and women in their twenties, whose incomes are much lower than the men's, to enter into romantic and sexual relationships, and most people think that this is as it should be. These relationships may lack complete mutual understanding and deep emotions, but even those among us who think that adulterous and promiscuous relationships should be outlawed are unlikely to think that it is the business of the law to ensure that all sexual relationships are accompanied by complete mutual understanding and deep emotions. Given that no one seems to be prepared to seriously argue that romantic and sexual relationships between people of radically different ages and/or social positions should be legally prohibited in general, it is not clear how a difference in age and/or social position could constitute a reason for legally prohibiting such relationships that happen to take place within a designated formal framework.

Indeed, some people would say that practically no personal relationships (including both romantic ones and nonromantic friendships) are ideally egalitarian, that in almost all of them one party tends to establish subtle dominance over the other. If one seriously thought that it is the proper business of the law to ensure that all personal relationships are completely egalitarian and free of such subtle forms of dominance, it would not be clear that any but a very few of our personal relationships should escape legal intervention.

Again, focusing on the differences in age and social status between the people concerned is not just something that somehow creeps into people's thinking about sexual harassment, despite its irrelevance. It is something that is explicitly invoked and exploited by those who wish to persuade us that the current approach to sexual harassment is justified. The already mentioned research report of the Working Women's Institute, for example, presents the fact that male harassers were, on the average, fourteen years older than the women to whom the conduct was directed, as if it were a part of what made the conduct wrong.[10] Another author writing on the topic says that "the sexual harasser uses his age or social position . . . as his weapons" and compares that with the way in which a rapist may use a gun or knife.[11]

It has also been claimed in the literature on sexual harassment that a relationship between an academic and a student should be regarded as suspect even when it leads to marriage, because "a faculty member's desire or willingness to marry a student does not necessarily imply equality in the relationship" and because "a faculty member's determination to marry his student may also have exploitative aspects."[12] These claims might or might not be true, but their place is surely in a discussion of what makes marriages and romantic relationships less than ideal. Their presence in the context of a discussion of sexual harassment only confuses the issues related to it.

This confusion is underwritten by the fact that feminists give very wide scope to the notions of power and domination. This has its justifications and may well be illuminating for some purposes. It, however, makes it all too easy to oscillate between discussion of very specific forms of institutional power that a boss has over a subordinate employee, simply in virtue of the rules that make one of them a boss and the other a subordinate employee, and discussion of other forms of (what such feminists would call) power that may exist between them. Such use of the word "power" enables feminists to overemphasize the similarities between cases in which a harasser abuses power of the first kind (say, by threatening not to rehire a subordinate employee if the employee does not comply with his sexual requests) and cases in which a person, consciously or unconsciously, uses power of the second kind to advance his sexual or romantic interests, that is, cases in which a person uses his experience, or the charisma that often comes with high social status, to make someone attracted to him. While it is fairly uncontroversial that abusing power of the first kind to advance one's sexual interests is seriously wrong and should be legally prohibited, the moral significance of the second form of power is not at all obvious.

For example, if someone makes a sexual advance knowing that he possesses a particular kind of charisma associated with high social status and that his possession of it increases the chances that the advance will be accepted, it is not at all obvious that he is *abusing* his charisma or, in general, that he is doing anything wrong. When a power is given to someone for a specific purpose, as is the case with formal power over a subordinate employee, then it is easy to see how using it for a different purpose, such as a sexual one, can constitute its abuse. But the power of the charisma that often comes with high social status is not bestowed on people for a specific purpose, and therefore it is not clear what could be meant by saying that someone is abusing it. It could be argued that a person who relies on that charisma in making sexual advances is not abusing anything but simply *using* an "asset" that increases his chances of being successful in sexual pursuits, and that there is no significant moral difference between him and people who make sexual advances knowing that they possess other kinds of "assets" that make them attractive (such as well-shaped bodies, wit, or good taste).

I am, of course, well aware that there is a line of thought that finds it troublesome, and regards it as an undesirable and eliminable feature of our culture, that such manifestations of power in the wide sense tend to be perceived as erotically attractive. That approach to sexuality is, however, in continuous conflict with the line of thought that regards power, broadly conceived, as intimately related to the timeless essence of erotic passion. Each of these two approaches to sexuality has a significant number of adherents in the society (as manifested, for example, by the high sales of *both* Catharine MacKinnon's and Camille Paglia's books), and it is unlikely that the conflict between them will be resolved in the near future. Given the highly controversial character of this issue, it seems unwise to use one of the opposed positions on it as a basis of public policy.

Moreover, even if one firmly embraced the first position and thought that regarding high social status as erotically attractive is undesirable and that we have a moral duty to work on eradicating that feature of the culture, it would still not follow that as long as social status continues to be erotically attractive to people, one would be justified in blaming (and still less in punishing) the individuals whose sexual attractiveness is thus enhanced. (Compare this point with the following: One may think that it is unjust or otherwise undesirable for medical doctors in the United States to be paid as much as they are. From that it does not follow, however, that there is anything blameworthy about an individual doctor, in the conditions of medical practice as they are at present, bargaining for and collecting the currently standard high fee.) Nor is there good reason to believe that punishing those who happen to profit from the erotic appeal of high social status is the most effective way to eliminate the appeal. If one seriously believes that the erotic appeal of such status is eliminable and that it ought to be eliminated, then it seems that one's course of action should be to try to persuade those who find social status and similar things attractive, to stop regarding them as attractive. It is only by following that path that one could possibly hope to achieve a stable result in this area.

The attributions of power in the wide sense in this context are based not only on the charisma of high social status but also on the possession of a certain kind of social skill that people often acquire with experience. A person who is old enough to have lived through quite a few sexual pursuits will usually have a better sense of what kinds of moves are likely to lead to what kinds of consequences in such interactions than someone much younger and less experienced. Thus, when an older, experienced person desires a sexual liaison with a younger, less experienced one who is initially reluctant, the older person will usually be able to profit from that experience in attempts to overcome the reluctance, while the younger one will not be able to draw on comparable experience. In such a case, chances are thus somewhat higher (other things being equal) that the older one will eventually overcome the younger one's reluctance than they would be if both people were of the same level of experience.

Again, it is entirely unclear why anyone would think that there is anything wrong with using social skills, acquired through experience, to advance one's sexual and romantic interests. There does not seem to be a morally significant difference between the use of such a social skill for that purpose and, for example, the use of adornment for the same purpose. Nor is there any clear reason for thinking that the use of such a social skill for that purpose is morally different from using other kinds of social skills for other purposes. For example, a person who has been through many job interviews in his life has thereby probably acquired certain skills that increase his chances of being successful at his next interview. If no one thinks that there is anything wrong with using that kind of experience in the pursuit of employment-related aims, why would anyone think that there is anything wrong with using an analogous experience in the pursuit of one's sex-related aims? The only possible answer is that the sex-related aims are somehow inherently more problematic than the employment-related ones. But if one makes that answer, then one effectively admits that it is not the imbalance of power that is morally significant here but rather the use to which the power is put. The argument thus gets transformed into something similar to the argument we have considered in the preceding subsection and thus is subject to similar counterarguments.

Moreover, once one begins to use the notion of power in the wide sense consistently, one finds that not only is it true that in many romantic relationships, both within and outside workplaces, educational institutions, and so on, one partner has power, in that wide sense, over the other but one can equally plausibly say that in many nonromantic friendships, sibling relationships, and even casual social interactions, one side has, in the same sense, power over the other. Thus, it follows that if we legally proscribed all instances of what can be regarded as manifestations of power in that wide sense, then very few of our personal relationships would remain legal. This seems to be a reductio ad absurdum of treating the fact that a particular interaction involves power in that wide sense as a reason for legal intervention.

The literature on sexual harassment occasionally attempts to boost the thesis that the difference in power, in the wide sense, between the people involved makes a sexual relationship between them morally wrong, by the argument that such a difference in power entails that the person with less power is not in a position to give genuine consent to the relationship. This argument attempts to assimilate the (alleged) wrongness of such sexual relationships (and of sexual harassment insofar as it involves such relationships) to the wrongness of nonconsensual sexual relationships, which is uncontroversial. One book on the topic, for example, under the heading "The Consenting Adult Myth," claims that "being attracted to an individual's role and consenting to a relationship are vastly different,"[13] while another author says that "truly consensual relationships are probably not possible within the context of unequal power."[14]

What I have said above can, however, be adapted to respond to this argument as well. There is an intelligible use of the word "consent," such that inequality of power, in the wide sense of "power," makes it impossible for a person with less power to "truly" consent to a sexual relationship (or, indeed, anything else). Just as it is, in discussing feminist ideas about power, supremely important not to forget the difference between the wide, feminist notion of power and the narrower, everyday notion of power, so it is, when the notion of consent is brought into the discussion, important to realize and keep in mind that the notion of "true" consent that appears in this argument is different from the everyday (or, for that matter, from the legal) notion of consent. This becomes obvious when we see how the argument is elaborated. One of the books mentioned above, for example, says:

> In a normal romantic situation, both the man and woman make efforts to assess each other's reasons for pursuing the relationship, to understand their true feelings and desires, and to predict their own and the other's future behaviors and attitudes. In a faculty-student relationship, the enormous role (and frequently age) disparity inhibits the woman so that she herself may have trouble understanding and predicting her feelings.[15]

But having trouble understanding and predicting one's emotions and feeling inhibited from analyzing them is a feature of all too many cases of passionate romantic involvement that would be regarded as perfectly consensual in the everyday sense of the word. It is certainly far from being unique to "faculty-student" relationships or, in general, to what is currently labeled as sexual harassment. The same book then goes on to pronounce:

> People who promote the consenting adult myth seldom mention that true consent demands full equality and full disclosure.[16]

But once the notion of consent is taken to demand "full equality," it turns out not only that it is impossible for secretaries to "truly" consent to sexual liaisons with their bosses or for students to "truly" consent to romantic involvement with their professors but also that very many of the transactions in our lives are not consensual in that sense. For example, if one is buying a car from a car dealer or a house through a real estate agent, one is, typically, dealing with people whose knowledge of the relevant matters and experience in this kind of transaction is vastly superior to one's own. In these respects, the relationship between an ordinary customer and a car dealer or a realtor is far from being one of "full equality." That, in itself, entails that buying a car or a house is typically not consensual, in the sense of "consensual" introduced by the present argument. Yet such transactions are, under normal circumstances, clear cases of something that is consensual in the everyday sense of the word.

Now, the thesis that sexual relationships that are not consensual are morally wrong is uncontroversial only if the word "consensual" is taken in its everyday sense. That thesis does not entail anything about whether relationships that are not consensual in the different sense outlined above are morally wrong. One, therefore, cannot prove the wrongness of sexual relationships between people of unequal power (in the wide sense of "power") simply by showing that those relationships are not consensual in that special sense.

The proponents of the line of argument I am criticizing here may respond to all this by acknowledging that their notion of consent is different from the everyday one and then proceeding to claim that although the thesis that sexual relationships that are nonconsensual, in that sense, are wrong is a controversial thesis, it is still a thesis that we should, upon thinking carefully about the matter, accept. However, even if that move is granted, for the sake of argument, it still cannot advance the discussion about the law on sexual harassment very far. Whatever the way in which such relationships are wrong might be, it all too obviously cannot justify a legal prohibition of these relationships, because far too many relationships would have to be prohibited if the reasoning were applied consistently. "Full equality" between potential sexual partners is rare not only within workplaces, educational institutions, and similar formal frameworks but also outside them. Moreover, "full equality" is equally rare in nonsexual dealings between people (think again of buying a car from a car dealer), and there is nothing in this pattern of reasoning about consent to limit its application to sexual matters. If the law were to prohibit all the dealings between people that are not based on "full equality," then very little of what we do in our day-to-day lives would remain legal.

The notion of power sometimes figures in discussions of sexual harassment in a way that is different from anything we have encountered so far. Sometimes it is said that sexual harassment involves power not because of any particular features of the people involved but rather because, in the kind of society we live in, men generally have power over women. However, even if, for the sake of argument, one accepts (together with a wide sense of the word "power") the general theory that entails that this is so, making this claim in a discussion of what should be done about sexual harassment is unhelpful. Saying that (heterosexual) sexual harassment involves power insofar as men generally have power over women fails to distinguish it from all other interaction between men and women. Once it is accepted that there is a general imbalance of power between men and women, it follows that all interaction between men and women takes place against the background of that imbalance and is likely to be colored by it. Yet, presumably, no one would say that all interaction between men and women ought to be legally controlled. In other words, if one is to agree that there ought to be *special* laws and policies about sexual harassment, one needs to be shown what makes sexual harassment different from other kinds of interaction between men and women. To show that it partakes of the general imbalance of power between men and women is to show what makes it similar to other kinds of male-female interaction and thus to undermine, rather than support, the thesis that it ought to be treated differently.

Before I move to my next point, I would like to recommend a simple antidote against most of the confusions in thinking about sexual harassment that I have outlined so far. Whenever one thinks about the issues related to sexual harassment, one should force oneself to take as one's paradigms the cases in which the person engaging in the relevant conduct and the person at whom the conduct is directed are similar in age, general life experience, and general social status and are both single and in which the harasser is neither promiscuous nor attempting to become so. Only features that can be detected in such cases can be relevant to the justification of anything like the present law about sexual harassment or provide a rational ground for the present movement aimed at eradication of sexual harassment. Arguments about sexual harassment that fail to work in such cases are not about sexual harassment as a type of conduct but really about something else that only happens to overlap with sexual harassment.

Sexual Harassment Causes Harm

An argument for the thesis that sexual harassment is morally wrong and ought to be legally prohibited that is, at first sight, much simpler and more difficult to refute than the other ones is the argument based on the claim that sexual harassment causes harm to those who are exposed to it. Thus, the early Working Women's Institute's study found:

> Almost all (96 percent) of the respondents reported suffering some type of emotional stress. Nervousness, fear, anger, and sleeplessness were mentioned most often. A majority of the women (63 percent) also developed physical reactions as a result of the tension of the situation. Most common were headaches, nausea, and weight losses and gains. In 12 percent of the cases the stress symptoms were so severe that the women sought therapeutic help to alleviate them.[17]

Another early researcher, quoted in Catharine MacKinnon's widely read book on sexual harassment, reported:

> The anxiety and strain, the tension and nervous exhaustion that accompany this kind of harassment take a terrific toll on women workers. Nervous tics of all kinds, aches and pains (which can be minor or irritating or can be devastatingly painful) often accompany the onset of sexual harassment.[18]

A more recent article on sexual harassment presents the following list of consequences which "may be experienced by student victims" of sexual harassment:

—general depression, as manifested by changes in eating and sleeping patterns, and vague complaints of aches and pains that prevent the student from attending class or completing work;

—undefined dissatisfaction with college, major, or particular course;

—sense of powerlessness, helplessness, and vulnerability;

—loss of academic self-confidence and decline in academic performance;

—feeling of isolation from other students;

—changes in attitudes or behaviors regarding sexual relationships;

—irritability with family and friends;

—fear and anxiety;

—inability to concentrate;

—alcohol and drug dependency.[19]

The truth of such observations is perhaps not too controversial. It is readily believable that some consequences such as those outlined above follow many cases of sexual harassment. In any event, I shall, for the purpose of this discussion, assume that such observations are, by and large, true. The question I want to focus on is what precisely follows about the moral wrongness of sexual harassment when such observations are taken as true.

In order to assess the real relevance of these facts to our issue, we need to remind ourselves of the more general and equally uncontroversial fact that sexual liaisons, and even mere attempts to establish them, all too often have unhappy endings. Since well before anyone even thought of the notion of sexual harassment, it has been a well-known fact of life that rejected lovers and would-be lovers often make themselves obnoxious by behavior that can range from tears to threats, and thereby cause considerable distress, distress that may well be accompanied by "nervousness, fear, anger, and sleeplessness" or "changes in attitudes or behaviors regarding sexual relationships." Moreover, one's knowledge that rejected lovers and rejected would-be lovers often behave this way can make one apprehensive that a specific person whom one has turned down might behave this way, and that apprehension can itself cause considerable distress, even if no such behavior actually occurs. In some cases, one may be distressed because of one's discovery that what one interpreted as expressions of emotion were, in fact, merely parts of a manipulative seduction game; such a discovery may easily lead to a "sense of powerlessness, helplessness, and vulnerability" or a "feeling of isolation." As if all this were not enough, our insecurities, our feelings of guilt, peer pressure, and unresolved traumas from our past can all find ways to complicate and amplify our emotional responses to experiences that involve sexuality.

Thus, it seems to follow that the harm caused by sexual harassment, undesirable and worrisome as it is, does not prove much about sexual harassment as a *type* of conduct, because much of that harm is of the same nature as the harm associated with other unsuccessful romantic relationships and unsuccessful attempts to establish sexual relationships. Given that the legal system is, in general, not preoccupied with unpleasant behavior of rejected lovers and would-be lovers or with insincerity in seduction, and with the harms that such behavior or insincerity causes, unless the behavior crosses the threshold of some independent category of legally prohibited conduct (such as assault), it is not clear how those harms could in themselves provide a justification for a legal prohibition of sexual harassment. The harms that ensue from sexual relationships (or attempts to establish them) when they go wrong are of the same nature regardless of whether the harmful conduct takes place within a formal framework (such as that of employment or education) or outside it. Therefore, they cannot provide a reason for treating the behavior that causes them within a formal framework differently from otherwise identical behavior that occurs outside a formal framework.

The claim that unpleasant behavior of former lovers and rejected would-be lovers or of insincerity in seduction, which take place within formal frameworks (and which amount to sexual harassment) causes harm, thus turns out to be analogous to the claim that such behavior causes harm when it takes place on odd-numbered days. Both claims are true, but confusing and misleading. Such behavior on odd-numbered days does cause harm, but so does such behavior on even-numbered days. There is thus no reason for being specially concerned about the behavior of that kind that takes place on odd-numbered days. Analogously, such behavior does cause harm within workplaces, educational institutions, and so forth, but so does such behavior outside them. The harm, therefore, does not provide a reason for being specially concerned with it when it occurs within them, that is, when it comes within the extension of the concept of sexual harassment.

In response to this, it will probably be argued that sometimes the harm caused by the conduct that is classified as sexual harassment exceeds the typical harms that stem from unsuccessful romantic relationships or unsuccessful attempts to establish romantic relationships. But as long as it is acknowledged that this happens only *sometimes*, it follows that the roots of the additional harm (and thus, arguably, of the additional moral wrongness) are not the features that make the conduct an act of sexual harassment, but some further features. So, again, we do not have an argument in favor of the special laws or other special organized activities aimed at eradicating sexual harassment as such. If some conduct of rejected lovers and rejected would-be lovers causes more harm than other such conduct, then we should try to isolate the features that cause the extra harm and focus our attention on them, rather than think of the matter in terms of the unhelpful notion of sexual harassment, which does *not* isolate those features. And once we do isolate the features that make some acts of sexual harassment specially harmful, it will probably turn out that these are features that fit the definition of some independent legal category, such as assault or intentional infliction of emotional distress, and that there already are well-established legal mechanisms for dealing with the conduct.

The authors of the literature on sexual harassment often manipulate their readers by presenting the sufferings of some harassment victims vividly, but in isolation, without comparing them with the sufferings that are caused by similar romantic misfortunes that do not amount to sexual harassment. Take, for example, the following use of a woman's testimony as to her traumatic experience of losing her virginity in her professor's bed, which appears in a book on sexual harassment in education:

> The only thing I remember now is finding myself in his apartment and seeing dirty dishes on the table. I thought, "So this is it," and I'm sure that everything that happened I wanted to happen. Only it wasn't the way I thought it would be at all. He didn't talk much. I guess I wanted him to say he loved me or something. Remember I was pretty young. All I remember is that it hurt and there was blood and I was embarrassed because I didn't know what to do about the sheet.
>   . . . And you know, even after all this time, I don't remember anything that hurt worse.[20]

There is no doubt that this woman's experience was traumatic. What makes it all too believable that it was traumatic is that it was an experience of losing one's virginity with a man who turned out not to be particularly loving and caring, and apparently, not even considerate, while the woman was up to that point under the illusion that he was at least somewhat emotionally involved, and was (as we understand from the remainder of her testimony, which the book quotes at length) generally insecure, as well as someone who had received a "strict" upbringing likely to trigger feelings of guilt in connection with almost any sexual experience. What is important to notice is that none of the features I have just listed has anything to do with the fact that the man in question was her professor. We can easily imagine an alternative sequence of events in which this same woman meets a man who is similar to her professor, except that he has no contact whatsoever with the university, and who similarly gives her the illusion that he is emotionally involved but at the crucial moment turns out not to be so, and indeed not to be even considerate. It is hard to believe that the experience of losing her virginity with that man would have been any less traumatic for the woman. The parts of her testimony that I quoted above would have read exactly the same if they had been descriptions of that alternative sequence of events. But if this is so, then it is gratuitous to include her testimony in a book that is supposed to be a book on sexual harassment, as if the testimony proved something about sexual harassment itself (i.e., about sexual harassment as a type of conduct).

Sexual Harassment Involves Discrimination

How the Sexual Harassment Law Came into Being

In the preceding subsections, we considered some of the reasons that seem to motivate the support for the existence of the sexual harassment law among the general public and/or some theoreticians working in the area. However, the body of law that is generally referred to as the sexual harassment law does not even purport to be based on any of these reasons. Within the legal system itself, the only ground for the existence of the sexual harassment law in its present form is the claim that sexual harassment constitutes discrimination on the basis of sex.

In order to fully understand that point, one needs to know how the sexual harassment law came into being. Contrary to what one may expect, the prohibition of sexual harassment did not first become law through its enactment by some legislative body. No democratically elected representatives of the people had any opportunity to consider such a prohibition or vote on it before it first became law.

What happened, rather, was that in the mid-seventies, lawyers inspired by certain branches of feminism started taking on cases that involved what later came to be referred to as sexual harassment. They argued before federal courts that such conduct constituted discrimination in employment on the basis of sex, and that it thus ought to be treated as a violation of Title VII of the Civil Rights Act of 1964, which had prohibited such discrimination. At first, courts dismisses their arguments,[21] but then, in 1976, one court accepted such an argument.[22] Others followed suit and made similar decisions, and in a few years a body of case law emerged in which sexual harassment was treated as discrimination on the basis of sex. These developments received the endorsement of the Supreme Court when, in 1986, the Court decided its first sexual harassment case, *Meritor Savings Bank v. Vinson*.[23]

The sexual harassment law at the federal level is thus a creation of the courts, not of the Congress. The statutory basis for that case law is the Civil Rights Act of 1964, which prohibits discrimination on the basis of (among other things) sex in very general terms, without saying anything specific about sexual harassment or any similar topic. The legal legitimacy of the whole body of federal law that governs sexual harassment in employment hinges on subsuming sexual harassment cases under that very general prohibition of sex discrimination. If that subsumption turns out to be unwarranted, then the whole (by now rather substantial) body of law that has been built on it will turn out to be without proper foundation within the legal system.

The federal law about sexual harassment in education is much less developed than its counterpart concerning sexual harassment in employment, but it also hinges on subsuming sexual harassment cases under a statute (Title IX of the Education Amendments of 1972) that prohibits discrimination on the basis of sex in very general terms, without saying anything explicit about sexual harassment.

After the federal U.S. law about sexual harassment had become well entrenched, some state legislatures, as well as some foreign jurisdictions, enacted their own laws about sexual harassment in the form of explicit statutory provisions. In these jurisdictions, legal regulation of sexual harassment is thus not solely a matter of case law, as it is at the level of federal U.S. law. In many other respects, the law in these jurisdictions is, however, typically modeled after the federal U.S. law on the matter. One of the ways in which that influence shows itself is that the statutory provisions about sexual harassment usually appear among statutory provisions regarding discrimination. Thus, even in these jurisdictions, the law appears to be informed by the idea that sexual harassment is a form of discrimination.

The fact that the law subsumes sexual harassment under the notion of discrimination on the basis of sex means that the considerations discussed in the preceding subsections, while they may be of great importance to those who are observing the operation of the law from the sidelines, carry little weight in the structure of the law itself. From the viewpoint of the law, even the fact that a victim of sexual harassment has suffered harm is not in itself a ground for providing a legal remedy, no matter how grave the harm might be. This is something that very few people, other than specialists in the field, are aware of. That lack of awareness causes a great deal of confusion in thinking about sexual harassment. The courts dealing with sexual harassment will, of course, often hear evidence of the harm suffered by alleged victims of sexual harassment. However, the ultimate question that a court dealing with such a case needs to resolve is not "Has the plaintiff suffered harm?" but, rather, "Has the plaintiff, in suffering the harm, been discriminated against on the basis of sex?" The evidence of the harm suffered by the victim is legally relevant only insofar as it can contribute to answering the latter question.

Before we scrutinize more carefully the idea that sexual harassment is a form of sex discrimination, we should acknowledge that looking at it in this way does avoid one crucial problem that we have seen with all the arguments about sexual harassment that we have considered so far. A fault we have found in all the preceding arguments is that they do not make any reference to the feature of the concept of sexual harassment that restricts its applicability to designated formal frameworks, such as those of employment and education, and that they are, therefore, incapable of explaining why sexual harassment should be treated differently from otherwise similar conduct that takes place outside such formal frameworks. Subsuming sexual harassment under the notion of sex discrimination solves that problem because antidiscrimination laws apply only within employment, education, and similar formal frameworks. If sexual harassment is a form of sex discrimination, then it ceases to be puzzling why the law should prohibit such conduct only within designated frameworks.

Why is it thought that sexual harassment is a form of discrimination on the basis of sex? There appear to be three possible reasons for that belief. The first is that in practically every case in which complaints of sexual harassment are made, the conduct in question is directed to people of only one sex, not both. And it is not just that the conduct happens accidentally to be directed to people of only one sex; rather, the motivation for the conduct is typically such that individuals of the other sex simply would not be, from the viewpoint of the person engaging in the conduct, suitable targets for it. Someone who directs harassing conduct to females typically does so precisely because he wants to direct such conduct to females and is not at all interested in directing it to males.

The second reason for believing that sexual harassment constitutes sex discrimination is that in the society as a whole, people of one sex, namely female, are exposed to such conduct far more often than people of the other sex. Unlike the first reason, which takes each case of sexual harassment separately, the second reason can be applied only when we consider the overall pattern of sexual harassment in a given society. Someone who accepts the first reason believes that a particular case of sexual harassment is discriminatory because of something about that particular case considered on its own. Someone who accepts the second reason believes that a particular case of sexual harassment is discriminatory because it is a part of a pattern that is discriminatory on the whole.

The third reason that people may have for regarding sexual harassment as sex discrimination is that a typical instance of such conduct affects individuals of one sex, namely female, more profoundly than similar conduct would affect individuals of the other sex. On that basis, it can be argued that even if, in a particular case, the conduct in question were directed to both males and females, the females would still be discriminated against in that they would suffer more as a result of it. Some people may accept two, or all three, of these reasons at the same time, but they are still distinct reasons and need to be examined separately.

Of these three possible reasons for regarding sexual harassment as a form of discrimination on the basis of sex, it is the first that has played the central role in the actual development of the sexual harassment law. However, the other reasons may need to play the crucial role in those rare cases in which both men and women have been subjected to similar treatment. On the other hand, while the first reason applies both to the cases where the victim is female and to the cases where the victim is male, the other reasons may be invoked only in cases in which the alleged victim is female. It should also be noted that although, within the law itself, the first reason is the central one and the others play, at most, a supplementary role, the nonlegal theoreticians who write about sexual harassment often appear to believe that the second and third reasons are of great significance.

In scrutinizing these alleged reasons, it is important to be clear about what precisely is the issue that needs to be resolved here. Our issue is not simply whether it might be defensible to regard sexual harassment as discrimination. The issue is whether subsuming sexual harassment under the notion of sex discrimination can play the central, or at least a significant, role in providing an account of what is wrong with sexual harassment. What should ultimately interest us about the three alleged reasons is not whether they provide some kind of a ground for regarding sexual harassment as sex discrimination but whether they point to a significant source of the wrongness of sexual harassment.

With that in mind, let us examine each of the three alleged reasons in turn.

The First Alleged Reason

At first sight, the first alleged reason seems impossible to challenge. Surely, it could be argued, if someone deliberately, systematically, directs a certain kind of conduct only to people of one sex and never to those of the other, then it follows that he discriminates on the basis of sex when engaging in that conduct. The very meaning of "discriminate" seems to render that conclusion unavoidable.

We need, however, to remind ourselves of the difference between the original sense of "discriminate" and the sense it has acquired in political contexts. In the original sense, "to discriminate" means simply to distinguish, treat differently, or differentiate, without any suggestion that there is anything wrong about the activity to which the word is applied. Thus, for example, an instructor reading student essays discriminates, in that sense, between essays that possess certain features and those that do not, and a wine taster may discriminate between wines that possess certain qualities and those that do not. Although the word has been, and still often is, used in that wide sense, in contemporary political contexts it is usually used only for *wrongfully* different treatment. Thus, when someone says that an employer which systematically avoids hiring black candidates for jobs is discriminating against them, it will normally be understood that what has been said implies that such differentiation between black and other candidates is wrongful. When it is shown that someone systematically treats only people of one sex, and never those of the other, in a certain way, then it certainly does follow that he discriminates on the basis of sex in the original sense of the word "discriminate," but without further argument, it does not follow that he discriminates in the current political sense of the word, namely, that he wrongfully treats the two sexes differently.

Not all discrimination on the basis of sex, in the first sense of "discrimination," is discrimination in the second sense. For example, when a male visitor to my department asks me where the nearest washroom is, I will normally point him in the direction of the men's washroom. When a female visitor asks me the same question, I will point her in a different direction, namely, the direction of the women's washroom. In responding to the question as to where the washroom is, I thus treat men and women differently. In the original sense of the word, I discriminate on the basis of sex when responding to that question. Yet no one would seriously argue that there is anything wrong about my treating men and women differently in that particular respect. It would certainly be ludicrous to argue that my directing men and women to different washrooms is in any way inconsistent with my commitment to the principle that sex discrimination ought to be eradicated. In that principle, the word "discrimination" is used in the narrower sense of wrongful differentiation.

What follows from all this is that simply pointing out that in almost all sexual harassment cases, the conduct at issue is deliberately directed at members of only one sex is not sufficient to subsume sexual harassment under the general principle prohibiting discrimination on the basis of sex. That prohibition is against wrongful discrimination, that is, against discrimination in the narrow sense of the word, while pointing out that the conduct is directed at only one sex merely shows that those who engage in it discriminate in the wide sense of the word. Therefore, if the treatment of sexual harassment as a violation of the principle prohibiting discrimination on the basis of sex is to be justified, it needs to be proven that the differentiation between the sexes that is characteristic of sexual harassment is wrongful.

At first sight, the task of proving its wrongfulness seems easy. In some cases of sexual harassment, it is indeed glaringly obvious that we are dealing with wrongful differentiation between the sexes. These are, for example, the cases, which usually occur at workplaces that have until recently been exclusively male, where the conduct in question is clearly motivated by hostility toward the presence of women in the workplace. The harassment in these cases consists in various kinds of insults of a sexual nature, which are directed at the women with the definite purpose of making them feel embarrassed, humiliated, and intimidated, and sometimes with the hope that a campaign of such insults will eventually drive them out of the workplace. The conduct is in such cases directed at women, and not men, because it is motivated by hostility toward the presence of women, and not men, and because its purpose is to embarrass, humiliate, and intimidate women, and not men. It is fairly unproblematic that the differentiation made between men and women in such a case is wrongful. It is thus fairly unproblematic that such cases can be regarded as violations of the general prohibition of discrimination on the basis of sex.

However, not all cases of sexual harassment are like that. The current notion of sexual harassment covers a great deal of conduct that is not motivated by such hostility toward people of a particular sex or, indeed, by any hostility toward anyone. Much sexual harassment consists of sexual advances, that is, acts intended to lead to some kind of further sexual interaction between those who make them and those to whom they are directed. Sexual advances may end up amounting to sexual harassment when there is a promise of employment-related benefits for accepting them or a threat of negative employment-related consequences for rejecting them. Cases of that kind are usually referred to as quid pro quo harassment. More often, sexual advances become sexual harassment because they end up, contrary to the intentions of those who make them, offending their recipients.

The question we need to consider now is whether the sexual harassment that consists of such sexual advances is justifiably regarded as a violation of the prohibition against discrimination on the basis of sex. In trying to deal with that question, it is tempting to reason in the following way. First, it could be said, the conduct that we are dealing with in such cases is wrong. The wrongness of quid pro quo harassment is uncontroversial. The wrongness of sexual advances that just, unintentionally, end up being offensive may be debatable in some cases, but people tend to agree about it when the advances in question are particularly gross, crude, and vulgar. In such cases, it could be argued, even though the person making the advances may not have intended them to be offensive, it was still wrong-fully careless of that person to make them without considering the likeli-hood of their being offensive. Let us, at this stage of the discussion, simply set aside any cases that may be problematic, and assume that we are dealing only with the sexual advances that are wrong, whatever they are. The sec-ond thing that can be pointed out in this tempting, but ultimately falla-cious line of reasoning is that in each case of sexual harassment that con-sists in sexual advances, the advances are likely to be directed only to people of one sex, and not both. What we are dealing with in such cases thus involves differentiating on the basis of sex. Given that the conduct in question, first, is wrongful and, second, differentiates on the basis of sex, it follows, according to this line of reasoning, that it wrongfully differenti-ates on the basis of sex. If that is accepted, then it must be accepted that such conduct, at least prima facie, violates the prohibition against discrimi-nating on the basis of sex.

Although this reasoning may well seem plausible, it is, in fact, defective. Let us look back more closely at the claim that such cases involve differen-tiation on the basis of sex. The claim, as it stands, is undoubtedly true, but let us ask ourselves why people who engage in such conduct differentiate on the basis of sex. Why would a person, for example, direct sexual ad-vances that unintentionally end up being offensive, only to people of one sex, and not both?

The answer is that their reason is exactly the same as the reason people generally differentiate between the sexes in deciding to whom to direct their sexual advances. Why does a heterosexual male always direct his sex-ual advances to women and never to men? Simply because he is a hetero-sexual male. When heterosexual males make advances that turn out to be offensive, the reason why they direct them to women and not to men is the same: they are heterosexual males. They make these advances in the hope that they will lead to some sexual experience that will be pleasurable to them, and because they are heterosexual males, it is only sexual experi-ences with women that they find pleasurable. Mutatis mutandis, the same applies to heterosexual women and homosexuals.

The fact that a particular sexual advance ends up being offensive is un-doubtedly important, but it is not in any significant way related to the fact that the advance involves differentiating between the sexes, because offensive and nonoffensive sexual advances involve differentiating between the sexes in exactly the same way and for the same reasons. Similarly, the fact that quid pro quo offers or threats accompany someone's sexual advances is unrelated to the fact that the advances involve differentiating between the sexes, because they involve it in exactly the same way and for the same reasons as any other sexual advances. The reason heterosexual quid pro quo harassers have for directing their harassing advances only to people of the opposite sex is the same as the reason all heterosexuals have for directing their advances only to people of the opposite sex. The reason homosexual quid pro quo harassers have for directing their harassing advances only to people of the same sex is the same as the reason all homosexuals have for directing their sexual advances only to people of the same sex.

The differentiating between the sexes involved in the cases of sexual harassment we are considering here is thus simply the differentiating that is inherent in being a heterosexual or a homosexual. Now, everyone would agree that there is nothing wrong with being a heterosexual. Many people nowadays would also agree that there is nothing wrong about being a homosexual. (Those who do not agree are invited to simply set aside the cases of homosexuals and concentrate on the ones involving heterosexuals.) No one would seriously argue that people are under obligation to become bisexuals. The cases we are considering, therefore, do not wrongfully differentiate between the sexes, despite the seeming plausibility of the argument to the contrary. They differentiate between them only in the way that straightforwardly follows from the fact that those who make the advances are heterosexual or homosexual, and that kind of differentiation is not wrongful.

Where the argument to the contrary goes wrong is in assuming that the fact that something is wrongful and the fact that it is a case of differentiating between the sexes entail that it is a case of wrongfully differentiating between the sexes. That is a fallacy. An act may be wrongful in virtue of some of its aspects and differentiate between the sexes in virtue of some completely distinct aspects. In such a case, the act can be characterized as both wrongful and differentiating but not as wrongfully differentiating. That is precisely what we have in the cases of sexual harassment that involve sexual advances. What makes these acts wrong (for example, the carelessness about causing offense) is something completely distinct from what makes them differentiate between the sexes, namely, the heterosexuality or homosexuality of those who engage in them.

The subsumption of these cases under the notion of sex discrimination is, therefore, not at all justified by the first of the three reasons that purport to justify it. The right to be free from discrimination is not the right to be free from both heterosexuality and homosexuality.[24]

The Second Alleged Reason

What about the second reason that purports to justify treating sexual harassment as sex discrimination, namely, the reason that consists in pointing out that when the pattern of sexual harassment in the society as a whole is considered, women are far more often its victims than men? We have already noted that the second reason applies only to the cases of sexual harassment in which the victims are female. Some people may regard its being restricted to cases involving female victims as a weakness, but some may regard it as a strength or, at least, not as a significant weakness. The political movement against sexual harassment is, after all, primarily aimed at protecting women, not men, from such conduct.

The second reason is unconcerned with the aims, motivations and intentions of the individuals who engage in the conduct in question. Thus, it is immune to the criticisms that have been made against the first reason. Even if what guides these individuals is something inherently innocuous, such as their heterosexuality or homosexuality, their conduct can, if one accepts the second reason as sound, be regarded as discriminatory, simply in virtue of belonging to a pattern that is, on the whole, discriminatory. The second reason, so to speak, makes individual cases of sexual harassment borrow their discriminatory character from the way in which such cases are distributed across the society as a whole. This enables the second reason to avoid the argument that has been used above against the first one, but it creates doubts about the significance of the second reason. Most people, when looking at a given instance of sexual harassment that they regard as wrong, think of it as something that is wrong even when considered on its own, independently of the way in which similar acts may be distributed across the society. They think of each instance of, for example, quid pro quo harassment or some blatantly offensive sexual conduct as something that would have been wrong, in more or less the same degree, even if the pattern of distribution of such acts were different. That means that the second reason does not capture the core of what is perceived as wrong with such conduct. Even if the second reason for treating sexual harassment as discrimination is sound, it, at most, points to a relatively insignificant source of the wrongness of such conduct, a source that operates in addition to some independent main source.

Indeed, it could be said that treating the second reason as if it were the main reason for regarding such conduct as wrong would be insulting to the victims of the conduct because it would imply that what happened to each of them individually does not count in itself, but gains its moral significance only in virtue of being a part of a larger pattern. If we took the second reason as central to the account of the wrongness of sexual harassment, then we would expect an individual female victim of sexual harassment to think of what she was exposed to, not as an injustice to *her*, but merely as an exemplification of some larger injustice done to women as a group. Many female victims of sexual harassment may regard that as a distortion of their experience.

Moreover, if the second reason were accepted as central to the account of the wrongness of sexual harassment, then it would be puzzling why the legal response to it should take the form of giving individual victims the right to sue for and, if successful, collect the damages. If the wrong of sexual harassment is essentially a collective wrong, a wrong done to women as a group,[25] which is the way the second reason presents it, and if individual victims are to be thought of as wronged only insofar as what is done to them partakes of that collective wrong, then it becomes unclear why the principal legal remedy for sexual harassment should consist in forcing employers to compensate individual victims. A primarily collective wrong calls for a primarily collective remedy. The collective remedy could, for example, take the form of forcing the employers found responsible for sexual harassment to pay a substantial amount into some fund for the betterment of the position of women. If we seriously thought of the wrong of sexual harassment as primarily a collective wrong, then we would find it natural to think of something like that as a more appropriate remedy for it than payments made to individual victims. The fact that most people do not find it natural to think of such collective remedies as more appropriate than the present, individual ones suggests that most people do not really think of the second reason as capturing the main ground for regarding sexual harassment as wrong.

The above shows only that the second reason would have, at most, a relatively insignificant role in the overall account of what makes sexual harassment morally wrong. I now want to show that the second reason is incapable of playing any role in such an account, because it is in fact unsound. The second reason, like the first one, may well appear sound if one focuses only on a certain kind of case. For example, if some women at a particular blue-collar workplace are subjected to a campaign of insults of a sexual nature by male coworkers who wish their workplace to return to being all male, then a part of what makes one morally concerned about that particular case of sexual harassment may well be that similar incidents are occurring at similar workplaces throughout the society and that the particular incident thus belongs to a pattern, which pattern is, in turn, morally worrisome because it adversely affects the employment opportunities of women.

But as we had an opportunity to observe before in discussing the first reason, not all sexual harassment is like that. Let us look at the cases of sexual harassment that consist of sexual advances that end up being offensive to their recipients. It would be difficult to deny that women are exposed to such sexual advances far more often than men. But before we rush to the conclusion that this uncontroversial empirical fact proves that such advances constitute discrimination against women, we need to take into account another, equally uncontroversial empirical fact. This is the fact that women, overall, receive many more sexual advances (including both offensive and nonoffensive ones) than men. For a very long time, it has been a social convention among heterosexuals that all sexual advances should be made by men and that women should only accept or reject such advances but not make any themselves. That convention is now dying, at least among educated people in major urban centers, but looking at the society as a whole, it is far from being dead yet. As a result of the remaining influences of that convention, many more sexual advances are made by men and directed at women than are made by women and directed at men.

When that fact is taken into account, then the fact that women receive offensive sexual advances more often than men can be seen as merely its by-product: women receive more sexual advances that are offensive, simply because women receive more sexual advances in total. Once the number of offensive sexual advances directed at women is seen in that light, that number does not provide any ground for claims of discrimination. The absolute numbers of offensive advances received by men and by women seem far less relevant for the issue of discrimination than the ratios between the number of offensive advances and the total number of advances received by each sex. While such ratios are difficult to ascertain with any precision, there is no good reason to believe that they differ radically between men and women.

The argument I have just made will undoubtedly receive the response that the convention according to which heterosexual sexual advances should always be made by men and directed at women is itself a form of discrimination against women. There are two comments to be made about this response. The first is that it is not at all clear that the convention constitutes discrimination against women. Many men would be ready to testify that the supposed privilege that the convention confers on them is, in fact, a burden and they consequently rejoice in the weakening of the convention and hope its complete demise is imminent. This is not to deny that the convention also imposes a burden on women. But if the convention is burdensome to both sexes, then it follows that it is not a form of discrimination against one sex, however undesirable it may be on other grounds.

The second comment is that even if it is accepted that the convention does discriminate against women, it does not seem that this is of great relevance to the issue. The issue, let us remember, is whether the second reason for regarding sexual harassment as sex discrimination is convincing when applied to sexual harassment that consists in offensive sexual advances. If we are not left with anything more than the claim that offensive sexual advances are discriminatory insofar as male-to-female sexual advances are, in general, discriminatory, then we, after all, do not have any special reason for regarding that form of sexual harassment as discrimination. In other words, if this response to my argument against the second reason were accepted, the point would still hold that the second reason does not provide us with justification for treating sexual advances that constitute sexual harassment differently from sexual advances that do not. Arguing that the general convention about sexual advances is discriminatory, therefore, cannot provide support for the sexual harassment law in anything like its present form.

At the end of this discussion of the second reason, it may be useful to note that the second reason belongs to the general approach to discrimination that is known as the "disparate impact theory," unlike the first reason, which belongs to the "disparate treatment theory." The disparate treatment theory ascribes discriminatory character only to rules and policies that *explicitly* differentiate between the relevant groups, and it is relatively uncontroversial. There is, however, in discussions of discrimination, a recurring controversy as to whether we should, in addition to the disparate treatment theory, accept the disparate impact theory. The latter theory ascribes discriminatory character to rules or policies that affect different relevant groups in significantly different ways, even if those rules or policies are formulated in terms that are, on the face of it, neutral between the groups. For example, requiring all candidates for a job to pass a certain test of physical strength that does not in any direct way involve the candidates' sex, but that is, in fact, passed by a significantly higher percentage of male than of female candidates may be regarded as discrimination on the basis of the disparate impact theory, but not on the basis of the disparate treatment theory. Because the second reason belongs to the controversial disparate impact theory, rather than the relatively uncontroversial disparate treatment theory, this reason can be challenged not only by arguing as I have above but also by challenging the disparate impact theory in general. I shall not, however, pursue that challenge here, because it would lead us too far into the general issues of equality and discrimination.

The Third Alleged Reason

We are now left with the third reason that can be invoked in support of treating sexual harassment as a form of discrimination: An individual instance of such conduct (it is alleged) typically has a different, more adverse, effect on a woman than similar conduct would have on a man. It is useful to note here that formulations such as "sexual harassment has worse effects on women than on men" are ambiguous as to whether they express the second or the third reason. The difference between the second and the third reason is that the second reason claims that sexual harassment has worse effects on women than on men insofar as women, as a group, are exposed to *more* cases on such conduct, while the third reason claims that it has worse effects on women than on men in that an *individual* case of it typically has worse effects on a woman than it would have on a man. Like the second alleged reason, the third one applies only to cases of sexual harassment in which the victims are female, but, as has been observed in the above discussion of the second reason, that, in itself, need not be regarded as a problem.

Although it is widely assumed that a typical case of sexual harassment has worse effects on a woman than similar conduct would have on a man and although I am happy to accept that assumption for the sake of argument, it may be worthwhile to note that the amount of formal research on the matter is fairly limited. While quite a few studies about sex differences in the perception of sexual harassment have been conducted, most of them are about a question subtly different from the one relevant here. In such studies, the respondents are typically presented with third-person descriptions of various kinds of conduct, in which the sexes of the people involved are specified, and are then asked to assess the conduct. The investigators then proceed to analyze whether male and female respondents, on the whole, differ in their assessments. Asking whether men and women differ in their assessments of such conduct when they imagine it to be directed toward other individuals, whose sex is given, is a different matter from asking whether there are differences between the impact that such conduct has on male and female recipients. To summarize the research by saying something like "there are gender differences in the perception of sexual harassment" obscures whether the thesis is about the differences between men and women as disinterested assessors of such conduct or as recipients of the conduct. Most of the research is about the former; what is relevant here is the latter.

But in any event, as I said, I will be happy to treat it as proven that a case of sexual harassment *typically* has worse effects on a woman than similar conduct would have on a man. In investigating whether such an empirical thesis can support treating sexual harassment as a form of discrimination, we need to notice one crucial word in the formulation of the thesis: the word "typically." The thesis has plausibility only if we take it to be that such conduct typically has worse effects on a woman. It would be all too obviously false to say that all women would have one reaction to certain conduct of a sexual nature, while all men would have another, different reaction to it. The plausible thesis can only be that percentages of men and of women who would have a certain reaction to a particular sexual conduct differ or that men's and women's reactions are, on the average, different. Facts involving percentages and averages are, of course, facts about groups, not about individuals. Thus, the thesis is that women, taken as a group, differ in these respects from men, taken as a group.

This means that the third alleged reason is importantly similar to the second one. Although the third reason makes reference to a characteristic that can be possessed by individual instances of sexual harassment (unlike the second, which appeals only to the overall pattern of such conduct in the society), it, in fact, tries to base the discriminatory character of such conduct on a fact that involves *average* instances of such conduct. Speaking about an average instance of some conduct in a given society is, however, simply a way of speaking about that conduct in the society as a whole. Like the second reason, the third one makes the discriminatory character of an individual case of sexual harassment depend not only on the features of the case itself but crucially on certain patterns in the society as a whole. The fact that a particular woman was exposed to suffering of such and such intensity in a case of sexual harassment is not sufficient to bring the third reason into operation, no matter how high the intensity is. The third reason can be applied to an individual case only when the suffering of the woman is compared with the average suffering of women in such situations and contrasted with the average suffering of men in analogous situations. If one regarded the third reason as central to one's account of the wrongness of sexual harassment, one would thus have to think that what happened to a particular victim of sexual harassment is of little moral significance on its own: one would have to regard it as something that, as it were, borrows its moral significance from the pattern to which it belongs. One would have to say that the suffering of such and such specific woman who was exposed to a particular instance of sexual harassment does not really matter in itself; what matters is that her suffering is typical of women, and not of men, in such situations. As we have noted in the discussion of the second reason, people do not generally think in this way of a case of sexual harassment that they regard as wrong; rather, they think of it as something that is wrong even when considered on its own, independently of any pattern to which it may belong. The third reason for treating sexual harassment as a form of discrimination, therefore, even if sound, does not capture the main ground for regarding such conduct as wrong.

The implausibility of taking the third reason as a significant part of an account of what makes sexual harassment morally wrong can be made even more vivid if we reformulate it. Saying that, on the average, an instance of sexual harassment has worse effects on a woman than such conduct would have on a man is equivalent to saying that such conduct, on the average, does not have as bad effects on a man as on a woman. When we think of a serious case of sexual harassment with a female victim, it is hard to believe that its moral wrongness crucially depends on how much *a man* would have suffered under similar circumstances and that if facts changed and men came to suffer more in such cases, then the conduct would cease to be wrong. A female victim of such conduct may find it particularly insulting to be told that the moral wrongness of what she was exposed to depends on such facts about men. And yet this is precisely what we would be committed to telling her if we took the third reason to be central to what makes sexual harassment wrong.

Finally, it should be noted that the third reason, like the second one, belongs to the disparate impact theory of discrimination and thus shares with the second reason the vulnerability to the attacks that can be made against that theory in general.

Why Sexual Harassment Cannot Be a Form of Sex Discrimination

Having shown that the reasons for regarding sexual harassment as sex discrimination are either unsound or, at best, provide only an insignificant part of an account of what makes sexual harassment morally wrong, I now wish to move to a more general argument against the thesis that looking at sexual harassment as a form of sex discrimination can generate a plausible account of what is wrong with it. The argument will develop some of the points that have already been hinted at above.

Let us remind ourselves that what is needed, if the sexual harassment law and related activities are to be justified, is an account of what is wrong with sexual harassment as a *type* of conduct. I have already acknowledged that sex discrimination may well be an aspect of what is wrong with some cases of sexual harassment, such as campaigns of deliberate insults motivated by hostility toward the presence of women at a particular workplace. That the wrongness of some instances of sexual harassment can be accounted for in that way, however, does not prove that the wrongness of sexual harassment as a type of conduct can be accounted for in that way and, therefore, does not justify the way in which sexual harassment is currently dealt with. As long as it can be shown that the wrongness of other kinds of sexual harassment is not captured by classifying them as sex discrimination, it follows that an account of what is wrong with sexual harassment as a type of conduct cannot be produced by treating it as a species of sex discrimination.

The reason why it is generally misguided to think of sexual harassment as sex discrimination is that the wrong of discrimination is an essentially comparative wrong, while the principal wrong committed in many cases of sexual harassment is an all too obviously noncomparative wrong. In order to understand that point, let us, for a moment, consider a paradig-

matic case of sex discrimination. Let us suppose that John and Mary work
for the same employer, perform exactly the same work, and have the same
education, experience, dedication to the job, and so on. Yet John's salary
is fifty thousand dollars, while Mary, simply because she is a woman, receives the much lower salary of thirty thousand dollars. Most people would
readily agree that the way Mary is treated is seriously wrong and that what
makes it wrong is that it involves discrimination on the basis of sex. In this
case, our assessment that Mary is treated wrongly is crucially based on a
comparison between the way she is treated and the way John is treated.
There is nothing apart from this comparison that could justify us in saying
that she is treated wrongly. Receiving thirty thousand dollars a year is not
a bad thing in itself; in fact, considered on its own, it appears to be a good
thing. What makes her being paid that salary morally wrong is not the
absolute amount she is paid but, rather, the fact that she is paid so much
less than John. This is what is meant by saying that the wrong of discrimination is an essentially comparative one.

In that respect, being wronged by discrimination is different from many
other ways in which one may be wronged. The wrong of being beaten up,
for example, is a clear example of a noncomparative wrong. In order to be
justified in saying that someone who has been beaten up has been treated
wrongly, I do not need to compare the way he has been treated with the
way other people have been treated. When one gets beaten up, it is usually
true that one has been treated worse than others, but that is not normally
the morally crucial thing about being beaten up. Being beaten up is something that is bad even when considered on its own and is thus unlike
Mary's receiving thirty thousand dollars, which is, considered on its own,
not a bad thing.

A good test for whether we are dealing with a comparative or a noncomparative wrong is this. When the wrong is comparative, then it can be
eliminated by improving the treatment of those who are worse-off, by
worsening the treatment of the better-off, or by some suitable combination of the two. Thus, in the example of John and Mary, the wrong of
discrimination can be eliminated by raising Mary's salary to fifty thousand
dollars, by reducing John's salary to thirty thousand dollars, or by some
combination of increasing Mary's salary and reducing John's, so that they
are both paid some intermediate amount, say forty thousand dollars. So
far as the goal of eliminating discrimination is concerned, all these ways of
dealing with the problem are equally good. If, in a particular real-life situa-

tion of this kind, we regard some of these ways of eliminating discrimination as preferable to the others, that could only be because we think that some other goals are at stake in addition to eliminating discrimination. We simply cannot rationally prefer some of these ways over others with reference to the goal of eliminating discrimination, because they all accomplish that goal perfectly. As long as we think of such a problem as purely a matter of discrimination, we should be indifferent among these different ways of dealing with it.

On the other hand, when the wrong is a noncomparative one, then it cannot be eliminated by worsening the position of those who have not suffered it. If a group of hooligans have beaten up Mary, the matter cannot be rectified by their beating up John, or anyone else, as well. If, after beating up Mary, they move on to beat up John as well, we will not think of them as annulling the wrong they have done to Mary. Quite the contrary: we will think that in beating up John they are committing an additional wrong.

Let us now apply this test to sexual harassment. Suppose that women at a particular workplace have been subjected to quid pro quo harassment: their superior has requested (to use the legal euphemism) "sexual favors" from them and has threatened them with negative employment-related consequences if they do not comply. Clearly, these women have been wronged. But it does not seem plausible to say that the wrong committed against them would be rectified if some men at the same workplace were subjected to analogous requests, accompanied by similar threats. Subjecting the men to such treatment would not annul the wrong that has been done to the women. And not only would subjecting the men to such harassment fail to make things better, but most people would say that it would make things worse, that it would be an additional wrong. This means that the principal wrong committed against the women in this example is a noncomparative wrong. Its being a noncomparative wrong, in turn, entails that it is not the wrong of sex discrimination.

Or to take another example, suppose that women at a particular workplace have been exposed to some gross, crude, vulgar sexual advances and that they have been offended by this. Most people would agree that these women have been wronged (although in many such cases there may be disagreements about how serious the wrong is). Again, it does not seem that the wrong committed against them would be annulled if some men at the same workplace then came to be subjected to similar advances. If one believes that similar advances are unlikely to cause the same degree of offense to men as to women, one may want to also consider the possibility of subjecting the men to whatever advances (perhaps more crude ones) are likely to cause them offense similar to the offense that has been caused to the women, but it still does not seem that subjecting the men to such advances would rectify the matter. If men came to be subjected to such advances, in addition to women, there would be more crudeness and vulgarity in the workplace, and it seems clear that this would make things worse rather than better. As before, the fact that the wrong committed against women is not rectified when men are subjected to analogous treatment (whatever precisely is thought to be analogous here) entails that the wrong suffered by the women is a noncomparative wrong, and thus cannot be the wrong of discrimination. Given that the above two examples are representative of much of the conduct that is at issue in sexual harassment cases, it can be concluded that it is misguided to subsume sexual harassment, as a type of conduct, under the notion of sex discrimination.

The Right Reasons for Opposing the Fight against Sexual Harassment

In the preceding section, I have shown that the arguments that may appear to support the law and the movement against sexual harassment do not, in fact, support them. What I have presented there does not, strictly speaking, on its own constitute an argument *against* the law and other organized action aimed at eradicating sexual harassment. It does, however, become an argument against the law if one adds to it the widely accepted background assumption that the state may not create laws that restrict individual freedom unless there is a good reason for creating them. The prevailing view in Western societies is that with respect to any possible law that restricts individual freedom, the burden of proof is on those who uphold it, to show that there are good reasons for its existence. It is a standard liberal principle that if the burden is not discharged, then having such a law is a bad thing. What the preceding section shows is that with respect to the law about sexual harassment, the burden has not been discharged. That, together with the background assumptions of the liberal political culture, amounts to an argument against the law.

Although the preceding section constitutes, in that way, an argument against the law, it is quite possible that some people will agree with what I said there and still remain unmoved by it. They may accept the arguments of that section as sound, they may agree that there is no good reason for supporting the law and even agree that it is, in a way, a bad law and yet shrug their shoulders to all that. Their reaction may be articulated as follows:

> So what? Perhaps this law should not have been created, but the fact is that it has been created. Perhaps its existence is, in the light of general liberal principles, a bad thing, but nothing that has been said so far shows that it is bad enough that it would be worth my while to participate in any political action against it.

Because I suspect that this kind of reaction may be rather widespread, I shall devote this section of the essay to showing that there are serious problems with the law about sexual harassment, and to a certain extent with other activities aimed at eradicating sexual harassment, that go beyond the mere absence of good reasons for supporting them.

The Demarcation Problem

The rules against sexual harassment are generally understood to prohibit only some of the conduct of a sexual nature that occurs within workplaces, educational institutions, or other designated frameworks. In other words, it is generally thought that there are some kinds of sexual conduct within such frameworks that are not affected by the prohibition, that the rules on the matter still leave people free to pursue their romantic and sexual interests within the designated frameworks in some ways. Most people's acceptance of the sexual harassment law depends on their understanding the law in that way. While there may be some people who would be happy to endorse a complete ban on conduct of a sexual nature within such frameworks, most people would be upset by such a ban. The main reason is, of course, that workplaces and educational institutions typically bring together people who have a great deal in common, and people generally value opportunities to seek romantic partners among those with whom they have a great deal in common. In addition to that, some people may find it inherently disturbing that the state would restrict their freedom in this way, independently of how much interest they presently have in engaging in such pursuits. Thus, quite a few people who now accept the law would probably become opposed to it if they started perceiving it as a ban on all conduct of a sexual nature within designated frameworks.

In this subsection, I argue that contrary to appearances, the law does, in fact, amount to such a ban. In order to see that, we need to examine the concept of sexual harassment more closely.

The definition of sexual harassment that is typically followed by federal courts dealing with sexual harassment cases is the one that has been formulated by the U.S. Equal Employment Opportunity Commission (EEOC) in 1980:

> Unwelcome sexual advances, requests for sexual favors, and other verbal or physical conduct of a sexual nature constitute sexual harassment when (1) submission to such conduct is made either explicitly or implicitly a term or condition of an individual's employment, (2) submission to or rejection of such conduct by an individual is used as the basis for employment decisions affecting such individual, or (3) such conduct has the purpose or effect of unreasonably interfering with an individual's work performance or creating an intimidating, hostile, or offensive working environment.[26]

This definition has also been widely influential outside the federal law. The definitions of sexual harassment in state laws and even in foreign jurisdictions tend to be quite similar to it, with words such as "unwelcome" and "offensive" playing the crucial role.

On the face of it, this definition indeed covers only some, and not all, conduct of a sexual nature that occurs within a designated formal framework. However, one's understanding of a legal rule is never complete without putting oneself in the shoes of an individual who is trying to follow the rule. Thus, in order to see what the prohibition of the conduct covered by this definition really amounts to, we need to look at it not only from the viewpoint of courts and other observers but also from the viewpoint of individuals who wish to engage in some conduct of a sexual nature without violating the prohibition. Such an individual needs to find out whether certain conduct would violate the prohibition *before* engaging in the conduct. That means that such an individual needs to be able to determine in advance whether the conduct is covered by the definition.

In some cases, that will be easy. When the conduct one is contemplating involves threatening a person with adverse job-related consequences if the person does not comply with one's sexual requests, it is clear that the definition applies and that the conduct is prohibited. Similarly, if the conduct involves deliberate insults of a sexual nature, it is fairly easy to predict that the conduct would be unwelcome and would contribute to an offensive working environment and thus would be covered by the definition.

But what if the conduct involves a sexual joke made in the hope that it will be funny to the recipient or a sexual advance made in the hope that it will be accepted and lead to some mutually satisfying sexual interaction? Human sexuality being what it is, it is impossible, at least in present-day Western civilization, to predict with anything approaching certainty whether or not a given person will find such conduct unwelcome and offensive. The same sexual jokes that some people find funny, others find unwelcome and offensive. The same sexual advances that some are longing to receive, others find unwelcome and offensive. Yet the people who have such different reactions to sexual conduct are often indistinguishable in terms of the information that is likely to be generally known among their colleagues. Thus, it seems that often the only way to find out whether someone would find certain conduct of a sexual nature unwelcome and offensive is to ask the person.

But here is the catch: asking a person about such matters is itself verbal conduct of a sexual nature that may easily be unwelcome and offensive and thus come under the definition of sexual harassment. Notice that the definition of sexual harassment makes the concept apply as soon as the conduct has the effect of causing "an intimidating, hostile, or offensive working environment," regardless of whether that effect has been intended or not.

Given that for practically any conduct of a sexual nature, there exists a possibility that it will be unwelcome and offensive to its recipient, and that any attempt to find out whether it will be so received may itself turn out to be unwelcome and offensive, it follows that the only way in which a person can avoid running afoul of the prohibition of sexual harassment is by abstaining from any conduct of a sexual nature within a workplace, educational institution, or other formal framework covered by the law. From the viewpoint of an individual who wishes to engage in some conduct of a sexual nature, the prohibition of sexual harassment thus amounts to a prohibition of all conduct of a sexual nature within designated formal frameworks. Moreover, given that in Western societies, much of the conduct aimed at establishing nonsexual friendships is, in its early stages, indistinguishable from conduct aimed at establishing friendships with a sexual component, this prohibition of all conduct of a sexual nature is bound to have a chilling effect on the pursuit of nonsexual friendships as well.

Finally, it should be mentioned that even the minority of people who think that prohibiting all conduct of a sexual nature in designated formal frameworks is a good thing should not be happy about the feature of the law that has been outlined in this subsection. If one thinks that such a prohibition is a good thing, then it is reasonable to expect that one would want the prohibition to be clear and explicit. The sexual harassment law, I have argued, amounts to such a prohibition, but it does not make it clear and explicit that this is what it amounts to. Therefore, the argument of this subsection provides practically everyone with a reason to oppose the law.[27]

The Conflict with the Freedom of Speech

If one looks at the definition of sexual harassment quoted in the preceding subsection, one sees that it covers, among other things, "verbal conduct" of a certain kind. "Verbal conduct" is, on any reasonable interpretation, synonymous, or almost synonymous, with "speech." Much of the conduct that is complained of under sexual harassment rules falls under that part of the definition: it consists of speech that creates "an intimidating, hostile, or offensive working environment."

Legally proscribing speech creates a serious problem in a society that is, as all Western societies are, deeply committed to freedom of speech, that is, to the principle that speech, in general, ought not to be prohibited by law. The problem is particularly serious in the societies, such as the United States, in which such a principle is enshrined in a written constitution. This is not to deny that the speech that is treated as sexual harassment is often quite nasty and hurtful. In the United States, however, its nastiness has to be looked at against the background of a legal system in which the courts have consistently defended the freedom of very nasty people to say very nasty and hurtful things, by appealing to the principle of freedom of speech, embodied in the First Amendment to the Constitution. The problem is exacerbated by the fact that the speech covered by the concept of sexual harassment consists not only of inarticulate person-to-person insults but also of the expression of general views about the proper role of women in society or about the desirability of their pursuit of certain occupations. Remarks to the effect that women cannot make good police officers, made within a police station, can certainly create a hostile working environment for female officers at that station. However, such views, no matter how crudely formulated, are political views, and political views are generally thought to be at the very center of what the principle of freedom of speech protects.

The principle of freedom of speech, as articulated in the judicial interpretations of the First Amendment, does admittedly have some exceptions. The prohibition of sexual harassment cannot, however, comfortably fit under any of these exceptions. Without getting into the intricacies of First Amendment scholarship in detail, here is the main reason why. The First Amendment, even when all the qualifications and exceptions are taken into account, precludes the state from prohibiting expressions of one political view while permitting expressions of the opposite view. When the state is allowed to restrict certain forms of speech, say noisy manifestations at certain times or locations, it must ensure that the restrictions apply equally both to proponents of a particular viewpoint and to its opponents. If the state prohibits noisy rallies of antiabortionists under such and such circumstances, then it must prohibit noisy rallies of proabortionists under the same circumstances. If it prohibits noisy rallies of Democrats under certain circumstances, then it must prohibit noisy rallies of Republicans under the same circumstances. There is no exception to the principle of freedom of speech that would ever allow the state to prohibit rallies of Democrats under circumstances under which it permits rallies of Republicans, or vice versa. The state must never, ever use legal restrictions of speech to favor one viewpoint on a given issue over the opposite one. Whatever precisely it is that the First Amendment prohibits, it most definitely does prohibit the state from interfering in the marketplace of ideas in that way.

The prohibition of sexual harassment, insofar as it includes speech, is, however, precisely a prohibition that applies to expressions of a certain viewpoint without applying to expressions of the opposite viewpoint. Through the sexual harassment law, the state prohibits people from expressing the views, for example, that women are not capable of being good surgeons or police officers or that women are, in general, inferior to men, under circumstances under which the state allows people to express the views that women are capable of being good surgeons or police officers or that women are, in general, equal to men. The state thus favors one viewpoint over the opposed one by restricting the expressions of the latter.

That is precisely what the principle of freedom of speech, as it has been understood so far, does not allow. It is thus doubtful that one can consistently be committed to the principle of freedom of speech and endorse the present sexual harassment law. It is also doubtful that the sexual harassment law, insofar as it applies to speech, is consistent with the First Amendment. Up to the time of writing, whether the sexual harassment law *itself* is consistent with the First Amendment has not been tested in the courts, although a few First Amendment challenges to specific *applications* of the law have been successful.[28]

The Fight against Sexual Harassment Causes Harm

One thing that one definitely needs to take into account in deciding whether to support or oppose the law and other measures aimed at combating sexual harassment is that they cause avoidable harm. Pointing out the existence of such harm does not on its own constitute a conclusive argument against such measures, but it does supplement the arguments made elsewhere in this essay.

One kind of harm that such measures cause is obvious from the argument presented above in the subsection entitled "The Demarcation Problem." We have seen there that from the viewpoint of individuals who might wish to engage in conduct of a sexual nature, the prohibition of sexual harassment really amounts to a prohibition of all such conduct. Someone who does not wish to risk being guilty of sexual harassment has to abstain from all conduct of a sexual nature, wherever the rules against sexual harassment apply, because it is impossible to be certain in advance that such conduct will not turn out to be unwelcome and offensive.

Sexual conduct is, however, not always unwelcome and offensive: sexual jokes are sometimes funny to those who hear them, and sexual advances sometimes do lead to sexual relationships that are fulfilling to both of the people involved. The rules against sexual harassment, by forcing people who take them seriously to abstain from all conduct of a sexual nature, preclude at least some of such joyful sexual interaction from taking place. Given that personal relationships with a sexual component are, for many people, the source of a more intense sense of fulfillment than anything else in their lives, closing down the opportunities for such fulfillment is, for many people, a serious harm. The harm is rendered particularly serious by the facts that people who work together tend to have a lot in common and that romantic relationships between people who have a lot in common are, other things being equal, more satisfying than between people who do not.

It has to be understood that closing down the opportunities for fulfilling sexual and romantic relationships is not just some kind of an unfortunate, easily eliminable by-product of the fight against sexual harassment. The roots of this problem go to the very core of the desire to eliminate unwelcome and offensive sexual conduct. It is in the very nature of sexual advances that at the moment when a sexual advance is made, it is unknown to the person making it whether it will be unwelcome and offensive or will be accepted and lead to further mutually satisfying sexual interaction. Because of that, it is simply impossible to prohibit unwelcome and offensive sexual advances without affecting the ones that lead to mutually satisfying sexual interaction.[29] Also, as has been hinted at above, the prohibition of sexual harassment affects people's opportunities for nonsexual friendships at workplaces, educational institutions, and so on. The prohibition leads people to abstain from making attempts at establishing nonsexual friendships within such frameworks whenever there is a risk, as there often is, that their attempts may be interpreted as manifestations of sexual interest.

Of course, not all people go through the steps of reasoning outlined in the subsection on "The Demarcation Problem." Because they do not think much about the rules against sexual harassment, many people do not perceive them as rules that prohibit all conduct of a sexual nature. Such people continue to pursue their sexual interests in their workplaces, educational institutions, and so forth, in spite of the existence of rules against sexual harassment. In order to see what kind of harm the law can do to them, let us consider the following scenario.

Peter is attracted to his coworker Paula and would like to get to know her better. Believing it to be a suitably nonthreatening way to proceed, he invites her for lunch. Paula is not at all interested in Peter and does not wish even to have lunch with him. Moreover, she is completely unprepared for his invitation, so at the moment when he utters it, she panics. What she ends up answering is "I am really very busy this whole week, but maybe next week." She does not in fact have the slightest intention of actually going out for lunch with Peter next week or ever. She utters those words because they are the words that first come to her mind as something that can get her out of the present awkward situation smoothly. Not knowing her well, Peter is unable to notice her feeling of awkwardness and takes her words literally. He walks away looking forward to the next week.

As the next week arrives, Peter begins to linger around Paula's office, to go to the photocopier when she is likely to be there, and in general to seek every opportunity to run into her, all in the hope that he will thus be able to reissue the lunch invitation (he does not wish to bother her by phoning her). Her "maybe next week" is very vivid in his mind. She, on the other hand, wishes to avoid running into him, because she knows that he would take the opportunity to reissue the invitation and she dreads having to explicitly turn it down. So she begins to deliberately avoid getting her work to the photocopier when he is there, walking past his office, and in general doing anything that might get her in contact with him. A few days into the week, she begins to notice that Peter spends more time than would be normal in the vicinity of her office. That significantly amplifies her nervousness. She begins to feel besieged in her office. She suddenly remembers reading in a popular magazine about respectable-looking men who turn out to be maniacs who stalk and eventually violently attack women they are attracted to. Peter begins to look like a serious menace. In the meantime, Peter is blissfully unaware that his lingering around Paula's office has been noticed. He thinks that their not having run into each other is just an accident. He therefore continues to wait patiently for an opportunity to invite Paula for lunch, still vividly remembering that she said "maybe next week."

This story exemplifies the kind of miscommunication that is not infrequent in romantic pursuits. Although the behavior of both individuals is easily understandable, the result is most unfortunate. The story of Peter and Paula is a sad story. Various versions of it have been playing themselves out in real life for a very long time. But the introduction of the concept of sexual harassment makes it possible for such stories to become much sadder. Paula may remember the pamphlet about sexual harassment that her employer has dutifully provided to all employees, which probably contains something like the EEOC's definition of sexual harassment. That may lead her to think of what is going on as sexual harassment. After all, Peter is engaging in some conduct of a sexual nature here: it is obvious that he is motivated by sexual interest in Paula, isn't it? His conduct has the effect of making her working environment intimidating, doesn't it? So it looks as if the definition is satisfied. Paula may thus go to discuss her problem with the officer of her company who is in charge of such matters. As a result, a whole cumbersome bureaucratic machinery will suddenly descend on both Peter and Paula.

For the purpose of my argument here, it does not particularly matter what eventually happens to Peter. It is quite possible that he may be able to escape a formal punishment, but it is certain that he will not be able to escape bureaucrats investigating his very intimate desires and pursuits. Regardless of its ultimate disposition, Paula's is a prima facie viable complaint, and the company is under legal obligation to take any such complaints seriously and investigate them thoroughly.

Bringing in bureaucracy to deal with subtle miscommunications in a delicate area of people's lives is as wise as bringing a bull into a china shop. There is no good reason to believe that bureaucratic intervention in such miscommunication produces beneficial results in the long run. It is true that Paula may, at the cost of involving herself with the bureaucratic machinery, obtain relief from the tension that Peter's behavior is causing to her. But bureaucratic intervention is extremely unlikely to make either Peter or Paula better equipped to avoid such misunderstandings in the future, to understand their sexuality, and that of others, better, or to trust people of the opposite sex. Quite the opposite result is likely. The experience will almost certainly leave both Peter and Paula profoundly distrustful of the opposite sex. For many years into the future, both Peter and Paula will likely be quite tense about almost any interaction with members of the opposite sex. For them, "opposite sex" will not merely be a conventional way of referring to the sex other than one's own: the incident will make them think of the opposite sex as in a very strong sense opposite, and indeed opposed, to one's own. The lives of the Peters and Paulas of the real world thus end up being significantly poisoned by their encounters with sexual harassment bureaucracies. The friends in whom they confide and others who come to know about such incidents will also have a seed of distrust of the opposite sex planted in them.

In thinking about this argument, it is important not to be misled by the fact that many institutions give those who complain about sexual harassment the choice between dealing with the matter "formally" or "informally." The so-called informal procedures for dealing with such complaints are, in fact, quite formal. Indeed, they have to have a considerable level of formality because what happens under these procedures may be relevant to the question of the institution's legal liability if the case should ever reach the courts. There is something self-contradictory about providing for a procedure in an official document and appointing special officers for carrying it out and then calling the procedure "informal." In any event, the fact that such a procedure is called "informal" does not annul the fact that it consists in people who are total strangers to oneself prying into one's most intimate desires. Nor should that label make one forget that these people have *formal* power to conduct such "informal" investigations in virtue of their *formal* positions in the bureaucracy of the institution and that the "informal" procedures are always backed up by the availability of the (more) "formal" ones.

Similarly, one should not allow oneself to be befuddled by the facts that the bureaucrats who deal with sexual harassment complaints often have nonthreatening-sounding titles, such as "mediator," and that their education may have been in disciplines such as counseling. These facts should not distract one from appreciating that the ultimate reason for these officers' employment is to ensure that their employer does not find itself in court. Indeed, those who get enmeshed in sexual harassment investigations may find it additionally disorienting that these officers tend to use a counselor's jargon and style of conduct while exercising what is ultimately a law enforcement function.

The Fight against Sexual Harassment Invades Privacy

The argument of the preceding subsection that the rules against sexual harassment lead to bureaucrats investigating very intimate details of people's lives may be expressed by saying that these rules lead to invasion of privacy in a broad sense. However, the procedures discussed in the preceding subsection are still ultimately triggered by the action of one of the people involved, namely, by the complainant's making the complaint. That is not, however, the end of the effects that the law has on people's intimate lives.

Even if two people who work together are in a sexual relationship that is mutually satisfying and neither of them has the slightest inclination to complain about anything, they may still find their intimate lives scrutinized by bureaucrats. This is because the concept of sexual harassment has been interpreted in such a way that it applies to conduct of A that is directed to B, if the conduct creates "an intimidating, hostile, or offensive working environment" for C, a third party who happens to witness it or otherwise to come to know about it, even if the conduct does not at all create such an environment for B, the person to whom it is directed.[30] If C chooses to complain, the law makes it necessary to take the complaint seriously, investigate the matter, and sometimes impose punishments on those involved. Thus, two people who are pursuing a perfectly happy sexual affair may find the privacy of their interaction invaded by the sexual harassment bureaucracy if someone else, who is for whatever reason upset by their affair, chooses to complain.

Nor is that all. The law about sexual harassment in employment does not just force employers to have in place the mechanisms for responding to any complaints of sexual harassment that its employees may see fit to make. It is possible for an employer to be legally liable for sexual harassment even if no internal complaint has been made. This means that the law gives the employer an incentive to maintain constant alertness to any sexual harassment that might be going on, so that it can be responded to even if no internal complaint is made. Given that any conduct of a sexual nature within the workplace may turn into a case of sexual harassment, that means that the employer has to maintain awareness of any sexual activity between its employees. As one manual of advice about sexual harassment has put it:

> An employer is . . . required to monitor interoffice dating . . . . As [the law] becomes more inclusive, an employer will be required to monitor more and more conduct previously considered private and beyond the legitimate interests of an employer.[31]

Such "monitoring" of the intimate aspects of people's lives may well appear to quite a few people to be a rather serious invasion of privacy. That the law would encourage such invasion of privacy is not only inherently worrisome but also at odds with the general trend in recent decades of giving employees considerably more protection of privacy relative to their employers than has been usual in the more distant past.

As if all this were not enough, the nonlegal literature on the topic sometimes goes even further than the law in encouraging invasions of privacy. An article about empirical research on sexual harassment in universities, for example, says:

> Faculty members need to take responsibility when they see their colleagues engaging in harassing behaviors. To ignore these behaviors is unethical for those of us in areas where emphasis is on the welfare of the individual.[32]

Given that sexual harassment is not readily distinguishable from other conduct of a sexual nature, urging academics to "take responsibility" for their
colleagues' "harassing behavior" amounts to urging them to spy on, and
presumably report, any conduct of a sexual nature that their colleagues
might engage in within the framework of the institution.

Lack of Respect for Autonomy

One recurring theme in the nonlegal literature on sexual harassment is
that many of those who are, in the authors' opinion, victims of sexual
harassment, do not think of themselves as victims of sexual harassment or,
for that matter, as victims of anything. One previously quoted, widely
read, book on sexual harassment in universities, issues the following warning to students:

> If a student is having a personal relationship with a professor and is sure that
> sexual harassment has nothing to do with her situation, she should think
> again.[33]

This is based on the authors' finding that

> a frequent coping tactic is refusal to acknowledge that harassment exists.
> Some students are either too naive or too self-deluded to admit that sexual
> exploitation can occur in their relationships with teachers. The students ex-
> plain their intimate relationships with faculty in idealistic terms. They use
> hyperbole to describe the professor—he has "given life meaning," he has
> taught them "what it is to be an adult." They may know the definition of
> harassment, but what happens to them is "different" or "special."[34]

Another study has

> found that 50 percent of the female students . . . surveyed reported having
> experienced at least one incident of harassment when specific behaviors meet-
> ing legal definitions of harassment were described to them without the use of
> the term harassment. However, when asked directly if they had been ha-
> rassed, only one percent indicated that they believed they had been sexually
> harassed.[35]

The remedy that the authors of such literature typically propose for this
discrepancy is that in deciding who is a victim of sexual harassment, the

views of psychologists, counselors, and similar experts should override the views of the putative victims who deny their victimhood:

> If a student reports being the recipient of sexual overtures but does not define them as harassment, should these events be defined as harassment by the person to whom they are reported? It would seem appropriate to label this experience harassment.[36]

The experts should then work on making the putative victims accept the label and thus "encourage receptivity to a range of support services available to counteract the isolation typically experienced by harassment victims."[37]

The crucial difference between characterizing something as having "given life meaning" and characterizing it as sexual harassment is that the first characterization implies that it is something highly desirable while the second implies that it is highly undesirable. A disagreement about whether something is desirable is not a disagreement about a scientifically ascertainable fact. Expertise in an empirical science does not give one any special authority on such matters. The view of an expert on such an area that a certain course of events (say a particular sexual involvement of a student with a professor) was undesirable and the view of the putative victim that it has "given life meaning" are therefore on a par: there is no reason to assume that the first is somehow correct and the second mistaken. In fact, respect for people's autonomy is normally taken to imply that adults should be left to lead their lives in accordance with their own ideas as to what is desirable (as long as that does not harm others).

To say that an adult person who sees a particular personal relationship as having "given life meaning" (and thus as something highly desirable) should be made to stop seeing it that way and start thinking of it as an instance of sexual harassment (and thus as something highly undesirable) involves considerable disrespect for that person's autonomy. It implies that in such cases, one should be made to stop enjoying what one enjoys and desiring what one desires. One is to be made to reinterpret one's actually lived experiences in the light of the experts' theories. One's deeply felt desires are to be replaced by the desires implanted by the experts, including the desire to use "support services" provided by the experts. The experts are in possession of a theory that implies that people are not supposed to desire certain kinds of sexual experiences, and when they encounter actual people whose desires do not fit the theory, their response is that the people need to be therapeutically molded until their desires come to fit the theory. It never occurs to them that the discrepancy between people's actual desires and the theory just might be an indication that something is wrong with the theory.

The fact that these experts approach the matter in this arrogant manner would still not constitute a specially worrisome problem if they were merely one of the many "sects" seeking converts to their views of sexuality, in fair competition with proponents of various other views on such matters. But these experts are not simply offering their view of the matter in the marketplace of ideas. They seek to obtain, and these days generally succeed in obtaining, offices, paid positions, and other resources with which to transform people who do not regard themselves as victims into people who think of themselves as victims in need of "support services," while no such offices, paid positions, or other resources are available to people with alternative views of sexuality to enable them to seek converts to their views.

The Structure of the Sexual Harassment Law

The legal systems of contemporary Western societies make a distinction between criminal and civil law. The distinction is accompanied by a set of well-established traditions that limit what the state may do to its citizens within the field of criminal law. One of these traditions is that the state may impose criminal sanctions only for conduct that is engaged in intentionally, knowingly, or at a minimum, recklessly. Criminal codes normally do not impose liability for mere negligence or strict liability. (Rare exceptions are normally thought to be in need of special justification.) Moreover, a criminal sanction may be imposed on an individual only if the individual's guilt has been proven beyond a reasonable doubt. The proof has to be made through an elaborate, carefully structured procedure that incorporates numerous safeguards.

The constraints that apply to the civil law are far less strict. Within the area of civil law, liability for negligence and strict liability are standard, and proof by a preponderance of the evidence is sufficient. These differences reflect the fact that being found guilty of a crime affects a person's life far more profoundly than losing a civil suit. Not only can a criminal sanction incorporate going to jail; even if one does not go to jail for a long time or at all, the mere fact that one has been found guilty of a crime may be enough to ruin one's life. Maintaining a respectable position in the community and pursuing a respectable career usually become impossible for such a person; the person comes to be generally treated as an outcast. None of that happens to those who lose civil suits. If one loses a civil suit, one may need to pay the damages, but otherwise one is free to get on with one's life and to maintain whatever degree of respectability one has had before.

Now, being found guilty of sexual harassment is, in its consequences, far closer to being found guilty of a crime than to losing a civil suit. Admittedly, sexual harassers do not go to jail, but in all other respects, one's life can be just as ruined by being found guilty of sexual harassment as by a criminal conviction. Those found guilty of sexual harassment are typically treated as outcasts, just as criminals are. If one is accused of sexual harassment, one stands to lose one's job (together with any chance of finding a respectable job) and one's respectability in one's community.

In spite of that, a person accused of sexual harassment does not enjoy anything that would come even close to the procedural safeguards that characterize criminal trials in civilized countries. Formal findings that the concept of sexual harassment applies to someone's conduct are often based on flimsy procedures carried out by people with less than a keen sense of what the rule of law is. Guilt does not have to be proven beyond a reasonable doubt or anywhere close to that. Moreover, what one is accused of need not be intentional or even reckless: it is, in fact, a matter of strict liability.

The law about sexual harassment in employment[38] thus affects people's lives in a manner that is normally reserved for criminal law without giving them the rights that criminal defendants normally have. The state has managed to accomplish this, without causing public uproar, by giving the law a two-level structure. At what I shall call the upper level, the state imposes on employers (usually corporations) the obligation to see to it that there is no sexual harassment within their businesses. The employers carry out that obligation by creating and enforcing various internal rules for their businesses that prohibit individuals from engaging in acts of sexual harassment. I shall call that the lower level.

This two-level structure means that the state does not deal directly with individuals accused of sexual harassment. When an individual is accused of sexual harassment, the individual's guilt is ascertained, and sanctions imposed, at the lower level. In spite of standing to suffer sanctions akin to criminal ones, the individual is not technically a criminal defendant or, strictly speaking, a party to any kind of legal proceeding. The state is not directly involved; the whole matter appears to be between the individual and the individual's employer. An impression is thus created that the traditions that constrain what the state may do to its citizens have nothing to do with what happens at the lower level. The state treats the sexual harassment law as civil, rather than criminal, in character because at the upper level, at which the state is directly involved, dealing with employers, the law indeed does consistently have the characteristics of a civil law. If an employer is sued for not having seen to it that there is no harassment in its business, the employer stands to suffer only a civil sanction.

As long as each of the two levels is looked at separately, it appears that the traditions about how the state may treat an individual are not violated. At the upper level, the state deals with employers (who are anyway corporations and not individuals) in the manner of the civil law; at the lower level, where individuals' lives are affected by the operation of the law, the state is not involved. That way of looking at the law, however, neglects the supremely relevant fact that what happens at the lower level happens because of the upper level. Employers do not enact and enforce their internal sexual harassment rules for reasons of their own; they do it because the state, at the upper level, requires them to. Thus, although the state is not involved directly at the lower level, it is still involved indirectly. It is misleading to describe the lower-level sanctions as simply imposed on individuals by their employers. Given that these sanctions are ultimately a result of what the state does at the upper level, what happens to individuals at the lower level should be regarded as imposed on them *by* the state *through* employers.

Once it is looked at in this light, the sexual harassment law turns out to be a rather worrisome violation of established traditions about what the state may and may not do to its citizens. The violation is additionally worrisome because it is not immediately obvious. By bringing employers into the operation of the law as intermediaries and by thus breaking up that operation into two levels, the state creates the illusion that these traditions have not been violated.

The two-level structure of the law has other undesirable consequences. In particular, it makes the law much harsher than it may appear to those who study only its upper level. At the upper level, courts impose liability on employers only if the conduct complained of has crossed the threshold of being "severe or pervasive," but the existence of such a threshold cannot percolate to the lower level. In order to avoid upper-level liability, employers have to stop the conduct that might generate liability *before* it reaches the threshold, and in order to have a margin of safety against liability they have to stop it *well* before it reaches the threshold. That means they are compelled to make punishable, by lower-level sanctions, even conduct that is well below the threshold.

The problems discussed in this subsection, unlike those discussed in the rest of this essay, have nothing to do with the specific content of the sexual harassment law: they stem solely from its structure. This means that even those who are not specifically interested in the topic of sexual harassment itself have a reason to take note of these problems. There is nothing in the two-level structure to prevent its application to entirely different kinds of content. If the problems associated with the two-level structure of the sexual harassment law are allowed to pass without comment, there is a danger that the state may be tempted to create other laws with the same structure. There is thus a danger that the state may try to use the device of a two-level law to control other kinds of individual conduct in a manner that violates the traditions that constrain the state's power, while creating the illusion that it is not violating them. Because the two-level structure is readily applicable to other kinds of conduct, the problems associated with it deserve the attention of everyone who is keen to preserve the liberal traditions that limit the powers of the state. The significance of these problems surpasses the significance of the specific issue of sexual harassment.

Postscript

The problems I have outlined in this essay are not the kinds of problems that can be remedied by simply changing this or that detail of the law about sexual harassment or the movement aimed at the eradication of sexual harassment. The arguments of this essay imply that the fight against sexual harassment is fundamentally defective. If one accepts these arguments, then the laws and other institutions that have been built around the concept of sexual harassment are beyond repair; the only reasonable course of action is to scrap them.

And yet, as I have repeatedly acknowledged throughout this essay, much of the conduct that is currently dealt with as sexual harassment is morally wrong, and at least some of it is wrong in a way that warrants some kind of official intervention. It is certainly true that the present law against sexual harassment and the related institutions have done a great deal of good by bringing welcome relief to some victims of such conduct. This gives rise to an important question. If the line of thought that I have been pursuing in this essay is generally accepted and followed to its ultimate conclusion and if the fight against sexual harassment is thus abandoned in anything like its present form, what is to be done about such conduct? Is there any way to reproduce the worthwhile accomplishments of the fight against sexual harassment while avoiding the problems discussed in the rest of this essay?

The preliminary response to this question is that much of the conduct that is currently classified as sexual harassment can readily fit under independently existing, well-established legal categories and can be dealt with as such. Some of the more egregious cases, for example, fit the legal definitions of battery and assault, others may satisfy the criteria for the tort of intentional infliction of emotional distress, in yet others a breach of contract can be found, and so on.

The interesting question, then, becomes whether there is a residue of cases presently dealt with as sexual harassment that do not fit any of the other existing legal categories, but are still wrong in such a way that they ought to be legally controlled. One possible response is to argue that there is no such residue. According to that line of thinking, after the cases of sexual harassment that can fit other legal categories have been subsumed under them, the sexual harassment that we will be left with will be nothing worse than mere rudeness. Such conduct should then be dealt with in the same way in which we deal with other instances of mere rudeness: through informal social mechanisms and not through the law or lawlike institutions.

An alternative line of response is to say that there are cases of what is now treated as sexual harassment that cannot fit any of the other legal categories and that are yet wrong in a way that calls for legal intervention. Therefore, this line of response goes, we need to try harder to produce an analysis that will capture the source of the wrongness of such conduct better than the analysis in terms of sexual harassment does. That will then enable us to create some new body of law for dealing with such conduct, a body of law that will avoid the pitfalls of the sexual harassment law that have been the subject of this essay and still preserve its worthwhile accomplishments.

Whether the first or the second of these two lines of response is ultimately more plausible is a difficult question, which I shall not attempt to answer. Trying to answer that question would go beyond commenting on the movement against sexual harassment as it actually is, which is what I took to be my task in this essay. Let me, however, without committing myself to it, try to indicate briefly how the second line of response might be developed.

At several points in the first section of this essay, I argued that seemingly plausible reasons for thinking that sexual harassment is wrong fail to explain why some problematic conduct within workplaces, educational institutions, and similar formal frameworks should be treated differently from otherwise similar conduct outside such frameworks. There is one difference between being within such a framework and being outside it that I have not considered there and that may be morally relevant. An essential feature of being employed or of being in formal education is that at certain times one simply has to be at certain places and communicate with certain people. This means that while at work or at school, unlike in other settings, one does not have at one's disposal some simple and effective ways of defending oneself from conduct that one finds annoying, obnoxious, offensive, or otherwise unpleasant: one cannot avoid the conduct by simply refusing to interact with the people who engage in it or by walking away. There is conduct of various kinds that is wrong but that clearly does not call for legal intervention when it takes place in other settings, because one can easily deal with it on one's own by avoiding its source: one can simply turn away and refuse to listen; if necessary, one can cross over to the other side of the street, room, subway carriage; one can hang up the phone. When exposed to similar conduct at work or at school, one is often unable to do anything like that. In such settings, it is often impossible to avoid communicating with certain people, because communicating with them is an essential part of one's job or education, and it is often impossible to remove oneself physically from them, because being at a particular place is an essential part of one's job or education. This means that the annoying, obnoxious, offensive, or otherwise unpleasant conduct within such formal frameworks is morally more problematic than similar conduct outside such frameworks.

It can thus be argued that within such frameworks, one needs some form of protection against such conduct that will act as a substitute for what one can otherwise accomplish by removing oneself from the source of the conduct or by otherwise avoiding interactions that expose oneself to it. It can also be argued that legal rules may be the way to provide such protection. In other words, it can be said that because being at work or in education essentially involves a certain lack of privacy, there need to be rules that will limit the impact of that lack of privacy.

Notice that although this line of thought, if developed further, might perhaps produce a justification for introducing some kind of law against intrusive behavior at workplaces or in educational institutions, which might cover a great deal of what is now classified as sexual harassment, it will not generate a justification for anything like the actual sexual harassment law or the movement to eradicate sexual harassment. In particular, although this line of thought does provide a reason for treating the relevant conduct within designated formal frameworks differently from similar conduct outside them, it does not provide any reason for treating intrusive conduct of a sexual nature differently from intrusive conduct of a nonsexual nature. There is also no appeal anywhere in this line of reasoning to the notion of discrimination. Given that the actual sexual harassment law has been built upon subsuming sexual harassment under the notion of sex discrimination, any line of reasoning that does not involve that notion is bound to lead to something very different from the present law. Moreover, given that this line of thought is centered around the idea that people should be protected against unnecessary intrusion into their lives, it cannot generate measures that create more intrusion than they prevent. It is thus built into this line of thinking that it will not create the problems of the kind discussed above under the heading "The Fight against Sexual Harassment Invades Privacy."

As I have already indicated, this line of thought is something that I merely wanted to hint at, without developing it further, and without attempting to resolve whether, if fully developed, it would turn out to be plausible or not. I thus leave it an open question what, if anything, should replace the present fight against sexual harassment. The openness of that question should, however, not distract us from appreciating the main conclusion of this essay, which is that the fight against sexual harassment is unjustified and ought to be opposed.

Notes

1. See, for example, Richard Wasserstrom, "Is Adultery Immoral?" and Frederick Elliston, "In Defense of Promiscuity," in *Philosophy and Sex*, ed. Robert Baker and Frederick Elliston (Buffalo: Prometheus Books, 1975), 207–21, 222–43. The Wasserstrom article also appears in several other anthologies.

2. Peggy Crull, "The Impact of Sexual Harassment on the Job: A Profile of the Experiences of Ninety-Two Women," in *Sexuality in Organizations: Romantic and Coercive Behaviors at Work*, ed. Dail Ann Neugarten and Jay M. Shafritz (Oak Park, Ill.: Moore Publishing, 1980), 68.

3. Jill L. Sherer, "Sexually Harassed," *Hospitals and Health Networks* 69, no. 2 (1995): 56.

4. Barbara A. Gutek, *Sex and the Workplace: The Impact of Sexual Behavior on Women, Men, and Organizations* (San Francisco: Jossey-Bass, 1985), 160.

5. Billie Wright Dziech and Linda Weiner, *The Lecherous Professor: Sexual Harassment on Campus*, 2d Edition (Urbana, Ill.: University of Illinois Press, 1990), 76.

6. Ann Levin, "UCSD Alters Sex-Harassment Policy," *Tribune* (San Diego), 26 August 1988.

7. Jan Crosthwaite and Christine Swanton, "On the Nature of Sexual Harassment," *Australasian Journal of Philosophy* 64, supplement (1986): 100 (footnote omitted).

8. Crosthwaite and Swanton seem to acknowledge that their account of sexual harassment does not straightforwardly entail what kind of legal regime we should have for dealing with it. Ibid., 103.

9. The publishers of Lin Farley's widely read book on sexual harassment, Lin Farley, *Sexual Shakedown: The Sexual Harassment of Women on the Job* (New York, Warner Books, 1980) have placed on its front and back covers staged photographs that are clearly intended to represent cases of precisely such a nature.

10. Crull, 'The Impact of Sexual Harassment," 68.

11. Kathryn Quina, "The Victimizations of Women," in *Ivory Power: Sexual Harassment on Campus*, ed. Michele A. Paludi, (Albany: State University of New York Press, 1990), 94.

12. Sue Rosenberg Zalk, "Men in the Academy: A Psychological Profile of Harassment," in *Ivory Power*, ed. Paludi, 160.

13. Dziech and Weiner, *The Lecherous Professor*, 74.

14. Louise F. Fitzgerald, "Sexual Harassment: The Definition and Measurement of a Construct," in *Ivory Power*, ed. Paludi, 39.

15. Dziech and Weiner, *The Lecherous Professor*, 74–75.

16. Ibid., 75.

17. Crull, 'The Impact of Sexual Harassment," 70.

18. Lin Farley, testimony before the Commission on Human Rights of the City of New York on 21 April 1975, quoted in Catharine A. MacKinnon, *Sexual Harassment of Working Women: A Case of Sex Discrimination* (New Haven: Yale University Press, 1979), 52.

19. Vita C. Rabinowitz, "Coping with Sexual Harassment," in *Ivory Power*, ed. Paludi, 112–13.

20. Dziech and Weiner, *The Lecherous Professor*, 75.

21. *Barnes v. Train*, 13 FEP Cases 123 (D.D.C. 1974); *Corne v. Bausch and Lomb*, Inc., 390 F. Supp. 161 (D. Ariz. 1975).

22. *Williams v. Saxbe*, 413 F. Supp. 654 (D.D.C. 1976).

23. *Meritor Savings Bank v. Vinson*, 477 U.S. 57 (1986).

24. An argument essentially the same as this criticism of the first alleged reason has been made, albeit in a highly condensed form, in F. M. Christensen, " 'Sexual Harassment' Must Be Eliminated," *Public Affairs Quarterly* 8 (1994): 8–9.

25. Cf. MacKinnon, *Sexual Harassment of Working Women*, 172.

26. EEOC, "Guidelines on Discrimination Because of Sex," *Code of Federal Regulations* 29, sec. 1604.11 (a) (1996).

27. The argument of this subsection, "The Demarcation Problem," is elaborated in my "Sexual Harassment in the Law: The Demarcation Problem," *Journal of Social Philosophy* 25, no. 3 (1994): 102–22.

28. *Johnson v. County of Los Angeles Fire Department*, 865 F. Supp. 1430 (C.D. Cal. 1994); *Silva v. University of New Hampshire*, 888 F. Supp. 293 (D.N.H. 1994). The argument presented in this subsection, "The Conflict with the Freedom of Speech" is based on Kingsley R. Browne, "Title VII as Censorship: Hostile-Environment Harassment and the First Amendment," *Ohio State Law Journal* 52 (1991): 481–550.

29. The implications of the impossibility of prohibiting unwelcome and offensive advances without affecting the ones that lead to mutually satisfying interaction have been developed in my essay "Sexual Harassment and Negligence," forthcoming in *Journal of Social Philosophy*.

30. The interpretation of the law that makes it apply to the conduct that happens to affect third parties in this way stems from *Broderick v. Ruder*, 685 F. Supp. 1269 (D.D.C. 1988).

31. Titus E. Aaron with Judy A. Isaksen, *Sexual Harassment in the Workplace: A Guide to the Law and a Research Overview for Employers and Employees* (Jefferson, N.C.: McFarland, 1993), 83.

32. Linda J. Rubin and Sherry B. Borgers, "Sexual Harassment in Universities during the 1980s," *Sex Roles* 23 (1990): 410.

33. Dziech and Weiner, *The Lecherous Professor*, 167.

34. Ibid., 84.

35. Mary Kay Biaggio, Deborah Watts, and Arlene Brownell, "Addressing Sexual Harassment: Strategies for Prevention and Change," in *Ivory Power*, ed. Paludi, 223, referring to L. F. Fitzgerald and S. L. Shullman, "The Development and

Validation of an Objectively Scored Measure of Sexual Harassment" (paper presented at the meeting of the American Psychological Association, Los Angeles, 1985).

36. Biaggio, Watts, and Brownell, "Strategies for Prevention," 223.

37. Ibid.

38. My argument in this subsection, "The Structure of the Sexual Harassment Law," concentrates on how the law operates in employment settings, but some of it can mutatis mutandis be applied to educational settings as well.

3

Response

Linda LeMoncheck

Readers with a predilection for postmodernism may well be smiling in silent satisfaction at this point, since the two previous essays' disparate philosophical perspectives on sexual harassment speak to the postmodern position that the "truth" about controversial moral issues is ultimately a matter of socially located world view: I take the perspective that sexual harassment is a violation of sexual integrity, which violation is politicized by organizational hierarchies, gender expectations, and cultural stereotypes that inform sexually harassing conduct as a type of inequality. As such, women who are sexually harassed by men deserve special protection under antidiscrimination law that interprets sexual harassment as both a personal injury against individual women and a social injustice against women as a class. I have argued that understanding sexual harassment in this way can provide clarity and credibility to the variety of women's experiences of, and reactions to, being sexually harassed. Consequently, sexual harassment policies and procedures can serve the socially responsible purpose of identifying the kinds of individually and culturally sensitive workplace and campus environments most conducive to creative and cooperative work in the absence of oppressive gender politics. Dr. Hajdin, on the other hand, takes the perspective that sexual harassment is a personal injury whose harm may be found in hostilities between women and men or in circumstances of sexual attraction gone wrong. As such, legal claims against sexual harassment are inadequately served by antidiscrimination law, which only obscures the usefulness of common-law torts or of the criminal law for handling personal injury cases. Moreover, according

165

to Dr. Hajdin, workplace and campus sexual harassment policies enforced under the auspices of antidiscrimination law not only hide the ways in which ostensibly civil legal procedures criminalize alleged harassers in the absence of due process but also generally make life miserable for persons whose only fault is that they tried to be friendly to their coworkers.

What I propose to argue in my response is that by assuming that the harm of sexual harassment is a personal and not a political one, Dr. Hajdin insures that the characterization of sexual harassment as a social injustice prohibited by antidiscrimination law will appear misleading and mistaken. When sexual conduct is confined to conduct between private individuals with equal moral rights against noninterference, Dr. Hajdin can guarantee that whatever may be morally wrong with sexual harassment is reducible to personal injury in otherwise egalitarian sexual relationships. Thus, he concludes that the concept of sexual harassment, understood in terms of institutionalized gender hierarchies and oppressive sexual politics, "is not a morally significant concept" (p. 100). Moreover, by making sexual harassment solely a matter of unpoliticized personal injury, Dr. Hajdin insures that any laws that might prohibit sexual harassment will appear suspect for their overly intrusive claim on individuals' personal lives. Indeed, I wish to argue that by assuming that the state cannot legitimately use employers to prohibit specific employee behavior to enforce federal law, Dr. Hajdin throws out the baby of protective social policy with the bathwater of potential violations of individual civil liberties, which such policies need not actualize.

In general, my strategy is to show that only by obscuring the culturally located gender hierarchies and sexual politics that expose the social injustice of sexual harassment can Dr. Hajdin succeed in painting a picture of the contemporary feminist movement against sexual harassment as misguided. In this way, Dr. Hajdin confirms my thesis that sexual harassment is a regenerating and interpretive process of sexual politics whose operative question is not *whether or not* a given act is harassing but by whom and under what cultural conditions the assessment of the conduct is being made. Thus, the relevant question under this model is not a definitional one but a political one, namely, "Who defines the terms and conditions of the moral and legal discourse on sexual harassment?" Recall that this model embraces the incommensurability of conflicting interpretations of sexual harassment and does not attempt to resolve the lack of consensus about what sexual harassment "is." From this perspective, sexual harassment is not a "capturable" phenomenon amenable to guidelines designed to encompass all appropriate cases but, rather, a dynamic and dialectical phenomenon whose meaning is interpreted and reinterpreted, generated and regenerated, depending upon the power of those who can appropriate its terms and conditions. I see my task as one of empowering the reader to recognize the danger of this appropriation when it disguises its partial and historicized interpretation of sexual harassment as objective and universal "truth." At the same time, I wish to argue that a gendered reading of sexual harassment as both personal injury and social injustice, while also partial and historicized, does not disguise its partiality but invokes it in order to socially locate men's harassment of women within the gender hierarchies that circumscribe it.

Let me begin with a review of Dr. Hajdin's major tenets and some of his reasons for holding them. I will then identify where and how Dr. Hajdin's construction of sexual harassment drives his specific arguments forward. The main thesis of Dr. Hajdin's essay is that current state and federal laws prohibiting sexual harassment as a species of sex discrimination, as well as current political movements to combat sexual harassment, which are either foundational to or inspired by such laws, are unjustified and ought to be opposed. Dr. Hajdin argues that the concept of sexual harassment that the current law and concomitant political movements invoke does not pick out a substantive or illuminating normative distinction among types of sexual conduct worthy of separate consideration by either morality, social policy, or the law. In Dr. Hajdin's view, using the concept as if it could pick out a significant moral category of wrong only obscures our understanding of the real grounds for the wrongness of the conduct in question. Thus, sexual harassment "as a type of conduct" (p. 100) cannot provide a moral foundation on its own account that would justify special laws or social policy prohibiting the conduct to which the concept of sexual harassment refers. Moreover, what ends up being wrong about sexual harassment is not something that in most cases we would want prohibited by law, since to prohibit such conduct, even when morally objectionable, would be overly intrusive into the personal lives of women and men.

Dr. Hajdin argues that the wrong of sexual harassment, when it is wrong (and he is very explicit in his assertion that much of what is currently classified as sexual harassment is indeed wrong), can be subsumed under other sorts of moral or legal wrongs that have the normatively significant content that the concept of sexual harassment lacks. The moral wrong of sexual harassment can be addressed through prevailing community standards of right conduct, while its legal wrong can be addressed through existing common-law torts, the criminal law, or some as yet unspecified law, which Dr. Hajdin hints in his conclusion may be of the sort explicitly protecting privacy. Specifically, since the wrong of sex discrimination cannot subsume the wrong of sexual harassment in the ways that many feminists think, Dr. Hajdin contends that interpreting sexual harassment as illegal under antidiscrimination law is both misleading and mistaken.

Dr. Hajdin also argues that current EEOC guidelines used to evaluate sexual harassment claims describe sexual harassment in ways that make it possible to avoid objectionable sexual conduct in the workplace only by refraining from all sexual or personally intimate conduct there. Moreover, such guidelines succeed in violating the privacy, freedom of expression, and autonomy of those who are bound by sexual harassment law and social policy; therefore, such guidelines as measures of the efficacy of both legal and social policy prohibitions on sexual harassment must be abandoned, along with any continued efforts to subsume sexual harassment under sex discrimination law. Indeed, it is contended that the state unjustly treats alleged harassers like criminals by prosecuting employers under federal or state antidiscrimination laws that are designed explicitly to handle civil suits but that have the potential to ruin the lives and reputations of those accused of sexual harassment, without any of the procedural safeguards that characterize criminal trials in the United States. This is accomplished without public censure because the law imposes only civil sanctions on employers for sexual harassment by their employees and requires employers, in turn, to impose their own in-house prohibitions and penalties on their employees to insure employers' freedom from legal liability. To the extent that some additional law might be required specifically to prohibit sexual harassment, Dr. Hajdin argues that any such law must be designed to protect against, instead of either encourage or require, unnecessary intrusion in people's lives. As such, it would very likely not refer specifically to sexual conduct per se, but would speak to the more general issue of individuals' rights to privacy within the workplace.

Everyday Experience and Formal Frameworks

Dr. Hajdin assures his readers that their knowledge of how to apply the concept of sexual harassment is knowledge they have acquired through "everyday experience" (p. 102) and as such, will be sufficient to follow his initial line of reasoning. My concern is whether Dr. Hajdin can identify our readers' various conceptions of sexual harassment in a concise enough way to be useful to him. Since Dr. Hajdin's arguments in the section entitled "The Wrong Reasons for Supporting the Fight against Sexual Harassment" are designed to show that the concept of sexual harassment is not a morally significant concept, the apparent legitimacy of his readers' understanding of sexual harassment must be shown to be illegitimate if their concept of sexual harassment is to be eliminated in favor of other, more illuminating types of moral concepts. This requires Dr. Hajdin to be able to identify his readers' concept of sexual harassment, the application of which they have learned through "everyday experience," so that he can say with certainty that this is the concept he has debunked.

However, if on Dr. Hajdin's own account, his readers have learned how to apply their concept of sexual harassment by using obfuscating and suspect legal and theoretical constructs, it is doubtful that Dr. Hajdin's readers will have a clearly defined or commonly held view of what sexual harassment is, without which Dr. Hajdin cannot isolate the concept of sexual harassment he wants to delegitimize. Even when social policy guidelines are explicit on the matter, sexual harassment is not understood or experienced in the same ways by everybody, or even by all women, by all black women, or by all women in the same workplace. Indeed, some women and many men will tell you that they have had virtually no experience of sexual harassment themselves or that they would not know exactly when they were being harassed unless the conduct were identified for them, and these are often the very people who find it difficult to understand the complaints of others or identify others' treatment as harassing. When a major part of the debate over what is wrong with sexual harassment is that people disagree about what kinds of conduct, if any, the concept should be applied to, I find it extraordinary that Dr. Hajdin would ground his initial arguments aimed at resolving this issue on what can at best be described as a Wittgensteinian family-resemblance concept whose parameters are contingent on the particular social location of individual users.

I became suspicious that Dr. Hajdin, in spite of his admission that sexual harassment is a contested moral concept, might be relying on a common and clearly defined understanding of sexual harassment when he suggested that while sexual harassment debates typically involve debates over the meaning of sexual harassment itself, debates over abortion or affirmative action are not debates over what abortion or affirmative action means; rather, he claims, the latter are debates over whether or not abortion or affirmative action is morally wrong. According to Dr. Hajdin, this is because terms like "abortion" or "affirmative action" have meanings that are commonly agreed upon: "[W]e all know what it [the concept of abortion] stands for . . . . [I]t has been a part of *our everyday conceptual framework* for a fairly long time" (p. 98, emphasis added). On the contrary, I suggest that debates over abortion and affirmative action are heated precisely because intelligent and well-meaning people cannot agree on what the concepts mean: Is abortion the murder of an unborn child or the excision of lifeless human tissue? Is it a violation of a person's right to life or an exercise of a person's freedom of choice? Is affirmative action an example of reverse discrimination or of equal opportunity? Is it a quota system or a system of educational access? Indeed, the importance of recognizing these conceptual debates is that each side will fight to put its understanding of the issue on the table and to discredit the conceptual framework of the opposition, since the concepts themselves determine to a large degree the moral and legal evaluations individuals make of them. Similarly, Dr. Hajdin's and my disagreements over what is wrong with sexual harassment hinge on whether sexual harassment is conceptualized as a private and personal injury or (also) as a culturally located social injustice.

Dr. Hajdin goes on to say that "[t]he concept of sexual harassment can be applied to certain conduct only if that conduct occurs within a formal framework of a kind that is specified by law . . . . [T]he concept simply cannot be applied outside a designated framework; otherwise similar conduct that occurs outside a workplace, educational institution, or other designated framework does not constitute sexual harassment." (pp. 102–3) This stipulation is made explicit so that Dr. Hajdin can be sure that his readers will understand the meaning of sexual harassment the way he intends to use it. But why should I or any reader accept the stipulation that sexual harassment be confined to formally designated frameworks, when part of my own and many feminists' "everyday experience" is that sexual harassment is a pervasive and ubiquitous part of the American social landscape and not just a feature of workplaces or campuses? Indeed, many feminists contend that the expression "sexual harassment" serves the important purpose of providing a name to an otherwise nameless injury that if left nameless, would remain normalized and accepted because it is so pervasive a feature of social life. The only reason Dr. Hajdin appears to offer for why the concept cannot be applied outside a designated framework is that otherwise similar conduct that does not occur within a designated framework is not sexual harassment. However, this begs the question: I wish to know *why* similar conduct outside these frameworks should not constitute sexual harassment, not *that* similar conduct outside these frameworks does not constitute sexual harassment.

I contend that the "relevant formal frameworks" (p. 103) of employment and educational institutions to which sexual harassment law refers exist in virtue of the nature of sex discrimination law, not because of self-evident conceptual restrictions on the meaning of sexual harassment. Antidiscrimination civil rights legislation was written as applicable to the workplace and, ultimately, to educational institutions. Sexual harassment within such frameworks was then successfully shown to be a form of sex discrimination and thus became illegal within those frameworks. Feminists did not first confine the conceptual apparatus of sexual harassment to the workplace and academia, then plug that apparatus into preexisting law. (The expression "sexual harassment" came into the lexicon before the first successful Title VII sexual harassment suit was decided.) Indeed, Title VII includes discrimination on the basis of sex because conservative, Southern opponents of the Civil Rights Act thought that prohibiting such discrimination was so obviously ludicrous that the bill would go down in defeat. The bill was nevertheless popular enough during Lyndon Johnson's strong civil rights administration to be passed.[1] It is a mistake to think that many feminists' "everyday experience" of sexual harassment, prior to its acceptance by the courts as a form of sex discrimination, would have been confined only to formal frameworks of a law many people regarded as a joke or that feminists are only interested in condemning sexual harassment in current legally designated formal frameworks. Current sex discrimination law simply makes it possible to address directly, at a state and federal level, not only the personal injury of sexual harassment within the workplace and academia but the social injustice of unequal treatment that occurs there as well. This does not mean that there are no other contexts in which women are sexually harassed as a form of gender oppression or that sex discrimination is confined to organizational milieus. However, not every case of sexual harassment need be illegal, since not every violation of sexual integrity will result in the kinds of harm (to reputation, livelihood, or well-being) that requires legal intervention to resolve the matter. One of Dr. Hajdin's main arguments for his claim that sexual harassment is not a morally significant concept is that arguments for the special moral or legal wrongness of sexual harassment must justify why sexual harassment applies to some designated frameworks and not others. I am arguing that sexual harassment is a morally significant concept independently of the frameworks currently designated to legally prohibit the conduct and that the concept of sexual harassment needs no such formal frameworks to make sense of what is wrong with it.

I am also puzzled by Dr. Hajdin's apparent disapproval of the way sexual harassment law has come into being: "No democratically elected representatives of the people had any opportunity to consider such a prohibition or vote on it before it first became law . . . . The sexual harassment law at the federal level is thus a creation of the courts, not of the Congress" (pp. 121–22). Yet a wide variety of federal laws in the United States, including antidefamation law, obscenity law, and antisegregation law, are also "a creation of the courts," whose decisions have established legal precedents consistent with the Constitution and binding as law. Hence, sexual harassment law cannot be singled out, much less singled out as objectionable, because it was not legislated by Congress. Dr. Hajdin claims that if sexual harassment law is a function of sex discrimination law, then the significant or central wrong of sexual harassment must be that it is a form of sex discrimination. If it turns out not to be a form of sex discrimination, he argues, then there is no justification for sexual harassment to be subsumed under Title VII or Title IX. However, *congressional legislation* making sexual harassment a form of sex discrimination would also make proving sex discrimination necessary to proving unlawful sexual harassment, so I do not understand Dr. Hajdin's complaint about the origins of sexual harassment law.

Moreover, neither suffering sex discrimination per se nor suffering harm per se is itself sufficient to make a legal case against sexual harassment under current law; that is, sex discrimination is not, using Dr. Hajdin's words, "in itself a ground for providing a legal remedy" (p. 123) for sexual harassment, just as harm is not in itself such a ground. This is because, as Dr. Hajdin rightly points out, there is a difference between discrimination on the basis of sex and wrongful discrimination on the basis of sex, and Title VII requires proof of wrongful discrimination. In the case of Title VII, the wrongness of the discrimination has to do with discriminating with respect to "compensation, terms, privileges, or conditions of employment," which is thought to harm the discriminatees by, for example, economically disadvantaging them or adversely affecting their competitiveness or effectiveness in the workplace. Thus, contrary to Dr. Hajdin, I would argue that the wrongness of sexual harassment *requires* looking for the harm that informs sex discrimination, since such harm is precisely what makes sexual harassment *wrongful* sex discrimination.

There may be a variety of specific injuries that the courts may address in filling out the context of the wrongful discrimination of sexual harassment in the workplace, in the same ways that manipulation, threat, and sexual presumption may all be a part of the wrong of failing to treat the harassed as a moral equal. As I argued in my initial essay, such injuries are an important part of understanding the complexity of the wrongness of sexual harassment, as well as establishing ways of interpreting sexual harassment law that do not impose an unfair burden of persuasion on the claimant. I have argued for an understanding of sexual harassment in terms of both personal injury and social injustice, consistent with the law's provision of remedies for sexual harassment that speak to both these types of harm.

Gender Politics and Cultural Oppression

Dr. Hajdin suggests that many of the objections made against sexual harassment are actually complaints about men's adultery, promiscuity, or insensitivity in sexual relationships and that complaining about sexual harassment per se only confuses the matter. Moreover, it is contended that because adultery, promiscuity, and sexual insensitivity, when they are wrong, are wrong outside the workplace or academia as well as in it, these complaints cannot be used to justify special moral or legal attention paid to them qua sexual harassment. I have already argued that formally designated frameworks are an unnecessary conceptual tool for understanding the wrong of sexual harassment. What I would like to know is exactly who is making these kinds of complaints about sexual harassment. Feminists point out that many male harassers are married, because feminists want critics to recognize that sexual harassment is not merely a case of men in clumsy pursuit of female partnership. Sexual harassment law and social policy are not designed to sterilize a perfectly appropriate venue for meeting potential partners; rather, they are about making the workplace and campus safe from men whose economic and social status give them the power and authority to sexually harass women with impunity in the absence of formal prohibition of such harassment.

When feminists point out that many male harassers have serial affairs with the women they harass, their aim is to condemn the pervasiveness of sexual harassment in academic institutions whose interests in protecting the reputations of their faculty may inhibit female students from coming forward to identify repeat harassers. These are not professors relying on their personal charisma and intellectual charm to attract female students but men using their academic authority to coerce students into sex, to make sexist or inappropriately sexual comments to students under the auspices of autonomy in the classroom, or to pursue students sexually by exploiting a collegial relationship designed for intellectual stimulation and moral growth. Feminists are not complaining just because some professors use their considerable social status to win sexual brownie points with students. Feminists complain when those students are manipulated, threatened, or imposed upon sexually in virtue of an unacceptable sexual presumptiveness that intellectual status and authority confer on men in the academy. In such cases, women are not free and equal moral agents whose power to set the terms and conditions of the relationship protects them from injury, exploitation, or intimidation. I have argued that power in sexual relationships need not be egalitarian to be non-oppressive but that it must be shared so that women are not disadvantaged in ways conducive to their sexual harassment. I agree with Dr. Hajdin that if feminists want to free women from men's sexual power plays, we should start by teaching women and men to stop rewarding high social status with erotic appeal. Nevertheless, such appeal is no excuse for taking advantage of those individuals in positions of social, economic, or sexual vulnerability or for believing that female attention is a sexual come-on and that sexual pursuit is welcomed by the women pursued.

When sexual harassment is regarded as a violation of sexual integrity whose imposition or intrusion constitutes a failure to treat the harassed as a moral equal, complaints of adultery or promiscuity are beside the point. Women who have been sexually harassed are not responding with "Oh, did you say Tony was single? Then he can pinch my butt all he wants!" or "Are you certain that Randy has no other lovers, even though he keeps cornering me in the hallway? Then let me at him!!" If married men refrain from ogling attractive women at cocktail parties only when their wives are looking or only if their behavior will be reported in the local newspaper, then this is a sign that sexual harassers know that what they are doing is wrong and fear the moral censure that accompanies the exposure of wrongdoing. This is why a newspaper exposé is so telling—it is the unwillingness to risk being exposed for wrongdoing that is being revealed, not any "crucial" (p. 106) connection between sexual harassment and adultery or promiscuity.

Insensitivity in sexual relations is an important part of what is wrong with sexual harassment, and it is incorporated into my characterization of harassers as persons who fail to "world"-travel to the perspective of those whom they harass. However, the insensitivity of sexual harassment must also be understood in terms of the sexual oppression of women, which makes such insensitivity worthy of the separate moral and legal investigation that Dr. Hajdin would deny it. A gendered perspective exposes the larger picture of how men are stereotyped as sexually dominant and controlling in their sexual relationships and analyzes how sexual relations that disadvantage women socially and economically are normalized under patriarchy. As long as Dr. Hajdin privatizes sexual harassment as a case of sexual attraction gone wrong (e.g., adultery, promiscuity, sexual insensitivity), his analysis will fail to isolate the socially oppressive nature of the harm that justifies the inclusion of sexual harassment as an illegal form of sex discrimination.

Indeed, in virtue of Dr. Hajdin's approach, none of the ways that men as a class are sexually advantaged by a patriarchal culture get fleshed out. Dr. Hajdin thus loads the case against a gendered analysis of sexual harassment by refusing to identify the moral wrong of sexual harassment as a failure to treat women as moral equals, a failure that militates against the "full equality" to which Billie Dziech and Linda Weiner refer, as well as against the full disclosure of power-over advantages that make consent to sex less than free and informed. One of feminism's most consciousness-raising contentions is that individual men who live in a culture that confers institutional power and status to men as a class can use their gender-based authority, priority, and credibility to normalize otherwise unacceptable behavior, by defining the terms and conditions of what is normal. A woman's acceptance of her oppression is then construed as "consent" to apparently unobjectionable behavior. As long as sexual harassment remains a function of personal injury, and not a function of the gender hierarchies and cultural stereotypes that normalize the violation of women's sexual integrity, the social injustice that makes sexual harassment a pervasive and discriminatory form of the oppression of women will remain invisible.

Dr. Hajdin agrees that sexual harassers who make sexual advances toward others discriminate on the basis of sex, but he contends that this discrimination is morally unobjectionable: When making their sexual advances, heterosexual male harassers discriminate in favor of women and against men on the basis of heterosexual preference, and homosexual men discriminate in favor of men and against women on the basis of homosexual preference. Since there is nothing wrong with having a sexual preference for one sex and not the other ("No one would seriously argue that people are under obligation to become bisexuals" p. 129), such cases do not constitute wrongful discrimination. Dr. Hajdin's claim is that there is much that is wrong about sexual harassment and there is much that is discriminatory about sexual harassment, but that the wrong is not a function of the discrimination.

I must respond by reasserting that Dr. Hajdin has obscured the gender politics that makes sexual harassment a case of wrongful discrimination, that is, wrong in virtue of its discriminatory character. If the discrimination practiced by heterosexual male harassers is made solely a matter of personal preference, then it is no longer a social injustice whereby women are treated as less than moral equals in a culture that stereotypes women as the proper sexual subordinates of men, to be delegitimized, manipulated, threatened, or sexually presumed upon at men's discretion. Men's sexual harassment of women from this politicized perspective is an expression of the oppressive nature of the sexual stereotyping of women—an expression of how women's sexuality can be used as a vehicle for the oppression of women as a class. Men can violate women's sexual integrity with impunity when women are regarded as deserving no better as the natural and proper subordinates of men. "I was just trying to be friendly" and "I thought you'd like it" are excuses for presuming that the "right" sexual conduct toward women is whatever men believe is good enough.

In short, men sexually harass women because women's sense of themselves as sexual subjects in the world is regarded as less worthy of empathy and respect than the sexual subjectivity of men. As such, men's sexual harassment of women is "wrongful discrimination" on the basis of sex, prohibited by law in employment and educational institutions. It is a form of gender oppression that can preclude women from taking full and fair advantage of available social goods; where and when this occurs, sexual harassment should be illegal.

Moreover, lesbians and gay men harassed by homophobic or hostile straight women or men will say that there is something very seriously wrong with discriminating on the basis of sexual preference, that is, allowing one's sexual preference to inform a sexual prejudice against those who do not share the same sexual preference. From this perspective, a heterosexual male who directs insulting or crude remarks at lesbians in virtue of their sexual preference for women over men is wrongfully discriminating against such women on the basis of sexual preference. Indeed, lesbians and gay men have fought, thus far unsuccessfully, to include heterosexist sexual harassment under Title VII and Title IX, precisely because gays believe it is a form of social discrimination against an oppressed group that should be legally prohibited in employment and educational institutions in the same way that racism or sexism is. My point is that using sexual preference to discriminate in favor of one sex and not another is not inherently innocuous, though it may well appear to be innocuous, if the discrimination involved in sexual harassment is analyzed independently of its political context and is not regarded as a social injustice marked by a failure to treat persons as moral equals.

I believe that Dr. Hajdin's approach is particularly worrisome, since he has done nothing to differentiate among victims of sexual harassment distinguished by race, class, sexual orientation, or other social locations that would reveal any of the special reasons, motivations, or injuries involved in violations of their sexual integrity. This omission is consistent with his depoliticized perspective on sexual harassment, insofar as all persons appear to be free and equal moral agents unburdened by the particular kinds of cultural oppression that would differentiate, in morally significant ways, the types of sexual harassment they experience. But American society is highly politicized, insofar as it is a society that culturally identifies its members by race, class, gender, sexual orientation, and a variety of other categories, as a way of empowering some and disempowering others in virtue of that identification. This means that persons do not all share the same moral status, even if we *should* share such moral status. My claim is that if a moral and legal analysis of sexual harassment does not speak to the ways that discrimination maintains and reinforces the empowerment of some at the expense of others, its analysis of the harm done to victims of sexual harassment will be seriously and dangerously incomplete.

Dr. Hajdin argues that objecting to sexual harassment because it betrays a pattern of discrimination against women as a class does not capture what is perceived as wrong with such conduct, since "[m]ost people, when looking at a given instance of sexual harassment that they regard as wrong, think of it as something that is wrong even when considered on its own . . . [and that would still be wrong] even if the pattern of distribution of such acts were different . . . . [Treating this reason] as if it were the main reason for regarding such conduct as wrong would be insulting to the victims of the conduct, because it would imply that what happened to each of them individually does not count in itself" (p. 130–31). According to Dr. Hajdin, objecting to a pattern of male sexual conduct in virtue of which women as a class are treated offensively, either more often or with a greater intensity of offensiveness on average than men as a class, fails to speak to the suffering of individual women who are sexually harassed.

However, this argument fallaciously implies that the wrongness of an action is always or solely a matter of the violation of an individual's rights perpetrated by another individual with equal rights and not a matter, or not also a matter, of how larger social institutions can constrain individuals' choices in ways that confer rights and privileges to some and not others. Dr. Hajdin's argument suppresses the important feminist observation that when abusive behavior toward women or men occurs with enough regularity and consistency, it can generate a pattern of behavior that becomes naturalized and normalized in virtue of its being a pattern. Thus, harms against persons may also be a matter of social inequality that results from entrenched cultural attitudes or patterns of behavior that invest some with more social goods, more rights, or more freedom to exercise the rights they have, than others. Identifying the pattern of an institutionalized sexual subordination of women identifies the social inequality of the sexual harassment of women under patriarchal constraints. Not to recognize this pattern as harmful to individual women distorts and minimizes the nature of the harm of sexual harassment *to individual women*. This is why I continue to argue for a reading of sexual harassment both as personal injury and as social injustice and to maintain that ignoring the politics of inequality at the heart of sexual harassment in the way Dr. Hajdin has done will make laws designed to recognize the injustice of that inequality appear superfluous.

Dr. Hajdin also contends that women receive more sexually offensive advances from men than men from women because, given the current structure of heterosexual conventions, women receive more sexual advances in the first place. Therefore, women cannot complain that they are wrongfully discriminated against in virtue of the greater number of offensive advances made toward them, since statistically speaking, this greater number is just a by-product of the greater number of advances men make toward women generally. Dr. Hajdin suggests that both men and women have objected to the convention that men initiate sexual advances in heterosexual relationships, so that it is not the convention that is discriminatory and even if it were, this would be a comment about the offensiveness of male-to-female sexual advances, not a comment about sexual harassment per se.

However, this reasoning assumes that offensive sexual advances are symmetrical by gender, such that increasing the number of advances on each side will increase the number of offensive advances proportionally. I argued in my initial essay that sexual harassment is not symmetrical by gender in virtue of the very asymmetrical content of our culture's gender stereotypes, further complicated by race, class, sexual orientation, physical ability, and age, among other social locations. Sexual harassment is an offense that occurs against women more often than men because women as a class are characterized as appropriate and unconditional heterosexual objects in a way that men as a class are not. Thus, the sexual imposition on women that constitutes men's violation of women's sexual integrity will occur more frequently because of oppressive sexual expectations that men will dominate the terms and conditions of their heterosexual encounters. If women and men are not apprised of the power and pervasiveness of such expectations, then there will be, as Dr. Hajdin asserts, "no good reason" (p. 133) to believe that ratios between the number of offensive advances and the total number of advances differ radically between women and men.

Feminists would be more sanguine about the cultural convention that men, not women, should "make the first move" in sexual encounters if the way this move is made were not so often in violation of women's sexual integrity. As it is, the convention paints a picture of women as the sexual gatekeepers against men's raging hormones, which implicitly condones any behavior men can "get away with," since by convention, women are responsible for stopping men before they "go too far." Thus, it is a convention that is entirely relevant to the issue of whether sexual harassment is an instance of sex discrimination, since this convention maintains and reinforces the gender stereotype of women as men's sexual objects. The objection that women as a class are sexually harassed more often and with greater severity than men is a testament to the existence of a patriarchal status quo so threatened by women's increasing social power that it resorts to this pattern of treatment. Combine the relatively small number of women whose positions within organizations give them the power to extort sexual favors with women's culturally limited ability to turn men into their sexual objects, and the sexual harassment of men simply will not occur in the numbers and with the intensity that it occurs to women. Female victims of sexual harassment should be insulted when it is *not* pointed out how the greater number and intensity of individual sexual violations of women than of men are a function of the threat that increasingly independent women pose to a male-dominated status quo dependent upon individual women's economic, social, and sexual submission.

Sex Discrimination and Noncomparative Wrongs

Dr. Hajdin argues further that sexual harassment cannot be a form of sex discrimination, because the wrong of sex discrimination is a comparative wrong, while the wrong of sexual harassment is a noncomparative wrong. Dr. Hajdin cites the example of Mary, who is the object of sex discrimination by her employer. We are told that Mary receives a lower salary than her coworker John, not in virtue of any differences in their qualifications or abilities to get the job done but solely because Mary is a woman. According to the story, Mary's salary is a perfectly decent salary on its own account, but when compared to John's, it is a salary that reflects discrimination against Mary by her employer, since both John and Mary have been hired to do the same work and both have the same skills. Dr. Hajdin points out that "[s]o far as the goal of eliminating discrimination is concerned" (p. 138), it matters little how the problem of John's and Mary's salary differential is handled (lowering his salary, raising hers, or splitting the difference), so long as the result is that John and Mary are paid the same amount.

Dr. Hajdin then contrasts the comparative wrong of sex discrimination with the noncomparative wrong of Mary's being beaten up, where it matters quite a bit how the wrong is rectified, since it will not right the wrong done to Mary to beat up John. "Being beaten up is something that is bad even when considered on its own" (p. 138), needing no comparison to the way other people are treated to identify the harm done. It is contended that the wrong of sexual harassment is like the wrong of being beaten up and unlike the wrong of sex discrimination, since it matters quite a bit how the wrong of sexual harassment is rectified: subjecting men to the same or similar treatment will not rectify the harm done to women who are sexually harassed and will only succeed in inflicting additional harm on others.

I would respond by reasserting that sexual harassment is an example of sex discrimination but that Dr. Hajdin's description of the sex discrimination against Mary obscures the normative complexity of it. Dr. Hajdin does not believe it necessary to address whether or not it is wrong to reduce John's salary to Mary's, because the only wrong Dr. Hajdin is concerned about is the difference between the salaries of John and Mary. For Dr. Hajdin, the sex discrimination issue does not turn on how Mary is treated independently of how John is treated, since he contends that the discrimination against Mary does not constitute a noncomparative wrong. But is this the only way to understand the wrong of sex discrimination? I have argued above that the wrong at issue in sex discrimination law can be understood in terms of the harm in virtue of discriminating on the basis of sex. The reason the discrimination against Mary is *wrongful* discrimination under the law is not merely that she is being paid a different salary than John on the basis of her sex but that by being paid a different salary than John on the basis of her sex, Mary is being harmed in some way—in this case, by being economically disadvantaged relative to John for the same work. However, using Dr. Hajdin's own normative distinctions, Mary's economic disadvantage, even though dependent upon a comparison of Mary's salary to John's, is a noncomparative wrong, since it will not do to rectify the wrongful discrimination against Mary by economically disadvantaging John or anyone else relative to Mary for the same work, that is, by harming John the way Mary has been harmed. To recognize the harm in discriminating against Mary on the basis of her sex is to recognize the noncomparative wrong of sex discrimination.

Now suppose Mary is paid the same salary as John but she is being sexually harassed by John, who has continually intruded on her job assignments with requests for "some hot sex." In such a case, John is discriminating against Mary, since it is in virtue of being a woman that Mary is being harassed by John. However, the harm of this discrimination lies in the fact that Mary is being discriminated against in ways that inhibit her effectiveness and competitiveness in the workplace. She is finding it increasingly difficult to work under conditions in which she is constantly being reminded of her status as a man's seductive sexual object. Thus, she can take advantage of sex discrimination law to rectify her harassment because the sexual harassment of Mary is a matter of being harmed in virtue of discrimination against her at work. Courts do not recommend harassing John in order to right the wrong done to Mary, since harassing John would force him to work at a competitive disadvantage, which would incur an additional wrong. Sex discrimination law does not require employers found guilty of sexual harassment under the EEOC guidelines to have all of their employees sexually harass each other, just as racial discrimination law does not require employers found guilty of racism in employment to have all of their employees engage in racist behavior, because antidiscrimination law recognizes the noncomparative wrong that informs wrongful sex and racial discrimination. This recognition allows claimants to seek compensatory and punitive damages for personal injury and recommends that employers promote changes in workplace behavior so as to eliminate not just the discrimination, but any harm in virtue of that discrimination. Thus, I would argue that antidiscrimination law is ideally suited to provide an umbrella for sexual harassment law, since it recognizes both the personal injury and the social injustice of sexual harassment.

In short, as long as the sex discrimination in sexual harassment is assumed to be a wrong that is "purely a matter of discrimination" (p. 139) and not a matter of harm in virtue of that discrimination, then the discrimination complaint against sexual harassment will appear misplaced, since the wrong of sexual harassment will then have to be rectified by treating everyone in the same way, including harassing everyone. However, if sexual harassment is understood as harm in virtue of discrimination on the basis of sex, it matters morally and legally both how the harassment is rectified and that the harassment discriminates on the basis of sex. This is why the EEOC recommends making changes in workplace social policy to prohibit behavior discriminatory under Title VII, changes that do not involve subjecting both men and women to sexual harassment. This is why feminists can credibly argue that individual women with their own personally injurious, context-specific, and culturally located experiences of sexual harassment can still also make the charge of sex discrimination, since those individual women are being sexually harassed in virtue of the oppressive ways women as a class are sexualized in contemporary Western culture. No feminist with whose work I am familiar, who claims that sexual harassment is a form of sex discrimination, denies that sexual harassment is also an injury to individual women that no one should have to tolerate. What such feminists want all of us to recognize is that the nature of the injury and the pervasiveness of it are explicable in terms of the gender hierarchies and cultural stereotypes that characterize women as the proper sexual subordinates of men. Given Dr. Hajdin's apolitical perspective, it is not surprising that when he discusses what is wrong with sexual harassment and how it is wrong, its social injustice as a form of sex discrimination remains invisible.

The Possibility of Sexual Misconduct

Dr. Hajdin believes that sexual harassment law as currently constructed is bad law, in part because he believes that the federal EEOC guidelines that typically define the conduct to be prohibited put a de facto ban on all conduct of a sexual nature in the workplace. With the specter of a sexual harassment charge looming large in the background, it is contended that the mere possibility of offending a fellow coworker or colleague with whom one may wish to form a sexual relationship will put a damper on any willingness to pursue that relationship within the context of work. Indeed, from this perspective, the law also keeps people from forming close personal friendships within such contexts, since the ways sexual as well as nonsexual relationships get started often involve the same initial, and potentially offensive, overtures. According to Dr. Hajdin, simply asking a person whether particular conduct is unwelcome or offensive "'is itself verbal conduct of a sexual nature that may easily be unwelcome and offensive and thus come under the definition of sexual harassment'" (p. 143). Because, under current guidelines, the reaction of the harassed, not the intent of the harasser, determines whether or not conduct is sexually harassing, Dr. Hajdin argues that the very possibility of offense will inhibit anyone from even requesting permission to act in certain ways, not merely inhibit individuals from acting in the ways intended. He concludes that such a ban on conduct is an unacceptable restriction on individuals' freedom to strike up personal relationships, the most valued of which are often made within just the contexts where the conduct is prohibited;

therefore, the law ought to be opposed. In Dr. Hajdin's opinion, even if one believes that workplaces and educational institutions ought to be purged of all conduct of a sexual or personal nature, sexual harassment law does not make the nature of this restriction clear or explicit, when it should.

It might be useful here to adopt terminology borrowed from the philosophy of language, that is, the distinction between mentioning offensive speech by talking *about* it and using offensive speech in ways that offend others. This distinction allows me to ask you if you would prefer that I not tell "dumb blond" jokes, before I offend you by launching into the joke itself ("There was this dumb blond at a bar guzzling Shirley Temples . . ."). Of course, you may be the sort of person who is offended by the use of the expression "dumb blond" to describe jokes or anything else; however, the linguistic distinction between mention and use still holds here, since what you are offended by is not my mentioning such jokes ("You remember when I asked you about telling those 'dumb blond' jokes?") but my use of the expression "dumb blond" to describe them. For Dr. Hajdin, the latter problem hits the nail on the head; the mere possibility that I might offend you by asking your permission to tell "dumb blond" jokes means that I cannot even mention offensive conduct without the possibility of conducting myself in offensive ways. Thus, Dr. Hajdin believes that the EEOC guidelines collapse the important distinction between mention and use, even if they purport not to do so.

No one could deny that "for practically any conduct of a sexual nature, there exists *a possibility* that it will be unwelcome and offensive to its recipient, and that any attempt to find out whether it will be so received *may* itself turn out to be unwelcome and offensive" (p. 143, emphasis added). Mentioning offensive speech is not *always* offensive, even if this is sometimes true, yet the collapse between mentioning offensive speech and being offensive requires that the two are *always* equivalent. Under my characterization of sexual harassment, the wrongness of sexual harassment is determined by the conduct of the harasser, not the response of the victim. Asking permission of another person to conduct myself in ways that might otherwise be harassing to her can be the morally appropriate conduct of a "world"-traveler making an empathetic and respectful attempt to discern another's perspective on sexual conduct. The attempt is not sexually harassing, not because she is unoffended by my inquiries, but because my own conduct of "world"-traveling has not violated her sexual integrity. However, if Dr. Hajdin's reasoning is accepted, sexually harassing conduct under my characterization should be wholly determined, not by the occurrence of violation, but by the *possibility* of violation, since it is always possible that in attempting to "world"-travel, I will violate the sexual integrity of the person to whose "world" I have attempted to travel. In this instance, I believe that it is Dr. Hajdin who has collapsed the distinction between mention and use, not the EEOC.

To take a different tack, let us suppose that you and I are coworkers. If I suspect that any use of the expression "dumb blond" will offend you, then I may refrain from using the expression in your presence. If I do refrain, this may be due to common courtesy, rather than to some form of radical self-censorship imposed by sexual harassment policy. But suppose I have no such suspicions. I ask you about whether it would be acceptable to tell such jokes, not wanting to offend you, but succeed in offending you anyway simply by using the expression "dumb blond." My honest mistake in offending you by asking your permission to tell such jokes may not lessen the offense you take at my use of the expression, but my assurances that I will refrain from using the expression in the future are assurances that my conduct will not pass the "severe or pervasive" test the Supreme Court has used to identify hostile environment sexual harassment. You may go ahead and report me, with all of the attendant upset and controversy that accompany Paula's reporting Peter in Dr. Hajdin's scenario describing the potential horrors of in-house sexual harassment policy, but such results are not because of inadequacies in sexual harassment guidelines or sexual harassment social policy, but because of what can happen when people mistake each other's good intentions. Indeed, Paula could believe that Peter is stealing office supplies when she sees him continually grabbing stacks of pens and notebooks for a team assignment she knows nothing about. We can imagine that Paula's reporting Peter to management makes him jump through similarly embarrassing and convoluted company hoops in order to straighten things out. Yet no one would pin the blame for Paula's and Peter's miscommunication on the company's policy against stealing office supplies. In short, the mere possibility of offense does not empty the EEOC guidelines of usable content or eviscerate the importance of in-house sexual harassment policies for helping management and coworkers discover what kinds of workplace environments they find acceptable.

I agree with Dr. Hajdin that the EEOC's "unwelcome and offensive"

criterion for sexual harassment should be dropped, but for a different reason, namely, that this criterion makes sexual harassment discoverable in
terms of how the claimant responded instead of how the alleged perpetrator acted, forcing the claimant's conduct to go on trial in ways that unfairly
diminish her credibility by presuming the welcomeness of the conduct in
question and the unreasonableness of the alleged victim. Because Dr. Hajdin has asserted how wrong he thinks much of sexual harassment is, I wish
he had spent more time coming up with alternatives for protecting women
from it. As it is, he has left women and men bereft of any guidelines that
would help workplaces and educational institutions understand their diverse constituents' attitudes about sexual harassment, so that they might
formulate collaborative and user-friendly policies specific to the needs of
their organizations.

It is simply good business sense for policy administrators to admit that
honest mistakes will be made on either side of an accusation of violation
of company policy but that such mistakes will not be tolerated as excuses
for unacceptable conduct. Encouraging collaboration and cooperation
based on care respect certainly should not be abandoned because it *might*
offend someone. Asking women and men, "What sorts of conduct from
others are you looking for in your workplace?" is a question designed to
minimize the possibility of offensive conduct, which Dr. Hajdin seems
convinced will only be maximized by sexual harassment law. No one is
asking men to second-guess what women are offended by. Feminists are
asking organizations to listen to women's and men's concerns about sexual harassment as a way of identifying potential problems and preempting
their occurrence.

Nor do policy makers have to worry about freedom of expression issues
in the way Dr. Hajdin makes out. Despite the airing of one set of political
views, freedom of expression under the Constitution does not guarantee
the airing of their opposition, if those opposition views would, through
slanderous sexual comments, harm a woman's reputation or ability to earn
a living, would incite someone to commit a sexual crime against a woman,
or would create a "clear and present danger" to her. If political views
about women disseminated in the workplace or in academia result in the
economic or educational disadvantage of women, antidiscrimination law
can be invoked to prohibit the expression of such views.[2] Sexually harassing verbal conduct can create a hostile environment in any of these ways,
so it is a mistake to say that sexual harassment law violates freedom of
expression by suppressing political speech or that the prohibition of sexual

harassment cannot comfortably fit under any of the exceptions to the First Amendment. Peter-and-Paula scenarios of the kind Dr. Hajdin describes do, of course, occur. I am arguing that they need not occur with the gender-sensitive, culturally located, and "world"-traveling approach to understanding sexual harassment I have endorsed.

I do have a few more concerns about Paula and Peter: Why think that Peter's advances toward Paula would be regarded by her as *sexual*, especially if, as has been stipulated, she is well aware of her company's sexual harassment policy and expects that others are too? Indeed, if Dr. Hajdin is correct, Peter will avoid doing anything that explicitly or unambiguously indicates a sexual interest in Paula. Peter's invitation to lunch could be a strictly business invitation, yet still be "seductively" presented because it is one that he is anxious for Paula to accept. In this case, he wants her desperately on his design team to improve its output. Paula has heard rumors from her coworkers that Peter is intent on signing her up, but she dreads his approach. Suppose Paula knows Peter is a lousy team manager and steals everybody else's great ideas, but Paula also knows Peter has good business connections that could serve her well in the future, so she keeps putting him off with a less blunt "maybe next week" instead of a possibly offensive "no," even though she wishes he would just go away. Peter, as in the original scenario, takes Paula at her word, is "blissfully unaware" of her upset, and keeps hanging around her the following week, hoping she will accept his lunch invitation. Paula, who is still determined not to get on Peter's bad side, watches the quality of her work begin to slip badly as she spends more time trying to avoid Peter. Finally, she takes the problem up with her immediate boss, who has noticed Paula's recent difficulty meeting daily project deadlines. Her boss decides to give Peter a good tongue-lashing for trying to intimidate Paula into a project she does not want and thereby forcing Paula to get behind in her work. Paula's boss warns Peter to "leave poor Paula alone" or a formal reprimand will go into his personnel file. Peter, totally mystified by this turn of events, goes away vowing never to bring a woman onto his design team again no matter how talented she is.

This is certainly a case of unfortunate miscommunication, and it may happen more frequently in workplaces where management does not encourage the kind of open, honest, and safe communication about coworker and management needs that I have advocated. But as unfortunate, and indeed common, as such miscommunication may be, Peter's treatment of Paula is not a case of sexual harassment. Indeed, given what Paula knows about Peter's motivations for approaching her, it would be surprising and inappropriate for her to file a sexual harassment complaint. Of course, she may wish to falsely accuse Peter of sexual harassment in order to get him to leave her alone. But, then, she could also accuse him of stealing office supplies because she thinks that this will get him transferred, demoted, or fired, any of which would get him out of her hair. I mentioned above how the possibility of mistaking good intentions for offense cannot be used as a reason to pick out sexual harassment policy as deserving of special censure. Intentional false accusations of violations of company policy can also make life miserable for those falsely accused, but such accusations are not an automatic indictment of the policies themselves. Even if Paula does misconstrue Peter's business invitation as a sexual one, Peter has good reason to be sanguine in this case, since many of Paula's coworkers know of his intentions to court Paula strictly for business, which would be revealed in any preliminary investigation. If Peter thoroughly complicates my picture by sexually harassing Paula under the auspices of a business invitation, then she has every reason to report him.

Miscommunication at work can take many forms, each of which may result in economic, social, or psychological trauma totally unrelated to the content or efficacy of company rules and regulations, and many instances of what may appear to be cases of sexual miscommunication are miscommunication about something else entirely. Dr. Hajdin has criticized sexual harassment policy for its *potential* for ruining people's lives and relationships just as he has criticized the EEOC guidelines for their supposed prohibition of *potentially* offensive sexual behavior. I have argued that the actuality of such potentials is a function of persons' unwillingness to "world"-travel or to recognize the role of gender politics and cultural stereotypes in their treatment of one another, not a function of anything inherently wrong with the in-house prohibition of sexual harassment or with construing sexual harassment as sex discrimination. Collaborative and cooperative formulation and implementation of sexual harassment policy from the feminist perspective I advocated in my initial essay can and should be institutional goals.

Invasive Bureaucracies and Overbearing Feminists

Dr. Hajdin implies that the clumsiness and insensitivity with which in-house bureaucracies handle sexual harassment charges are the rule and not

the exception ("Bringing in bureaucracy to deal with subtle miscommunications in a delicate area of people's lives is as wise as bringing a bull into
a china shop" p. 149). According to this view, such bureaucracies have
the potential to devastate the trust in the opposite sex of those unfortunate
enough to be in the way of the bull's charge. But why think this? The
"machinery" of sexual harassment policy to which Dr. Hajdin refers need
not be profoundly violating in the ways he makes out, especially when
those men who are most fearful of false accusations or misunderstood intentions are included in the formulation of policy and the investigation
and evaluation of complaints. Liability of employers is the very thing that
can and does prompt preemptive sexual harassment sensitivity programs,
reviews of current law, and policy development and ongoing policy review
by all sectors of the organization. Overzealous monitoring will be its own
undoing when employees complain that it does not reflect employee feedback and can only push more blatant sexual harassment underground. Dr.
Hajdin does not mention the informal mechanisms of writing letters,
using friends or colleagues as mediators, or soliciting these same third parties as witnesses at meetings between accuser and accused, all of which are
much more informal than the programmatic review mechanisms alluded
to by Dr. Hajdin, and all of which can be incorporated into written sexual
harassment policy under an "options for settling disputes" clause. "Total
strangers to oneself prying into one's most intimate desires" (p. 150) is
by no means necessary to a workable and successful sexual harassment
policy. Yet in his account of the intractability of investigating offensiveness,
Dr. Hajdin makes it appear as if there were no alternatives that are not
themselves harassing.

The irony here is that "total strangers" may be precisely what is required when students present their cases before university review boards
whose members are the colleagues of the accused or the former instructors
of the accuser. Many victims of sexual harassment will not be comfortable
with formal in-house mechanisms, due to their possible bias and lack of
follow-up, but would go to the EEOC if pressed; therefore, a wide variety
of the kinds of informal mechanisms I have described is, in fact, more
likely to keep employers out of court. Indeed, the broader the spectrum
of publicized policies and procedures, the less likely that the EEOC will
bring charges on behalf of claimants who have sidestepped those policies
to make hostile environment complaints, considering that filing an in-
house grievance is often the only way that large organizations could or

should have known what is going on. Moreover, if the idea is to avoid the courtroom, it seems altogether reasonable not to begin with accusatory and confusing "legalese," but to begin with "where the client is" (as what Dr. Hajdin refers to p. 150 as social work "jargon" would put it), so that this "delicate" matter can be investigated within a framework of care respect.

Even if Paula and Peter are profoundly disappointed in, and alienated by, their experience with their company's sexual harassment policy, I do not understand why this should leave either Paula or Peter, according to Dr. Hajdin, "distrustful of the opposite sex" or why it would be an experience that would not help Paula and Peter "understand their sexuality . . . better" (p. 149). Paula may have two adoring feminist brothers and a boyfriend sensitive to gender politics (he was a student in Linda LeMoncheck's "Feminism and Philosophy" class in college), or she may have already encountered more than her fair share of blustering sexual buffoons but is committed to preventing them from blunting an active heterosexuality. Thus, Paula may actually be determined that her run-in with Peter *not* adversely affect her relationships with the opposite sex. At the same time, Paula may have learned a lesson in directness; she may now feel that "honesty," either by open and direct conversation or immediate confrontation from the relative safety of a supervisor's office, "is the best policy." On the other hand, Peter may now realize that one woman's "no way!" may be another's "maybe next week?" if the latter woman's practical interests would be better served by being more oblique, and especially if men expect women to be friendly, sociable, and good humored when men "hit on" them. There is, in fact, no reason why Paula and Peter would not discuss these very dynamics in the context of the sexual harassment investigation.

However, in my opinion, Dr. Hajdin has set up a case that artificially and unnecessarily alienates those whom sexual harassment policies are meant to serve. Indeed, he never mentions that the reason it is so important for employees to have legal recourse against a fellow coworker's "perfectly happy sexual affair" (p. 151) is that the affair can result in the coworker's gaining unfair advantage in the workplace from her more powerfully situated lover. Thus, at the same time that he pushes the Paulas and Peters of the world down a slippery slope of dissatisfaction with, and distrust in, the opposite sex, Dr. Hajdin would bar others, under the guise of an invasion of privacy between two lovers, from making legitimate complaints about workplace bias. This is yet another instance of how privatizing a very political sexual relationship can distort the need for sexual harassment law that prohibits the social injustice of unequal treatment in the workplace.

I have mentioned in my initial essay that the problems that Dr. Hajdin raises not only are not inevitable but also are straightforwardly avoidable with a variety of practicable policy safeguards, many of which are already in place in sexual harassment policies throughout the country. Only recently, the university where I have been teaching hired two lawyers who specialize in consultation regarding the formulation and implementation of sexual harassment policies at colleges and universities. Over several days, these women solicited, heard, and synthesized comments, complaints, and recommendations from all sectors of the campus community, in order to propose recommendations to the administration that would best serve the needs of our particular campus. There is no question that this sort of meeting of the minds needs to be happening at more campuses and workplaces and with greater regularity. My complaint is that to speak as if it cannot and is not happening, or cannot and will not be successful, is to do a disservice to the abilities of women and men within such organizations to work creatively and productively together.

Dr. Hajdin also claims that feminists violate women's autonomy by overriding women's assessments of what counts as sexual harassment and what does not. I disagree. The feminists to whom he refers are convinced that not enough women are identifying men's sexual conduct toward them as that against which women have moral and legal recourse. Understood in this light, feminists are giving women back their autonomy, not violating it, by identifying the ways that women's sexual harassment is a form of the sexual oppression of women, the success of which depends upon women's accepting sexual presumption and intimidation as normal. Such consciousness-raising involves encouraging female students to see sexual harassment of students by professors as abuses of academic power within institutions whose own reputations require consolidating and reinforcing the academic status and authority of their faculty, and not as a female student's tolerable or inevitable trade-off for gaining intellectual expertise herself. Many feminists are asking female students to think about the ways that the sexual attentions of their professors put the seduced student at serious risk of sexual exploitation: If things turn out badly, a professor's credibility can grossly outweigh a student's own, if only because universities do not want to stain their reputations. Also, a professor's status as an intellectual and a man of the world can be used to give a female student the impression that he is treating her as "special" ("You're too smart to be hanging around these immature college jocks") and thus to seduce her with the implication of emotional commitment when his chief goal is to get her into his bed, not his life. This is an objection *not* to faculty promiscuity, but to sexual manipulation and intimidation in ways that fail to treat students as moral equals.

Moreover, feminists are not implanting their radical agendas in moldable minds or making young women reinterpret their experience. In the passage in *Ivory Power* that immediately follows one Dr. Hajdin quotes (p. 153), sexually harassed women are reported to experience humiliation, embarrassment, and guilt. They may blame themselves for what happened until they are given a way of validating their feelings with a name for their suffering. No one is implanting these feelings in these women. These women are crying out for someone to help explain their feelings to them. If feminists had the power of mind control to make one "stop enjoying what one enjoys and desiring what one desires" (p. 153), as Dr. Hajdin implies, they would have convinced men to stop their violence against women long ago. Indeed, I wish more feminists committed to preventing sexual harassment were in the positions of organizational power on college campuses that Dr. Hajdin claims. However, the continuing sexual violation and victimization of women in educational institutions indicates that feminist voices on campus are still not powerful enough to be preventive enough. No feminist who has come to feminism with women's *liberation* in mind is interested in taking other women's autonomy away from them. What I have been advocating is that women's sexual harassment be understood in terms of a dialectic between oppressive gender politics and liberating sexual exploration, a dialectic that reveals what is, at best, an unstable relationship between the sex that women want and the sexual liberation that women want. Feminists can then work from within this dialectical framework to understand the variety of women's experiences of, and responses to, sexual harassment, in order to offer women personally satisfying and socially responsible ways of dealing with it.

"Criminalizing" Alleged Harassers

I have several comments regarding Dr. Hajdin's claim that sexual harassment law unfairly and intrusively impugns those accused of sexual harassment in workplaces and educational institutions. One of Dr. Hajdin's criticisms is that while sexual harassment law is civil law, it has the same potentially devastating effects on one's job and one's respectability in the community as being accused of a criminal offense, but without any of the procedural safeguards that accompany criminal accusations. Specifically, he remarks, "If one loses a civil suit, one may need to pay the damages, but otherwise one is free to get on with one's life and to maintain whatever degree of respectability one has had before" (p. 155). However, I would argue that losing a civil suit for such potentially devastating personal injuries as assault and battery can have a chilling effect on one's job and community respectability, since people often react not only to how an injury has been punished but to the nature and extent of the injury itself. When a battered woman wins a civil suit against her abusive husband but has not pressed criminal charges against him, he must still face the possibility of community censure even if he never goes to jail. Sexual harassment law is an appropriate use of the civil law precisely because it imposes serious social sanctions, although not criminal sanctions, on those found guilty of sexual harassment.

Second, I do not agree that "if one is accused of sexual harassment, one stands to lose one's job (together with any chance of finding a respectable job) and one's respectability in one's community" (p. 155). Clearly, Dr. Hajdin is not familiar with the phenomenon that Myra and David Sadker have described as the grade-school "mobile molester," a person who has been formally accused of sexual harassment by a student but who is asked to voluntarily leave the institution in which the alleged harassment occurred, in exchange for a letter of recommendation to another unsuspecting school district.[3] School administrators can thus often avoid costly, vituperative, and publicly damaging court trials, even if the school privately acknowledges the nature and extent of the harassment and even though the harasser has been formally accused of it. Thus, teachers who chronically harass their students may float from teaching job to teaching job without any obvious adverse effect on their careers, especially when there is no institutional record of the harassment in the perpetrator's personnel files. With no state requirements as to how school administrators should deal with their harassing teachers, administrators are free to "pass the trash" even after formal in-house investigations, having satisfied themselves and their communities that the sexual harassment has been exorcised. Indeed, military women have complained that their formal accusations of harassment have been met with *their* demotions, revocations of privileges, or other sanctions, while their harassers have gone on to promotion.[4]

Moreover, the fact that sexual harassment, under the EEOC guidelines, is not a function of what the harasser intended may place the burden so heavily on the accuser to prove unwelcomeness that her accusations appear too weak to be sustained. This problem would certainly explain administrators' hesitancy to involve their schools in sexual harassment cases, their fears of countersuits by alleged harassers, and their willingness to pass their trash. This problem is also why I have recommended interpreting sexual harassment law in terms of how the alleged perpetrator acted, not how the claimant responded to the conduct in question. Thus, it is clear that I have my own reservations about sexual harassment law as it is currently construed. I simply believe there are ways, in current law, to emphasize the importance of the personal injury of sexual harassment without undermining the importance of the social injustice of sexual harassment.

Third, it is important to note that while the possibility of either liability for negligence or the withholding of federal funds offers a strong incentive for employers to implement sexual harassment policies within their workplaces, I am unsure whether this counts as a legal requirement in the way that paying quarterly taxes is a legal requirement imposed on employers by the state. There is no official state or federal requirement, with which I am familiar, that private businesses implement sexual harassment policies, such that if no such policies are in place, the employer is in violation of the law. Employers who have well-publicized and fully implemented sexual harassment policies may not be held legally liable for the hostile environment harassment of their employees; therefore, it certainly behooves employers to see to it that such policies are in place. However, this is not equivalent to being required to do so by the state, since workplaces without such policies are not strictly in violation of the law. If this is true, then Dr. Hajdin's argument that the state imposes what amounts to criminal sanctions on employees under the guise of civil law is weakened, since there is no formal state *requirement* that employers implement the allegedly criminalizing policies.

Dr. Hajdin might respond by saying that insofar as employers are compelled by the state, for practical reasons, to implement policies that de facto criminalize those accused of sexual harassment, the law is unjust. He comments, "Given that these sanctions are ultimately a result of what the state does at the upper level, what happens to individuals at the lower level should be regarded as imposed on them *by* the state *through* employers" (p. 156, Dr. Hajdin's emphasis). Yet I still feel somewhat at a loss here: What is wrong with this two-tiered system? The federal Occupational Safety and Health Administration (OSHA) makes employers liable for violations of health and safety standards by their employees, which in turn "compels" employers (read "provides strong incentives" to employers) to enforce compliance with workplace rules and regulations for which employees may be punished if disobeyed. Indeed, an employer may fire an employee for serious noncompliance, and if such noncompliance is blatantly negligent or in willful disregard of the safety of others, such actions, if known, could certainly damage that person's future prospects for a job or for respectability in the community. Yet no one is accusing OSHA of criminalizing employees under the guise of civil law, or accusing employers of exploiting federal civil sanctions in order to fire employees at will. OSHA imposes sanctions on employers in order to protect employees from health and safety hazards that employers might not eliminate on their own. OSHA mandates often involve costs that employers would otherwise be hesitant to pay. Such mandates can also impose external reviews of workplace safety, which compel employers to enforce standards they might otherwise ignore.

My point is that in the liberal democracy Dr. Hajdin values, an important role of the state is to protect the life, liberty, and pursuit of happiness of its citizens in a society where self-interest can take a dangerous, abusive, or oppressive turn. Sexual harassment law qua sex discrimination law serves the purpose of protecting employees in ways that, without civil sanctions imposed on employers, employers might not commit to on their own. Not recognizing the function of the state to protect its citizens from social injustice is consistent with Dr. Hajdin's understanding of sexual harassment as a private affair between two autonomous adults, each of whose rights to noninterference, if violated, should be adjudicated as a matter of personal injury. I am committed to protecting women and men from sexual harassment by looking at the wider cultural framework that shapes it.

Avoiding Sexual Harassment

In his concluding remarks, Dr. Hajdin notes that outside of the organizational contexts of work or school, it is relatively easy to turn away from, or refuse to listen to, "annoying, obnoxious, offensive, or otherwise unpleasant" (p. 159) conduct. According to Dr. Hajdin, nonorganizational settings are unlike work in that they do not typically require close contact or constant communication with the very person from whom the harassed would otherwise be able to escape. He suggests, but ultimately rejects, that this feature of organizational settings might justify special laws to provide protection against sexual, as opposed to nonsexual, conduct that is offensive. (Notice he does not call "annoying, obnoxious, offensive, or otherwise unpleasant" conduct outside organizational contexts *sexual harassment.*)

I have already argued that sexual harassment is a coherent concept inside or outside organizational contexts and that it is illegal in the workplace and in educational institutions because of the restrictions specified by Title VII and Title IX, not because of any independent contextual conditions on sexual harassment. What I am concerned about here is that Dr. Hajdin does not seem to recognize that the violation of a woman's sexual integrity may happen instantaneously, unpredictably, or inescapably, such that simply in going about the business of living, a woman cannot avoid being harassed. Hanging up the phone on an obscene phone call will not prevent a woman from being harassed, because the harassment—the conduct that prompts her to hang up the phone—has already happened. Walking across the street to avoid crude sexual remarks may avoid future harassment, but not what has just occurred. The reason I would delete a threatening E-mail message is that I have already been threatened. It is insulting to women to ask them to deal with a humiliating, degrading, threatening, or embarrassing sexual comment simply "by avoiding its source" (p. 159), since by the time a woman has done so, she has already been harassed; indeed, the "source" may have walked away as well. And how exactly am I supposed to avoid a pinch on the buttocks at a baseball game, when its very occurrence is what constitutes the harassment? Imagine that I have waited three hours in line for World Series tickets and have just been goosed from behind. How "easily" (p. 159) will I be able to leave that line? How unnerving will it be for me to stay in line?

Let us also talk about the unavoidable but *known* harasser: How does a woman "easily deal with" a sexually harassing husband, whose hostility only increases when she "refuse[s] to listen" (p. 159)? (Consider the ways he may sexually harass her in bed at night.) Is it any easier for a woman to leave her marriage than it is to leave her job? An E-mail stalker can disguise his name and address after sending me his first harassing messages, so that even though I know he is out there, I end up reading his offensive stuff anyway. Or he can send me one thousand E-mail messages, all of whose listings I have to read through in order to get to my other messages. If the one-thousandth message is one of contrition, how will I know this if I do not read any of the harassing mail? I simply do not have any "simple and effective" (p. 159) way of dealing with such cases, and laws against intentional infliction of emotional distress will be ineffective when intent is difficult to prove ("I was just trying to tell her I was sorry") or the defense turns a victim's emotional distress into the rant of a technologically insecure woman who cannot deal with E-mail. Suppose an angry former boyfriend keeps following me in his car at night, which no legal restraining order can practically prevent. How will it help stop him if I "refuse to interact" (p. 159) with him? Refusing to interact with him may be what is motivating the harassment. Then there is the guy with the wolf whistle and the "Hubba hubba!" who hangs out at the subway station every day on my way to work. Telling a woman to get a new boyfriend, change her telephone number, stop her E-mail, or take a taxi misses the point of feeling trapped, terrorized, paranoid, and incensed at having to rearrange her life to try to avoid a harasser she cannot even be sure is being avoided. The social injustice of such harassment lies in the fact that women are subjected, often on a daily basis, to such treatment *because they are women*, sexually stereotyped in a way that encourages their sexual harassment by men.

In short, complaints about sexual harassment are not only or always complaints about conduct in an organizational setting by a known harasser whose harassment could be avoided except for the requirement of close contact. Complaints about sexual harassment are complaints about violations of sexual integrity, either inside or outside organizational contexts, whose occurrence qua violation cannot be "undone" by walking away. In fact, when walking away is considered possible or desirable, this is an indication that a violation may have already occurred. The terrorizing element of sexual harassment lies precisely in the fact that women cannot confidently predict, even of persons they believe they know well, who their harassers will be or how those harassers will strike. It thus matters little that at work, if one agrees with Dr. Hajdin, I am among persons with whom I have so much more in common than in a less intimate venue.

Indeed, I wonder why Dr. Hajdin is so convinced that the privacy of the harassed is the issue most pertinent to developing rules against sexual harassment *within* organizational contexts, when, as I have shown, not being able to remove myself from the source of the sexual harassment or otherwise avoid interactions that expose me to it can be as great a problem, and more often a problem, outside such contexts. Perhaps it has something to do with Dr. Hajdin's general commitment to reducing sexual harassment and sexual harassment social policy to matters of private harm and personal injury within designated formal frameworks; recall that one of Dr. Hajdin's complaints about an organization's sexual harassment social policy is that *harassers'* and *alleged harassers'* rights of freedom of expression and privacy are being violated, as well as those of lovers in the same workplace whose liaisons are broken apart by the intrusiveness of a sexual harassment complaint. As I have argued, any in-house or legal sexual harassment policy that emphasizes individual rights over social justice will fail to capture both the gender inequality and the sexual politics that is at the heart of men's sexual harassment of women. Thus, such policies are bound to fail to capture the ways in which the sexual harassment of women violates their sexual integrity *as women* by treating women as the normal and natural sexual subordinates of men. Such policies are also bound to gloss over the sexual stereotypes specific to race, class, or sexual orientation that further complicate the discriminatory treatment and vary the experiences of, and responses to, sexual harassment. This is why the sexual nature of sexually harassing conduct is so important to address, and why specific laws identifying sexual harassment as a form of inequality are crucial to identifying the personal and political injury of sexual harassment.

Notes

1. See William Petrocelli and Barbara Kate Repa, *Sexual Harassment on the Job: What It Is and How to Stop It* (Berkeley, Calif.: Nolo Press, 1992), 1/20 (authors' pagination: chap. 1/p. 20).

2. I wish to thank Julie Van Camp for helping me understand some of the complexities of, and limitations on, freedom of expression under the Constitution. Any errors in applying these limitations to the case of sexual harassment are my own.

3. Myra and David Sadker, *Failing at Fairness: How Our Schools Cheat Girls* (New York: Simon & Schuster, Touchstone, 1995), 114–15.

4. Kenneth R. Weiss, "Female Sailors Accuse the Navy of Retribution," *Los Angeles Times*, 2 July 1996.

4

Response

Mane Hajdin

Dr. LeMoncheck's initial essay can be usefully divided into two main parts. The first part, amounting to approximately the first half of the essay, consists of a survey of various views on sexual harassment that have already been expressed in the literature. Within that part, she first (in the section "Feminist Objections to Sexual Harassment: The Case against Patriarchy") presents the views that support the movement aimed at eradication of sexual harassment, and then (in the section "Fragile Flowers and Predatory Beasts: Do Feminists Victimize Women?") presents the views that are critical of it. The authors discussed in both sections typically call themselves feminists, and quite rightly so. Dr. LeMoncheck, quite rightly, refers to all of them as feminists, but it is in fact the authors of the kind discussed in "Feminist Objections to Sexual Harassment" who first come to most people's minds when the word "feminist" is used, rather than the authors of the kind discussed in the following section. (That the word "feminist" has, in the minds of many, come to stand for what is, in fact, only one species of feminist thinking is a regrettable fact, but nevertheless a fact that for the sake of clarity, needs to be acknowledged.)

Dr. LeMoncheck has made the first half of her essay admirably balanced by devoting approximately the same amount of space to presenting each of these two lines of thought about sexual harassment. Her effort to be fair in her allocation of space to the two sides of the issue within her survey of the literature may, however, inadvertently hide one fact to which the readers should be alerted, as this fact may be relevant for a full appreciation of that survey. That is the fact that the amount of existing literature of the kind discussed in "Feminist Objections to Sexual Harassment" is much greater than the amount of literature of the kind discussed in "Fragile Flowers and Predatory Beasts." The former section represents the general characteristics of a rather wide body of literature (both scholarly and popular), while the small number of specific works discussed in the latter section pretty much exhausts the pool of the available literature of that kind.

Dr. LeMoncheck has considerable sympathy for the views expressed in the existing literature that supports the fight against sexual harassment. However, she does not wish to simply endorse these views as they stand, nor does she wish to simply dismiss the views of the critics of that fight. Rather, she believes that what the supporters of the fight against sexual harassment have said so far can be improved upon in a way that will take into account the arguments of the critics. The task of making such an improvement is what she undertakes in the second half of her essay, where she develops her own arguments in support of fighting sexual harassment.

In devoting the first half of her essay to a well-rounded and balanced survey of the existing literature on the topic, Dr. LeMoncheck has provided a valuable service to the readers of this book. In responding to her, I shall, however, concentrate on her own, original views about sexual harassment, which are formulated and defended in the second half of her essay. I shall divide my response into seven sections. Each of the first four sections of my response corresponds to one of the four subsections of the section of Dr. LeMoncheck's essay that is entitled "Reconstructing a Feminist Dialogue: The Sexual Politics, Process, and Dialectic of Sexual Harassment." The next two sections of the response deal with two distinct topics discussed by Dr. LeMoncheck in the section of her essay that is entitled "Sexual Harassment Legislation, Policies, and Procedures: A Feminist Perspective," while the final section of the response corresponds to the final section of Dr. LeMoncheck's essay.

Power

In the subsection entitled "The Power of Sexual Stereotypes and the Sexiness of Power," Dr. LeMoncheck dissociates herself from the often repeated slogan that sexual harassment is about power and not about sex. She argues that sex itself is, within our culture, closely connected with power. The view she comes to defend could roughly be expressed by saying that sexual harassment is about power *because* it is about sex and that this, at least partially, explains what is morally wrong with it. According to her account, even if, in thinking about sexual harassment, we set aside the specific forms of power that one person may have over another in virtue of their relative positions within some institutional hierarchy or their ages, social statuses, and so forth, there still remains the power that stems from the fact that what we are dealing with is something sexual. Manifestations of that kind of power can, according to her account, be found in sexual harassment simply because it is *sexual* harassment, and they are unlike the other kinds of power, which, as I have pointed out in my initial essay (in the subsection "Sexual Harassment Involves Relationships of Unequal Power"), may be present in some cases of sexual harassment but clearly are not present in all of them.

What makes the kind of power that is closely connected with sex itself specially morally problematic, Dr. LeMoncheck claims, is that it involves an asymmetry between the sexes: it is power that men have over women. This asymmetry makes it possible to argue that sexual harassment is a form of sex discrimination and to regard the issue of sexual harassment as an issue that is of special concern to feminists.

The argumentative move that Dr. LeMoncheck makes in her subsection on power is effectively the same, although expressed in a different tone, as what Catharine MacKinnon has expressed:

> The way the analysis of sexual harassment is sometimes expressed now (and it bothers me) is that it is an abuse of power, not sexuality. That does not allow us to pursue whether sexuality, as socially constructed in our society through gender roles, is *itself* a power structure. . . . What is not considered to be a hierarchy is women and men—men on top and women on the bottom. That is not considered to be a question of power or social hierarchy, legally or politically. A feminist perspective suggests that it is.[1]

According to Dr. LeMoncheck, this problematic power that men have over women is bestowed on them by certain widely held beliefs that assign asymmetrical roles to men and women in sexual interactions. She refers to these beliefs as "stereotypes" and "myths," and claims that they include the following:

> Men chase and women retreat; men dominate and women submit. Sex turns men into "studs" and women into "whores" (who cannot get enough).

Women are the proper and unconditional sexual objects of men's use and abuse. Women who do not ultimately accept men's sexual advances are sexual neurotics (frigid, lesbian, paranoid). Sex is pleasurable, playful, and fun, but women have to be talked into "feeling okay" about liking it.[2]

Now, let us look more closely at these beliefs that Dr. LeMoncheck ascribes to people in "contemporary Western culture." Does anyone really think that "women are the proper and *unconditional* sexual objects of men's use and abuse"? Surely our culture is full of various conditions that limit when sex between a man and a woman is acceptable. These conditions vary from one segment of the culture to another: in some groups, a condition may be that the man and the woman are married to each other; in some others, the conditions may demand only that they have had at least three dates together, find themselves in a room that can be locked, have some contraception available, and are both in the mood for it. But in every group within the society, one finds some condition: as a minimum, everyone would agree that the legitimacy of a man's obtaining sexual satisfaction with a woman is *conditional* on her consent. That general condition, in turn, makes the legitimacy of the man's sexual satisfaction in a specific case subject to whatever specific conditions the woman sees fit to impose. I find it difficult to think of anyone who would seriously claim that women are "unconditional sexual objects of men's use and abuse."

As for the belief that "sex is pleasurable, playful, and fun, but women have to be talked into 'feeling okay' about liking it," I assume that it is the second part of it (that "women have to be talked into 'feeling okay' about liking" sex) that Dr. LeMoncheck finds problematic and that she does not wish to deny that sex is pleasurable. But that second part seems obviously true if it is taken to be about some women on some occasions. Some women do receive the kind of upbringing that makes it difficult to enjoy sex, and can become open to its pleasures only after they have been slowly eased into it. On the other hand, the second part is equally obviously false if it is taken to be about all women on all occasions, but it is again doubtful that many people hold the belief in that implausibly strong version.

That "sex turns men into 'studs' and women into 'whores' " is admittedly a kind of thing that some people do say. People who would utter such words are probably themselves not very clear about what precisely they mean by them: upon analysis such words *may* turn out to be nothing more than a vulgar way of stating the truth that some men and some women enjoy sex very much. But setting aside what precisely such words mean, it cannot be denied that it is only some people that would utter them; quite a few people, including quite a few men, would never ever say anything even remotely similar. It is utterly unclear why the fact that some people say such things would be taken by anyone to reveal some profound truth about the relationships between the sexes in general, rather than just something about the specific people who are prone to make such comments.[3]

Dr. LeMoncheck continues her argument that in sex, men have power over women by claiming that

> Boys who grab at, stalk, tease, and pull down the pants of teenage girls just discovering a sexual identity are communicating to such girls that their sexuality is accessible to boys without regard to what the girls want.[4]

But it is again far from obvious that the boys are, strictly speaking, *communicating* anything by such acts; quite possibly, they engage in them for whatever immediate thrill they provide, without attempting to make any general point about anything. It is, of course, possible that the girls, and adult observers of such incidents, will take these acts to somehow show that the girls' "sexuality is accessible to boys without regard to what the girls want." But there is nothing in the acts themselves that compels that they be taken that way. They may equally well be taken to show nothing more than that these *particular* boys are little jerks who may, if they do not get some serious talking to, grow into big jerks.

Dr. LeMoncheck's argument here is an instance of the style of argumentation that one frequently finds in contemporary feminist literature. That style of argumentation involves finding examples of conduct in which men are nasty to women, which are of course readily available, and then claiming that the examples reveal some fundamental truth that somehow underlies all interaction between men and women. Such arguments are unconvincing because we can, with the same amount of effort, find many examples in which men are supportive, helpful, and so forth toward women, as well as many examples of conduct in which women are nasty to other women. There is no good reason to treat the examples in which men are nasty to women as revealing more significant truths than the examples of these other kinds.

Dr. LeMoncheck links her general views about the connection between power and sexuality, with the topic of sexual harassment in the following way. Given that female sexuality has various unpleasant, humiliating aspects, over which women have no control (people think that sex turns women into "whores," girls have their pants pulled down by boys, women may be victims of sexual assault), to remind a woman of her sexuality, even in seemingly innocuous ways (as by a man's keeping a photograph of his bikini-clad wife in the office), is to remind her of something unpleasant and humiliating over which she has no control; it is to remind her of her lack of power (in the wide sense of "power"). That reminder of her lack of control over these specific aspects of her sexuality then somehow diminishes her power in whatever other interaction is going on (say, in some business-related discussion).

But it is again unclear why we should accept that move. While it is undoubtedly true that sexuality sometimes brings sadness, distress, humiliation, and pain to women and while we may also agree, for the sake of argument, that it does that more often for women than for men, it seems undeniable that it also brings to women a great deal of intense joy and profound happiness. It is entirely unclear why an average woman who is reminded of her sexuality would more readily think of its dark sides than of its pleasant, fulfilling sides. If a photograph of someone's wife in a bikini is to remind another woman of anything about her own sexuality at all, why would it more readily bring to her mind the possibility of being sexually abused than the possibility of having a romantic holiday somewhere with a lover of her choosing? No doubt, some women do have a pessimistic tendency to focus on the unpleasant sides of their sexuality more than on the pleasant ones (just as various people have analogous pessimistic tendencies in other fields), but there is no reason to regard such a pessimistic tendency as more warranted than the opposite one or as being specially relevant to how we should behave.

Like many other writers on sexual harassment, Dr. LeMoncheck believes that directing attention to a woman's sexuality somehow "eviscerates" her "professional status," which would, of course, be undesirable in many settings in which women are trying to interact with others professionally. That argument would be convincing if it were, as a matter of psychological fact, impossible for a man to appreciate a woman both as a sexually attractive being and as a professional. But there is, in fact, no reason to believe that there is anything in male psychology to make that impossible, and every reason to believe the opposite. Women in happy romantic relationships know very well that their husbands and boyfriends can and do, at the same time, admire both their sexual allure and their nonsexual talents. If their husbands and boyfriends have no difficulty combining the two, there is no reason to believe that their more casual admirers in the office cannot do the same. In fact, not only is it possible for an appreciation of a woman's erotic appeal to coexist with an appreciation of her erudition, business acumen, or creativity, but each of them can strengthen the other. Women who know all that have no reason to believe that the fact that their sexuality receives attention means they are not being taken seriously as professionals.

In saying all this, I am, of course, not denying that directing attention to a woman's sexuality can be used as a put-down, as in the example that Dr. LeMoncheck discusses in which a woman's serious argument about an important matter was apparently discredited at a Navy convention by invoking her alleged sexual experiences. What is crucial about that example is not simply that it involved the woman's sexuality but that references to her sexuality were used in a certain specific way. That directing attention to a woman's sexuality in such a way can be used as a put-down does not prove anything about female sexuality as such or about how it is generally regarded within the society. Just about anything about a person can be used as a put-down, given the right context, vocabulary, and the tone of voice. One can insult someone by calling him a "smart ass," but this does not imply anything about smartness itself or about how smartness is generally viewed in the society.

Incidentally, one of the many human features that can provide material for put-downs is male sexuality. Telling a man who stayed in the office late in the evening with a female coworker to complete an important project that he did it only because he was having or hoping to have an affair with her, telling a man that he is enthusiastic about a particular idea only because he is bedazzled by the feminine allure of the colleague who proposed it, or telling a man that in general "men think only with their dicks" can be every bit as disorienting and hurtful to him as put-downs involving female sexuality are to women.

If what I have said within this section is accepted, then we are again left without a satisfactory answer to the question that I raised in different ways in my initial essay: Why is the difference between sexual harassment and similar conduct that is not of a sexual nature supposed to be significant?

Why should insensitivity, rudeness, and nastiness in sexual matters be dealt with any differently from insensitivity, rudeness, and nastiness in nonsexual matters? Without a satisfactory answer to that question, the fight against sexual harassment remains unjustified.

Overlaps

In the subsection of her essay entitled "Overlapping Frames of Sexual Violation," Dr. LeMoncheck makes several claims that are, in fact, distinct and need to be dealt with separately. The one that is easily dealt with is that

> a continuum that grades such types of harassment by the severity of single violations [does not] account for the severity that is due to a repetition or combination of violations. "More and less serious" does not capture patterns of "less serious" conduct that, over time, becomes severe.[5]

That point is quite readily acceptable, and I do not think that anyone would disagree with it. In fact, the point has been incorporated into the case law on sexual harassment. As one federal court has stated it:

> [T]he analysis cannot carve the work environment into a series of discrete incidents and measure the harm adhering in each episode. Rather, a holistic perspective is necessary, keeping in mind that each successive episode has its predecessors, that the impact of the separate incidents may accumulate, and that the work environment created thereby may exceed the sum of the individual episodes.[6]

Immediately after that fairly uncontroversial claim, Dr. LeMoncheck, however, proceeds to make a distinct, somewhat more controversial claim that qualitatively different kinds of sexual harassment are *incommensurable*. "Which is 'worse' overall," she asks rhetorically, "One pinch on the buttocks or one breast squeeze? Three hard stares or two crude jokes?"[7] The issue that these questions raise seems to me to be an instantiation, within the context of sexual harassment, of the more general problem as to whether qualitatively different wrongdoings are commensurable. In discussions about the criminal law, it is, for example, sometimes asked whether it is possible to put all crimes on a single scale of severity: does it even make sense to ask whether rape is more or less serious than espionage? Similarly, in the context of torts, one may wonder whether there is any principled way of determining whether defaming someone is more or less severe than causing someone's arm to be broken. When one thinks about such matters in these other contexts, one is typically forced to agree that regardless of whether different types of wrongdoing are in some profound sense commensurable or not, one simply cannot escape treating them as commensurable. There are only so many different kinds of legal responses to wrongdoing that are available. While imaginative reforms may increase the range somewhat, it is, as a practical matter, impossible for legal responses to wrongdoings ever to mirror all the qualitative diversity of the wrongdoings themselves. When deciding how to respond legally to wrongdoings, we therefore simply have to translate the qualitative differences between them into merely quantitative differences between prison sentences or amounts of monetary damages, even if we think that these wrongdoings are in some sense incommensurable. Even if defamation and a broken arm are in some sense incommensurable, we still have to decide whether the plaintiff with the broken arm gets more or less money than the plaintiff who has been defamed.

The same reasoning applies to sexual harassment. Regardless of whether there is a sense in which different kinds of sexual harassment are incommensurable, we, as a practical matter, simply have to measure them against each other in deciding how to deal with them. Legal and other organized ways of dealing with sexual harassment are unlikely ever to mirror the qualitative differences among different kinds of sexual harassment itself. This means that those who believe, as Dr. LeMoncheck certainly does, that there should be legal or quasi-legal penalties for sexual harassment simply have to devise some way of translating the qualitative differences among different kinds of sexual harassment into quantitative differences between more and less harsh penalties, even if they think that different kinds of sexual harassment are, in some profound way, incommensurable. Whether one agrees or disagrees with Dr. LeMoncheck as to whether different kinds of sexual harassment are commensurable is, therefore, unlikely to make much difference to one's view on how sexual harassment should be dealt with.

Dr. LeMoncheck's claims that I have dealt with so far within this section do not involve the idea of overlapping and are not central to what she argues in the subsection "Overlapping Frames of Sexual Violation." What is central to it is that sexual harassment needs to be understood in terms of "overlapping conceptual and normative frames of sexual violation." Dr. LeMoncheck does not explicitly stipulate what precisely she means by "overlapping frames," although she does characterize these "frames" as "variable," as "dynamic, unstable," and as allowing for "flexibility and instability." Insofar as I understand the thesis about "overlapping frames," it appears to involve two distinct claims. One is that sexual harassment often overlaps with other kinds of wrongdoing, that one and the same act can instantiate both sexual harassment and a wrong of some other kind. The other seems to be that different grounds of wrongness overlap in making sexual harassment wrong. The latter overlap is within sexual harassment, while the former is between sexual harassment and something else.

Let us take the overlaps between sexual harassment and other kinds of wrongdoing first. The existence of such overlaps is what is illustrated by Dr. LeMoncheck's example of harassment of black women, which may often be, at the same time, harassment of them as women (sexual harassment) and harassment of them as blacks, and by her example of harassment of lesbians, which may often be simultaneously harassment of them as women (sexual harassment) and harassment of them as homosexuals (which, although it has to do with sex, is not covered by the concept of sexual harassment, as normally understood). It is easy to agree with Dr. LeMoncheck that such overlaps do exist; if one thought about it more, one could probably come up with many more examples of them. It is, after all, not uncommon for the courts to deal with suits in which the plaintiffs make claims both under the sexual harassment law and under some other legal provision with respect to the same conduct.

What is puzzling about Dr. LeMoncheck's observation that there are overlaps between sexual harassment and other kinds of wrongdoing is not whether it is true (it clearly is) but why she attaches so much importance to it. The existence of such overlaps is by no means peculiar to sexual harassment: almost any kind of wrongdoing can easily overlap with other kinds of wrongdoing. Suppose that I have promised to tell the truth and then proceed to lie. Lying and promise breaking, two distinct types of wrongdoing, will then overlap in one and the same act of mine. The same holds within legal contexts. One often finds distinct legal categories overlapping within the same acts. One and the same act may, for example, be both a crime and a tort. That such overlaps exist between sexual harassment and other types of wrongdoing, therefore, does not seem to be a specially noteworthy characteristic of sexual harassment.

As one continues to read through Dr. LeMoncheck's subsection on overlaps, one realizes, however, that she does not think simply that there are overlaps between sexual harassment and other kinds of wrongdoing, but that these overlaps are, at least sometimes, of a peculiar kind. The overlaps are, she says, such that sexual harassment and the other kinds of wrongdoing cannot be "parsed out," because they are " 'not additive, but interactive.' "[8] It is, however, not at all clear why we should agree with that. Even if, for the sake of argument, we agree that the different kinds of wrongdoing sometimes interact, and are not simply added to each other, it is not clear that this entails that they cannot be "parsed out." Quite the opposite seems true. The very use of the words "interactive" and "overlaps" commits us to there being distinct things that interact and overlap: we cannot legitimately use these words unless we are prepared to say what these distinct things are. Saying what they are and why we believe that they are at work in a particular case seems to amount precisely to "parsing" them out. If we can do that, then the overlaps between sexual harassment and other kinds of wrongdoing do not seem to be different from other overlaps between different kinds of wrongdoing, after all. On the other hand, if we really cannot do that, then our inability to do it provides an excellent reason for concluding that the concept of sexual harassment is hopelessly muddled and should be abandoned. Perhaps I am misunderstanding Dr. LeMoncheck, and perhaps she means something else by "parsing out" here, but if so, she owes us an explication of what that is.

Let us now turn to the other, distinct claim that Dr. LeMoncheck appears to be making in her discussion of "overlapping frames," the claim that different grounds of wrongness overlap in making sexual harassment wrong. I am not entirely sure that I am interpreting her accurately here, but if she is indeed making that claim, then I wholeheartedly agree with her. The claim that insofar as sexual harassment is wrong, it is wrong on a number of distinct grounds was, after all, at the very core of my criticism of the fight against sexual harassment in the first section of my initial essay. The reader may find it surprising that Dr. LeMoncheck and I, who are supposed to be defending opposed views on sexual harassment, could agree about such a supremely important matter. If the two of us agree about *that*, the reader may wonder, then how did we end up having opposed views on the issue?

The crucial difference between us here is that from the claim that very different grounds of wrongness ("overlapping normative frames" in Dr. LeMoncheck's terminology) are at work in making the conduct that is now called "sexual harassment" wrong, I draw the conclusion that the concept of sexual harassment is unhelpful, that we should dispense with it, and that we should instead think of the conduct in question in terms of the concepts that do capture the different grounds of its wrongness. Dr. LeMoncheck, on the other hand, does not make that further step in her thinking on the topic. The reason for her not making that further step is, so far as I can see, her belief that the different grounds of the wrongness of sexual harassment cannot be "parsed out." But again, it is unclear why we should agree with her about that. If it is accepted that there are distinct "normative frames" that "overlap" in making sexual harassment wrong, it is not clear what could be the obstacles to our enumerating these "frames," explaining why we think that each of them is at work in sexual harassment, and identifying the cases of sexual harassment in which each of them is at work. Our doing so seems to amount precisely to "parsing" them out. Once such "parsing" is accomplished, it will be more illuminating to think of the conduct in question in terms of the results of the "parsing" than in terms of the concept of sexual harassment.

It is important not to forget here, as Dr. LeMoncheck sometimes seems to, that the concept of sexual harassment is not a concept with diffuse origins: it did not come into being spontaneously, through everyday communication among ordinary people. It is a concept that has been created recently, by a small, identifiable group of people. It is a concept that has been, so to speak, authored. Whenever a concept is created in such a deliberate way, its usefulness needs to be established by argument. If its usefulness is not proven, we should not acquiesce to the introduction of the concept into our conceptual framework.

Toward the end of her subsection on overlaps, Dr. LeMoncheck makes the claim that "sexual harassment is not a 'capturable' phenomenon amenable to guidelines designed to encompass all appropriate cases."[9] If this is taken literally, it amounts to the claim that no one can tell us what on earth sexual harassment is, and that again seems to me to be an excellent reason for concluding that we should dispense with the notion of sexual harassment in our thinking about these matters. Dr. LeMoncheck, however, does not seem to have intended these words to be taken literally, because a few pages later, she does proceed to formulate her own guidelines, which, so far as one can see, do purport to "capture" the phenomenon that the concept of sexual harassment applies to.

Dialectic

Dr. LeMoncheck devotes a subsection ("The Dialectical Relationship between Sexual Object and Sexual Subject") to arguing that full understanding of sexual harassment needs to take into account "a dialectic between the gender politics of women's sexual objectification and the political liberation of women's sexuality."[10] It is difficult to be sure what precisely that means and what precisely is the point that this subsection is making. Insofar as Dr. LeMoncheck points out that in present-day Western societies, people hold very different views about female sexuality, it is impossible to disagree with her. It is also impossible to disagree with her insofar as she seems to be pointing out that the coexistence of such different views on female sexuality can make life difficult, because actions that are perfectly reasonable under the assumption that the people one deals with hold one set of views on the topic may end up causing all manner of trouble if it turns out that their views are, in fact, different.

It is, however, rather unclear what is supposed to be the role of the word "dialectic" in discussing such matters. Sometimes "dialectic" appears to be no more than a fancy synonym for "interactive" or "interaction," and insofar as Dr. LeMoncheck may be saying that the interaction among different views about female sexuality is relevant to the issue of sexual harassment, it is again easy to agree with her.

But Dr. LeMoncheck seems to mean more than that by "dialectic" when she claims that understanding sexual harassment as a dialectic process "negotiates the tensions" between the two opposed lines of thought that she has presented in the first half of her essay. Whatever precisely "dialectic" might mean, it is rather unclear how characterizing sexual harassment as dialectic could have that effect. The views of, say, Catharine MacKinnon and Ellen Frankel Paul are mutually *contradictory*: whoever accepts one of them must, as a matter of logic, reject the other. There is no magic word that can transform that contradiction into a noncontradiction. Thinking that the word "dialectic" could have such a magic power has a certain affinity with the Hegelian roots of the present-day philosophical usage of that word, but it is unlikely to seem plausible to anyone who has no sympathy for Hegelianism.

This points to a more general problem with Dr. LeMoncheck's essay. When she embarks on developing her own views on sexual harassment, she gives the impression that she will take into account the arguments of the critics of the sexual harassment law that are summarized in "Fragile Flowers and Predatory Beasts." But looking at Dr. LeMoncheck's essay as a whole, Katie Roiphe, Rene Denfeld, Ellen Frankel Paul, and their sympathizers are likely to have a feeling that very little of their views has, in fact, been taken into account.

The Practical Guidelines

Dr. LeMoncheck offers

> the following characterization of sexual harassment, which is designed to give some identifying parameters to the offending conduct: Sexual harassment is a dynamic, dialectical, and interpretive process of sexual politics in which the harasser's conduct, words, images, or other icons are regarded as a violation of the sexual integrity of the harassed. This violation constitutes a sexual imposition or intrusion upon the harassed, which is facilitated by organizational hierarchies or informed by cultural stereotypes or both, in ways that delegitimize, manipulate, or threaten the harassed or presume sexual access to her. As such, sexual harassment constitutes an abrogation of the responsibility of the harasser to treat the harassed as a moral equal whose sense of herself as a sexual subject in the world is as worthy of empathy and respect as any other person's.[11]

Dr. LeMoncheck presents this characterization in a way that suggests that she regards it as an important improvement over other analyses of the concept that have been offered. Moreover, she offers it under the heading *"Practical* Guidelines and Interpretive Frameworks," which presumably implies that it is supposed to assist those who might be uncertain whether some given conduct constitutes sexual harassment. Our examination of the characterization thus needs to ascertain whether it is, in fact, capable of providing such assistance to the perplexed and whether it is capable of providing better assistance to them than the already existing definitions of sexual harassment (such as the one incorporated in the EEOC guidelines that I have criticized in my essay).

The first move that we can make in examining Dr. LeMoncheck's analysis quoted above is to set aside its last sentence. In connection with any kind of wrongdoing, one can say, if one is into such terminology, that the wrongdoing fails to treat the victim "as a moral equal" or as someone whose sense of self "is as worthy of empathy and respect as any other person's." It is debatable what precisely these words mean, but regardless of what precisely they mean, they seem to be of no help in distinguishing sexual harassment from other kinds of wrongdoing. Dr. LeMoncheck goes on to say that the harasser's failure to treat the victim "as a moral equal" entails that sexual harassment is a form of discrimination. That is true insofar as the harasser is indeed treating the victim differently from others, but in that sense, again, any wrongdoing can be characterized as discrimination because every wrongdoing involves treating its victims differently from others. What is important in this context is whether sexual harassment constitutes discrimination *on the basis of sex.* Harassers' failure to treat their victims as "moral equals" (whatever precisely that means) does not in itself entail that it does.

Let us now look at the part of Dr. LeMoncheck's characterization of sexual harassment that says that it is "a dynamic, dialectical, and interpretive process of sexual politics." Some possible criticisms of that clause are already implied by what I have said earlier in this response. Further specific criticisms could be made, but there is a more basic problem with that clause, which eliminates the need for discussing the details of its content here. Regardless of what one believes about the content of the clause, one has to admit that the theoretical assumptions it brings into the characterization of sexual harassment are highly controversial. For example, while the idea that the conduct currently labeled "sexual harassment" is *political* may seem plausible to many feminist theoreticians, it is an idea that many other people, including intelligent, educated people who have made reasonable efforts to acquaint themselves with feminist arguments, simply disagree with. How are the people who disagree with it supposed to go about applying these "practical guidelines"? If sexual harassment is something we are all supposed to abstain from, then we all have to be able to determine whether something is or is not sexual harassment, independently of whether we agree or disagree with some controversial theories. It is important to separate here the *justification* of a certain prohibition and the *identification* of what is prohibited. Even if it is thought legitimate for a certain feminist theory to play a role in justifying the prohibition of sexual harassment, the identification of what is prohibited must be independent of the theory if both its proponents and its opponents are expected to comply with the prohibition. Suppose that some crimes were defined in the criminal code in terms of being offensive to God. We would surely be opposed to that, on the ground that we expect both religious and nonreligious people to obey the code and that therefore both religious and nonreligious people ought to be able to use the definition in the code in the same way to identify what is prohibited. Building controversial feminist theories into a definition of sexual harassment is analogous.

Continuing to read Dr. LeMoncheck's characterization of sexual harassment, we find the clause that "the harasser's conduct, words, images, or other icons are regarded as a violation of the sexual integrity of the harassed." This is the part of the quoted characterization that comes closest to being helpful in identifying what sexual harassment is. The first problem with it, however, is that the passive construction "are regarded" leaves one wondering: "Regarded by whom?" One possible interpretation of "are regarded" is "are regarded by the victim." That interpretation, however, creates what is essentially the same problem as the one I have discussed in the subsection of my essay entitled "The Demarcation Problem" (in connection with the definition of sexual harassment in the EEOC guidelines). In present-day Western societies, people differ widely about what they regard as violations of their "sexual integrity." The kind of sexual advances that some people are longing to receive, other people regard as violations of their sexual integrity; the jokes that some people find amusing, others regard as violations of their sexual integrity. The person who is considering whether or not to engage in such conduct, therefore, simply cannot know whether the conduct would be regarded by the recipient as a violation of sexual integrity and thus whether it would, according to Dr. LeMoncheck's characterization, constitute sexual harassment. The problem cannot be solved by inquiring in advance whether the intended recipient would regard the conduct as a violation of sexual integrity, because such an inquiry may itself be regarded as a violation of sexual integrity.

Dr. LeMoncheck attempts to avoid this problem by claiming that "a woman will welcome respectful inquiries . . . concerning her sense of how she would like to be treated in this context by this person."[12] This may seem plausible until one tries to imagine in some detail what such "respectful inquiries" would really look like. Suppose I want tell a sexual joke to a woman. Following Dr. LeMoncheck's advice, I respectfully ask the woman whether she minds sexual jokes. It is quite likely that her answer will be something like "It all depends on the joke. Some of them I find rather funny, but there are some that I find quite disturbing." What now? If I am to continue my quest for information about the woman's attitudes, it seems that my next step is to outline more specifically what I had in mind. But if I do that and if the woman regards the jokes of the kind I have in mind as violating her sexual integrity, chances are that she will also regard my description of that kind of joke as violating her sexual integrity (even if I do not proceed to actually tell any such joke). In other words, it is true that inquiries made in very general terms are unlikely to be regarded as violations of sexual integrity, but it is also true that they are unlikely to really provide one with the information one needs. An inquiry that is specific enough to be usefully informative is, on the other hand, almost as likely to be regarded as a violation of sexual integrity as one's actually doing what the inquiry is about.[13] In many cases, even the very distinction between a preliminary inquiry about something and what the inquiry is about is, in practice, impossible to maintain. Asking someone "Would you mind it if I were to ask you for a date of such and such kind?" is in most real-life situations going to be perceived as equivalent to "I (hereby) ask you for a date of such and such kind."

The only way in which one can make sure that one's conduct will not be "regarded as a violation of . . . sexual integrity" by the relevant person is, therefore, to abstain from all conduct of a sexual nature. This interpretation of Dr. LeMoncheck's characterization of sexual harassment thus puts the people who are trying to abstain from the conduct covered by the characterization in the same position as the EEOC guidelines.

Dr. LeMoncheck's formulation "are regarded" can also be interpreted as "are regarded by the society" or "are generally regarded." But these alternative interpretations are subject to a related problem. The fact that people differ in these matters as widely as they do means that there is not a definite view on what violates sexual integrity that can be said to be held generally or by the society. If one attempted to use the characterization, so interpreted, to determine whether or not this or that specific conduct constitutes sexual harassment, one would often get no answer at all.

When Dr. LeMoncheck, later in her essay, refers back to this characterization of sexual harassment, the words "are regarded" disappear, and she speaks of sexual harassment as something that *is* a violation of sexual integrity, rather than something that *is regarded as* a violation of sexual integrity. But the problems that I presented above do not disappear with the disappearance of the words. The fact still remains that people disagree over what constitutes a violation of sexual integrity and that there is no clearly prevailing view on the matter. Characterizing sexual harassment in terms of violations of sexual integrity is, therefore, of little help to an ordinary person who wants to know what it is that the prohibition of sexual harassment prohibits.

These problems are not alleviated by the remainder of Dr. LeMoncheck's characterization of sexual harassment. She says that sexual harassment is "a sexual imposition or intrusion," but that part of the characterization is subject to the same argument as the one about sexual integrity because people differ widely about what they regard as imposing in sexual matters. The words "delegitimize, manipulate, or threaten the harassed or presume sexual access to her" are similarly unhelpful. People disagree widely on when these terms apply. When a man is flaunting indications of his high social status in making a sexual advance toward a young and inexperienced person, is he thereby manipulating the person he is trying to impress? When a honey-mouthed suitor showers someone with persistent, carefully selected flattery, does he manipulate the object of his romantic interest? Different people will answer these questions differently. Even "threaten," a word with seemingly straightforward meaning, can give rise to such differences in this context. While people generally agree about what counts as an explicit threat, they differ widely on what conduct of a sexual nature carries an implicit threat. And whenever I direct conduct of a sexual nature at someone, it can be said that I "presume" that the conduct is legitimate and thus, given that the conduct is sexual, that I "presume sexual access" to the person. The phrase is thus, in principle, applicable to all conduct of a sexual nature. Some people may consequently choose to apply it to a wide range of such conduct, while others may decline to apply it to anything falling short of rape. Dr. LeMoncheck's characterization of sexual harassment thus re-creates all the problems that beset the existing definitions of it and, therefore, does not constitute an improvement upon them.

Much of what I have said above by way of criticism of Dr. LeMoncheck's characterization of sexual harassment, she herself acknowledges in her essay, but she does not regard it as a criticism. For example, she says "I am not suggesting that there will be consensus on what counts as a violation of sexual integrity or what may best be deemed delegitimizing, manipulative, or sexually presumptuous."[14] Her reason for not regarding that observation as threatening to her position is that "consensus has never been necessary for moral or legal prohibition."[15] There are two responses to be made to that argumentative move.

The first is that saying that there is no consensus on these issues, although true, is an understatement. On many of these issues, not only is there no consensus, but there is no clear majority either; in fact, on many of them, it is not even clear what the plurality is. The second response is that the seeming plausibility of dismissing the criticisms by saying that "consensus has never been necessary for moral or legal prohibition" is due to confusing two things: justifying a prohibition and identifying what is prohibited by it. It is true that we do not expect consensus about justification of a prohibition. But from a well-drafted prohibition we do expect that it will generate near consensus about what it applies to and what it does not apply to (so that even the dissenters about its justification will be able to conform their conduct to it). Of course, tricky boundary cases eventually do arise in applying almost any prohibition, but with respect to them we still expect that there will be a consensus that they are tricky boundary cases. Moreover, we expect that responsible drafters of a prohibition will try to anticipate as many of such boundary problems as possible and to disambiguate the prohibition with respect to all such problems that they do anticipate. We expect those who draft our laws and quasi-legal regulations not to knowingly leave room for disagreement about what these laws prohibit (notwithstanding that there may be disagreements about whether and why these laws are justified in prohibiting whatever they prohibit).

The stretchability of Dr. LeMoncheck's characterization of sexual harassment, incidentally, means not only that the characterization would be unhelpful to ordinary people who wish to comply with the prohibition of sexual harassment but also that it would not in any way contribute to alleviating the concerns of the authors whose views Dr. LeMoncheck surveys in "Fragile Flowers and Predatory Beasts." The victim mentality that these authors criticize could flourish just as easily under Dr. LeMoncheck's characterization of sexual harassment as it does at present. The propaganda machinery that now encourages women to perceive the widest possible range of conduct as offensive and to dwell on its offensiveness could continue to function in pretty much the same way if Dr. LeMoncheck's characterization were accepted. The propaganda could simply accept Dr.

LeMoncheck's terminology and encourage women to perceive the widest possible range of sexual conduct as violations of sexual integrity and to dwell on its constituting such violations. That would have the same impact on society as the present propaganda about sexual harassment does, the impact that authors such as Roiphe regard as pernicious. Someone who rejects the views of these authors altogether may not regard this as a problem, but it is a problem for Dr. LeMoncheck, who earlier in her essay left her readers with the impression that she would be responsive to the views of these authors.

Within the same subsection, Dr. LeMoncheck also tries to account for the wrongness of sexual harassment by arguing that harassers fail to engage in what she, borrowing the term from María Lugones, calls " 'world'-traveling." That phrase appears to stand for what would be, in a more ordinary way of talking, called "putting oneself in the shoes of another," that is, imagining the experiences of that person as one's own.[16] It is probably quite true that harassers often fail to put themselves into the shoes of their victims and that this failure may be, in some sense, at the root of what they do. But the same is true of murderers, of those who deface library books, and of wrongdoers of various other kinds; all of them often do what they do because they fail to put themselves in the shoes of those affected by their acts. The explanation of sexual harassment in these terms is thus far too general to be useful in this context. It does not tell us how serious a problem sexual harassment is, because both very serious and trivial wrongdoings (such as being late for an appointment without a special reason) may have at their root the wrongdoer's failure to put himself in the shoes of those affected by the act. It does not tell us whether sexual harassment should be legally controlled. Most crucially, it does not tell us anything about whether it is illuminating to think of sexual harassment as a *distinct type* of wrongdoing or whether "sexual harassment" is a concept we should dispense with because it confusingly jumbles together very different kinds of wrongdoing.

Let me hasten to add that although in many cases of sexual harassment, it is true that the harasser is "too full of his own self-importance"[17] to bother to imagine what his actions are like from the perspective of their recipients, sometimes people end up committing acts of sexual harassment not because they are unwilling to put themselves in the shoes of those affected but simply because they lack information about what the "shoes" are like. As I have argued above, there is often no way to obtain such information without risking that the process of seeking it will itself turn out to be harassing.

The fact that the account of sexual harassment in terms of "world"-traveling is not specific enough to be useful does not affect only the subsection of Dr. LeMoncheck's essay in which it is presented. It also casts a shadow over the sections of her essay that follow, because the account is referred to many times in these sections, in ways that assume its usefulness.

Evidence

In her section "Sexual Harassment Legislation, Policies, and Procedures: A Feminist Perspective," Dr. LeMoncheck criticizes the present law on sexual harassment for putting an undue burden on plaintiffs in sexual harassment cases. Because the legal definition of sexual harassment (unlike Dr. LeMoncheck's own characterization discussed above) involves the notion of unwelcomeness, plaintiffs have to prove that the conduct in question was, in fact, unwelcome. All manner of details of how the plaintiff behaved, not only at the time of the incidents in question but also before and after them, may be indications of whether the plaintiff welcomed the conduct of the alleged harasser or not. This means that the arguments and counterarguments about whether the conduct was unwelcome may sometimes turn into a very detailed scrutiny of the plaintiff's own conduct—the plaintiff may thus, metaphorically speaking, end up being put "on trial." Dr. LeMoncheck regards that as undesirable, and many people would agree with her, both because such scrutiny is inherently stressful and because the prospect of such scrutiny may discourage many victims from pursuing their claims. Dr. LeMoncheck's argument here is analogous to the standard feminist arguments against the way in which the rape laws sometimes operated, the arguments that have in recent years led to some reforms of those laws. She uses the argument as one of the reasons for replacing the current legal definition of sexual harassment with her own characterization.

It is debatable how much of a burden the requirement of unwelcomeness really places on plaintiffs. It seems to be an exaggeration to present the current law as requiring that plaintiffs prove that their conduct was "entirely unprovocative and appropriately off-putting,"[18] given that, for example, in one sexual harassment case the court determined that the unwelcomeness of specific conduct to the plaintiff was compatible with the fact that she "sometimes gave as much as she got"[19] by way of "raw sexual banter" in the workplace.

But let us, for the sake of argument, agree with Dr. LeMoncheck that the law, at least sometimes, does lead to investigations that are burdensome for the plaintiff, and that this is, other things being equal, undesirable. The question is whether replacing the current legal definition of sexual harassment with Dr. LeMoncheck's own characterization would solve the problem. I believe that it would not. While people disagree about what conduct constitutes a violation of sexual integrity, most people would probably regard the behavior of the person receiving the conduct as relevant for determining whether the conduct was such a violation or not. Surely, if the person positively encouraged such conduct, that counts against its being a violation of sexual integrity. On the other hand, if the person clearly expressed dislike of such conduct, that seems to strengthen the claim that it was such a violation. Similarly, the plaintiff's conduct may be relevant for determining whether the alleged harasser, in the words of Dr. LeMoncheck's characterization, "presumed sexual access" to the plaintiff (whatever precisely that means) or was, in fact, granted such access by the plaintiff. So all the questions about the plaintiff's conduct that are potentially relevant under the present law would re-appear under a law formulated in terms of Dr. LeMoncheck's characterization of sexual harassment.

The Structural Problems Again

In the continuation of her discussion of the law on sexual harassment, Dr. LeMoncheck says that

> if both the reasonableness and the unwelcomeness standards are dropped, courts can assume a credible claimant and a respectfully empathetic alleged harasser between whom the burden of persuasion as to the merits of the case is balanced.[20]

As the reader could have guessed, I believe that the idea that there needs to be a balance between the positions of the alleged victims and those of the alleged harassers is on the right track. Dr. LeMoncheck, however, does not appreciate that such a balance is impossible as long as the law retains its present, two-level structure, which I discussed in my essay. The courts cannot create such a balance between alleged victims and alleged harassers because courts typically do not deal with the alleged harassers directly: the law primarily operates through lawsuits in which the defendants are employers rather than alleged harassers.

Employers, on the other hand, simply cannot afford to engage, in the lower-level proceedings, in a delicate balancing of the positions of the two parties to the dispute. They are under the threat of upper-level legal sanctions, and it is consequently reasonable for them to want to have and enforce lower-level regulations that will give them a wide margin of safety against these sanctions. In fact, the wider the margin, the better, so far as the employer is concerned. An employer that ends up erring in favor of the alleged harasser, even if only slightly, may easily find itself in court, while an employer that errs in favor of the alleged victim is unlikely to find itself in similar trouble, unless the error is extreme. Employers are thus given an incentive to structure lower-level proceedings in such a way that errors in favor of alleged victims are more likely than errors in favor of alleged harassers. Engaging in delicate balancing of the positions of the two parties to a lower-level dispute would be, from the employer's viewpoint, unreasonable because it would bring the employer too close to making an error that could prove costly: it would reduce the margin of safety. The understandable wish of employers to create a margin of safety against upper-level liability means that nothing that the courts do at the upper level is likely to create a balance between the two lower-level parties.

In other words, the fact that an alleged victim who is dissatisfied with the results of lower-level proceedings can always move the matter to the upper level while an alleged harasser who is dissatisfied with the results of lower-level proceedings can sue the employer only in a very limited range of circumstances in itself creates a fundamental imbalance at the lower level. It is difficult to see how that imbalance could be rectified as long as the law continues to have a two-level structure. Dr. LeMoncheck's recommendation that there be a balance between the positions of alleged harassers and those of alleged victims in sexual harassment proceedings could, therefore, be implemented only in the context of some very radical restructuring of the sexual harassment law, restructuring that would amount to dismantling the whole body of the current law and building something entirely new in its place.

Dr. LeMoncheck's discussion of what she calls in-house sexual harass-

ment regulations suffers from the same lack of appreciation of the implications of the two-level structure of the law. She speaks of these regulations
as if they were something independent of the law. The thesis that she is
trying to establish appears to be that these regulations are something that
it is desirable to have in addition to the law. Speaking about the regulations in that way is, however, out of place within the context of the law as
it is. In the present system, in-house regulations are not independent of
the law: they exist *because* the law requires employers to see to it that there
is no sexual harassment within their businesses and threatens them with
legal sanctions if they do not. That is why, in my initial essay, I refer to
these in-house regulations as the lower level of the operation of the law.
As long as the law retains its present structure, employers do not need
Dr. LeMoncheck's or anyone else's encouragement to maintain in-house
regulations against sexual harassment; the law gives them enough of an
incentive to do so.

Dr. LeMoncheck's detailed recommendations as to what in-house regulations should look like are also out of place in the context of a law that
has this two-level structure. In the present system, employers simply cannot afford to listen to Dr. LeMoncheck's or anyone else's advice as to
what kind of in-house regulations on sexual harassment would be desirable
on some independent grounds. They have to institute the kind of in-house
regulations that will best insulate them from legal liability, not the kind
that may be desirable on some other ground.

Communication and Empathy

Dr. LeMoncheck ends her essay with a call for more communication and
empathy on sexual matters than there is at present. More communication
and empathy, she suggests, can in the long run significantly reduce the
incidence not only of sexual harassment but also of many similar problems.
That more communication and empathy in these matters would be desirable is, again, something that it is easy to agree with. The problem is that
Dr. LeMoncheck presents the current lack of communication and empathy as primarily the lack of them *between men and women* and that she
consequently ends up recommending more explicit discussion on these
matters *between the sexes*. There is, however, no good reason to accept that
part of her argument.

A man and a woman who are both fundamentalist Christians already understand each other's outlooks on sexuality quite well, simply in virtue of their shared religious background (which incorporates a fairly specific sexual morality). Each of the two already knows perfectly well what the "sexual integrity" of the other involves. The fact that one of them is a man and the other a woman poses no obstacles to their understanding each other in that respect. They do not need any further discussions to enhance their understanding of each other in sexual matters. Similarly, a man and a woman who are both dedicated, experienced practitioners of sadomasochism are unlikely to have great problems understanding each other's sexuality. Within each such group, there is no special obstacle to understanding between men and women. The barriers to communication and empathy in sexual matters are primarily barriers between such groups, and these barriers have nothing to do with the sex of the people involved. The fact that a woman who is a fundamentalist Christian and a woman who is a practitioner of sadomasochism are both female does not create any special bond of understanding between them. Fundamentalist Christians of either sex are unlikely to know much about sadomasochism, and are unlikely to empathize with its practitioners,[21] regardless of their sex, and vice versa.

The number of such groups in present-day Western societies is enormous. Not only are there fundamentalist Christians and sadomasochists, but there are also those who think that adultery is a profound betrayal of one's partner, those who think that it is "no big deal" as long as it is kept discreet, and those who are in open marriages. There are those who think that homosexuality is a wholesome preference on a par with heterosexuality, those who think that it is okay but should not be flaunted, and those who think that it is an abnormality. There are those who think that pornography is degrading and who would not come anywhere near it, and those who regularly view pornography with their sexual partners as a prelude to their own sexual activities. The reader can probably easily think of numerous further examples. Within a group of people who hold a specific outlook on sexual matters, men and women already understand each other's sexual preferences well and generally have no difficulty respecting the sexual integrity of others. It is between one such group and another that communication and empathy are often lacking. That lack of communication and empathy can easily cause problems when people belonging to different groups end up working or studying next to each other, as they often do.

It is tempting to conclude from all this that what is needed is more communication and empathy among these different groups. But the matter is not so straightforward, because we encounter here a variation on the problem I have presented before in this debate. A part of many people's attitudes on sexual matters is their deeply felt abhorrence of views significantly different from their own, which involves their wanting to insulate themselves from these views. Such people do not want to know too much about these other views, and do not want even to be reminded of their existence. Their refusal to communicate and empathize may be so deeply entrenched that any attempt to overcome it would itself amount to violating their sexual integrity. A fundamentalist Christian may not wish to have his peace of mind disrupted by hearing what it is like to be a practicing sadomasochist. People who regard exclusivity in sexual relationships as highly important and are determined to pursue it in their own lives may not wish to have their resolve undermined by hearing about people who have found fulfillment in open marriages. A feminist who believes that pornography is a tool of the oppression of women may regard it as a betrayal of the cause to empathize with those who regularly view pornography and who think that viewing it is nothing more than innocent entertainment. Proponents of such views (and, again, more examples can be easily thought of) simply do not wish to be drawn into any kind of open discussion on sexual matters with the people whose outlooks on such matters they abhor. Dragging them into such a discussion would for them be a violation of their sexual integrity. Calls for more communication and empathy, sensible as they are, are therefore unlikely to be effective in resolving the tensions that underlie complaints of sexual harassment.

Notes

1. Catharine A. MacKinnon, *Feminism Unmodified: Discourses on Life and Law* (Cambridge, Mass.: Harvard University Press, 1987), 89 (emphasis in original).

2. P. 43 of this volume.

3. Cf. Igor Primoratz, "What's Wrong with Prostitution?" *Philosophy* 68 (1993): 180.

4. P. 43 of this volume.

5. Ibid., 49.

6. *Robinson v. Jacksonville Shipyards, Inc.,* 760 F. Supp. 1486, 1524 (M.D. Fla. 1991).

7. P. 50 of this volume.

8. Ibid., p. 52, quoting Celia Kitzinger, "Anti-Lesbian Harassment," in *Rethinking Sexual Harassment,* ed. Clare Brant and Yun Lee Too (London: Pluto Press, 1994), 133.

9. P. 55 of this volume.

10. Ibid., 56.

11. Ibid., 59.

12. Ibid., 61.

13. In fact, such inquiries can sometimes make things worse than they would have been otherwise. A woman may work at a place where there are pornographic calendars on the walls without paying much attention to them: they may simply not register in her mind as anything that is worthy of attention, and certainly not as something that violates her sexual integrity. But if she is then "respectfully asked" whether she minds the calendars, she may feel that the question "puts her on the spot" in a way that does violate her sexual integrity. She may feel that the question forces upon her some kind of a connection with the calendars, which the calendars themselves have not imposed.

14. P. 61 of this volume.

15. Ibid.

16. Some philosophers may regard this use of the phrase " 'world'-traveling" as not only unnecessary but, in fact, misleading because what one imagines when one puts oneself in the "shoes" of another actual person is not really another possible world (in the sense of "possible world" that is established in contemporary philosophy) but merely another perspective on the very same, actual world. Lugones is aware of that, and that is presumably why she puts "world" in quotation marks throughout her article. María Lugones, "Playfulness, 'World'-Traveling, and Loving Perception," in *Women, Knowledge, and Reality: Explorations in Feminist Philosophy,* ed. Ann Gary and Marilyn Pearsall (Boston: Unwin Hyman, 1989), 275–90.

17. P. 60 of this volume.

18. Ibid., 69.

19. *Lynch v. City of Des Moines,* 454 N.W.2d 827, 834 (Iowa 1990).

20. P. 69 of this volume.

21. Fundamentalist Christians may, of course, empathize with sadomasochists in a very general way, in which they empathize with all human beings, but such nonspecific empathy is not what is under discussion here.

Epilogue

We have been engaged in a debate that could easily be continued. Each of us could offer further arguments in reply to the other's response. In fact, as the manuscript of this book goes to the publisher, the two of us are exchanging correspondence containing further points and counterpoints on the issues that have been raised in the book.

The book itself, however, ends here because its main purpose is not to provide an outlet for the arguments of two specific individuals. Its main purpose is to stimulate its readers to develop their own arguments on the topic. Thus, we hope that the question that each of our readers is asking at this stage is not "How would the two authors further respond to each other?" but rather "What further arguments would *I* make on this topic? How would *I* go about refuting the arguments presented in this book that I do not find plausible? Are there, within the views that I find implausible, insights that are nevertheless worthwhile? How can I profit from what has been said in this debate to articulate my own views on the topic?"

Sexual harassment and the practices aimed at combating it affect, in some way or other, practically all of us. In discussions about it, views and arguments from a broad range of perspectives, therefore, deserve to be heard and considered seriously. We both think that serious public debate about sexual harassment has not been as vigorous as it should be, and we are dismayed that such semblance of public debate as can be found has all too often amounted to people dismissing their opponents, rather than considering their views seriously and responding to them in reflective and responsible ways. On the preceding pages, we both did our best to consider the views of our respective opponents (which, for each of us, included both the other author of this book and various other people who have published on the topic) as carefully and as attentively as was possible in a book of this size and to respond to them by counterarguments. We hope that the book will inspire its readers to approach the arguments of their respective opponents in the same spirit.

We agree that thinking responsibly about the problem of sexual harassment requires that one consider the matter from the viewpoint of everyone concerned: the actual and potential victims of sexual harassment; those who have been or might be, truly or falsely, accused of it; the people who run the institutions within which sexual harassment might take place; and finally, those who may be affected in various roundabout ways by sexual harassment itself or by the measures we may take to combat it. These are all people to whose "worlds," in the terminology used by one of us, we need to "travel" or as the other one of us would say, into whose "shoes" we need to put ourselves, when we think about sexual harassment. The fact that the two of us, after trying our best to do that, have reached radically different conclusions attests to the complexity of the matters involved.

We also both think that the problem of sexual harassment cannot be successfully dealt with in isolation. In other words, we think that reaching a fully thought-through position on sexual harassment requires that one compare and contrast the phenomena called "sexual harassment" with various other phenomena. When each of us engaged in such comparing and contrasting, the results reached ended up being quite different, though. A comparison that may have struck one of us as the key to the whole problem all too often struck the other as insignificant. But despite these disagreements in our conclusions, we do think that anyone who wishes to think seriously about sexual harassment would do well to ponder such questions as these: What are the similarities and differences between sexual harassment and other forms of sexual immorality? How is sexual harassment different from, how is it similar to, and how does it interact with, say, racial harassment? How does sexual harassment relate to the established general patterns of male-female sexual interaction?

The readers have probably noted that, although one of us thinks that the law about sexual harassment is, in general, on the right track while the other thinks that it is seriously misguided, neither of us is entirely happy with its current shape. We both think that the law is in need of more critical scrutiny than it has received so far, although each of us, of course, has very different hopes for the final results of that scrutiny. We urge our readers to accept the responsibility that they, as citizens of a democratic society, have for the current shape of the law and to try to influence its future development by joining the public debate about it.

Linda LeMoncheck
Mane Hajdin

Index

231

About the Authors

Linda LeMoncheck is a freelance writer and lecturer in philosophy, specializing in women's social and political issues. She has taught at California State University, Long Beach; Occidental College; University of Southern California, Los Angeles; and University of Southern California. Lemoncheck's publications focus on the role played by current conceptions of gender in women's sexual and reproductive lives. She is the author of *Dehumanizing Women: Treating Persons as Sex Objects* (Rowman & Littlefield, 1985) and *Loose Women, Lecherous Men: A Feminist Philosophy of Sex* (Oxford University Press, 1997). Her current research focuses on the relationships between rape, sexual harassment, and woman battering. She lives in Seal Beach, California, where she supports local women's organizations.

Mane Hajdin has taught philosophy at McGill University, University of Papua New Guinea, and University of Waikato (in New Zealand), and has been a research associate at the University of California, Berkeley. He specializes in ethics, philosophy of law, and social and political philosophy. His philosophical research is within the analytic tradition and covers both theoretical and applied aspects of these branches of philosophy. He is the author of a study in ethical theory, entitled *The Boundaries of Moral Discourse* (Loyola University Press, 1994), and a number of scholarly articles. His contribution to this volume is a by-product of his work on a more extensive study of moral problems associated with the law on sexual harassment.